THE POWER OF AN ATLAS

THE POWER OF AN ATLAS

AN IMMIGRANT'S TALE
A MEMOIR

SARDUL SINGH MINHAS

atmosphere press

© 2022 Sardul Singh Minhas

Published by Atmosphere Press

Cover design by Kevin Stone

No part of this book may be reproduced without permission from the author except in brief quotations and in reviews.

atmospherepress.com

To Rosemary:
My Anchor
The Love of My Life

Contents

PROLOGUE - 3

CHAPTER 1. An Atlas - - - - - - - - - - - - - - - - - - 9

CHAPTER 2. A Family of Risk Takers - - - - - - - - - - 18

CHAPTER 3. University Bound - - - - - - - - - - - - - 41

CHAPTER 4. Panjab University - - - - - - - - - - - - - 45

CHAPTER 5. IIT - 59

CHAPTER 6. Golden Dome - - - - - - - - - - - - - - - - 76

CHAPTER 7. Big Apple - - - - - - - - - - - - - - - - 103

CHAPTER 8. Westchester - - - - - - - - - - - - - - - 124

CHAPTER 9. Yardley - - - - - - - - - - - - - - - - - 157

CHAPTER 10. Hornet's Nest - - - - - - - - - - - - - - 177

CHAPTER 11. Old Dominion - - - - - - - - - - - - - - 196

CHAPTER 12. Pinnacle - - - - - - - - - - - - - - - - 209

CHAPTER 13. Retirement - - - - - - - - - - - - - - - 230

CHAPTER 14. Immigration—
        The Demagogue's Playground - - - - - - 249

EPILOGUE - 268

PROLOGUE

A hesitant, somewhat awed young man landed at Chicago's O'Hare Airport in September 1965. Nothing functioned smoothly in the country he had just arrived from. He had seen only two other airports in his life, in Delhi and Bombay, where the planes would stop on the tarmac and passengers would be bused to the arrivals building. But O'Hare was different. The plane pulled right to a gate at the arrivals building.

He had a fair command of written English, but the accents all around him were unfamiliar and terribly confusing. He traipsed to the head of the long immigration check line. The officer on duty was a tall, burly man with piercing blue eyes and a shock of brown hair. The young man was so absorbed in taking in the officer's appearance that he momentarily forgot the business at hand.

"Your ID, bud," barked Blue Eyes.

The young man was startled. Confusion washed over his face. "Excuse me," he stammered.

"Your identification, your passport," clarified the immigration agent in a softer tone.

He handed over his passport and was waved through with no further fanfare. The halls of the airport were immense, the ceilings high. Every surface shimmered. The floor was spotless, as were the countertops. It seemed magical how all surfaces in such an airport could be kept so clean.

Here was such a rush of people, most of them white. Their hair colors covered a full spectrum—black, brown, blond, red. And he had never come across black people in India. It required considerable effort not to stare. Amazingly, the lines of people moved smoothly. There were the moving walkways; he almost fell as he stepped off one. Trolleys carrying older or infirm people seemed to come right at you and swerved just in time. Everybody walked to their right; he didn't see a single person break this rule. This was weird to him. In the country he had left behind, people seemed to walk everywhere all at once, requiring very deft navigation. Not at O'Hare.

He had grown up in the northwestern Indian state of Punjab. His small village was a smattering of primitive mud houses, with no power or running water. He read books by the dim light supplied by kerosene lamps, books that would allow him flights of imagination such as visiting distant lands. His family drew water from an open well. Their life was close to the elements. His family, along with all others who lived in the village, made do without a school, a doctor, a hospital, or paved streets. Narrow muddy paths led out of the village, to the nearby town, to the paved road, to the cities. Villagers had to become particularly adept at trudging through ankle-deep mud after it rained.

Life was grueling. Working the land, tending to the cattle, and being aware of the lack of even elementary facilities, which he knew existed in nearby cities, fed the young man's determination to get a good education as the ticket to a good life.

His childhood flashed in his mind as he surveyed this marvelous airport. His mind juggled emotions as he made his way through the airport to the luggage pickup area. As he moved through the vast corridors lined with shops and restaurants, he felt alone in the airport, a place that teemed with humanity. He was a fully bearded, turbaned Sikh, the only one as far as he could see. He felt conspicuous and self-conscious, as if the people moving past were all staring at him.

He recovered his luggage. He had never before seen a baggage carousel. Bags appeared magically at the top, moved down on the sloping feeder, and went round and round on the carousel, to be plucked by their owners. Nothing like that existed at the airports in Delhi and Bombay.

When he stepped out of the airport, he had fifty dollars in his pocket. He hailed a cab to the Illinois Institute of Technology in Chicago. As the cab pulled away from O'Hare, the young man started a new phase of life: a journey in the United States of America. Two days later, he would board a bus to South Bend, Indiana. Three and a half years on, he would finish at the University of Notre Dame with a PhD in chemical engineering.

***

As you may have guessed, that young man was me. I have been toying with the idea of telling my story for quite some time. The vague idea turned into resolve when Donald Trump rode a wave of anti-immigrant sentiment to a devastating victory in the 2016 US presidential election. It offended me deeply that he would callously demonize the immigrant community and seek to nullify its contributions to American society and its economy. I noticed some of his exuberant supporters among the customers at my local Starbucks proclaim how Trump would rid the country of immigrants "who were sucking up America's precious resources." They didn't bother to distinguish between legal and undocumented immigrants. For that matter, even undocumented immigrants make a net contribution to America and do the jobs native Americans won't do.

In the half-century since my arrival in America, the

country has made very significant progress in ridding itself of racial and anti-immigrant bias. Trump threatened to reverse both and take us back to square one. The story below will give the reader an idea of the societal mores at the time I arrived.

***

One night in the fall of my second year at Notre Dame, in 1966, I went barhopping in South Bend with two undergraduate friends. Jorge had come to Notre Dame from Bogotá, Colombia. The other guy, Arun, was originally from Mumbai and had been in the US for only a few months.

Jorge was both a white guy and a Latino. Going back a few generations, his family in Bogotá was pure Spanish. He spoke English without a Spanish accent, so people mistook him for a white American. Arun and I, in contrast, spoke accented English and were easily identifiable as immigrants from India.

We first went to a common hangout for Notre Dame students. It was a weekday and attendance at the bar was sparse, so we decided to try another bar.

Jorge had gone in the past with another friend of his, a car repairman, to a bar that could only be described as seedy. But this bar drew a crowd on weekdays, too. It was located on the eastern outskirts of South Bend, close to Mishawaka. Jorge suggested we head out there.

I would normally have had foreboding about going into a "blue-collar" bar. I was concerned about how we, as non-white immigrants, might be treated once we stepped out of the safe bubble of American academia. But the drink I had at the first bar had affected my judgment. Though he was quite sensitive, Jorge couldn't put himself into the shoes of two non-white immigrants unable to "pass." Arun was rash and had a gung-ho spirit. So off we went.

While Jorge and I nursed our drinks at one corner of the

bar, Arun spotted a couple of pretty women on the far corner. A white guy had been trying to engage their attention, without too much success. When Arun spied that the women were no longer speaking with this guy, he trotted over and introduced himself.

He hit it off with them. After a while, the man who had earlier been rejected addressed Arun aggressively.

"I am a white man. I don't like you talking to the white ladies here."

"Excuse me. It is none of your business who I speak with." Arun stood his ground.

"Oh, you talk funny too. Where did the cat drag you from?"

"Again, none of your business." Arun was getting rattled. Jorge and I went over to him.

"Hey, Arun. Don't you remember we promised to meet Steve at the West End Bar at eleven p.m.? We need to hurry," said Jorge with a note of urgency. That gave Arun a way to disengage while saving face, and we left.

We didn't talk of this incident later in any detail. But I was mortified, even though I had only observed and not experienced the racial offense. We had witnessed unfettered white privilege, the expectation that white men didn't have to, or shouldn't have to, compete against non-whites—that everything by right belonged to white men, including the women in the bar.

The final joke was on the hateful man in the bar. The women had rejected him, but one of them pressed her phone number on Arun.

I had been in the United States for a little over a year. This was my first observation of racism directed against an Indian person. The man's comments revealed the double edge of bigotry—Arun was non-white *and* an immigrant.

***

Immigrants to America have put in incredible hard work and sacrifice. They have had their share of disappointments. But quite often, they have had a sense of satisfaction and accomplishment. What hurts me most was how some Americans, like my fellow customers at Starbucks, have been egged on by Trump to see immigrants as threatening outsiders who encroach on their jobs and resources. I want my story to show how immigrants have overcome many obstacles on their way to becoming productive Americans. With the election of President Joseph Biden, I believe immigrants have a fresh opportunity to tell their stories.

Immigration has been part of the nation since its founding. Some immigrants' stories start with this or that. My story begins with an atlas. I landed in America with the dream of becoming a productive American, a journey that began much earlier and has continued for fifty-six years since that day.

CHAPTER 1

AN ATLAS

Nothing happens unless first we dream.
- Carl Sandburg, "Washington Monument at Night," 1922

Winters in Punjab are very pleasant. Days are glorious, bathed in bright sunshine. Temperatures may shoot upward of ninety degrees Fahrenheit but rarely, only for a brief swath of the day, and usually don't dip below forty degrees at night. Rains chase away the sun for a couple of weeks in December. These rains are heavy and a lifesaver for the most important crop of the Punjabi farmer—wheat. But the rains end quickly, the countryside dries up, and the leisurely pace of peasant activity resumes.

We called our father Bauji and our mother Bhabiji. The affix *ji* after a name in India is an indicator of respect, very much like *san* in Japan. "Bau" is an adaptation of the word *babu*, clerk. Bauji's initial assignment after joining the army as a private included the duties of a clerk. He rose through the noncommissioned ranks performing clerical and office management duties. He came to be called Babu by his army mates. The designation oozed out, as it were, to the outside world and into my family, where it got simplified to Bauji.

Young people in Indian households call their sisters-in-law Bhabiji. Bauji's much younger brother and sister followed tradition and called my mother Bhabiji. Since my older siblings grew up in the joint family, which included their uncle and aunt, they too started calling our mother Bhabiji. Neither Bauji nor Bhabiji used the family name of Minhas. My father was Chanan Singh and my mother Chint Kaur.

When I was nine, our family moved from our ancestral village of Daroli Khurd to another village, Dhandaur, in mid-1952. Our family had been allotted new farming land at Dhandaur, only a couple of miles away, in lieu of the land we lost in the province of Sindh, which had become a part of Pakistan after the 1947 partition of the country. I well remember the day we relocated. Our belongings were loaded on a couple of bullock carts. It was in the middle of the monsoon season and the rains were coming down hard, turning the rutted pathway to mud. The two-mile trip took upward of four hours!

Bauji planted the critical wheat crop on close to forty acres of land in October. What followed for our family and our neighbors in the village was a long-sought rest through early April, when harvesting would begin in earnest. Some chores continued unabated through the winter break. The cattle had to be tended to. Our herd included several water buffaloes, which we relied on for milk products. We had a mare, getting on in years, though she was still producing foals into 1954. We would occasionally saddle her up and ride her. My brother Ranbir, two and a half years older than me, and I would handle the domestic chores.

Bauji would take a well-earned vacation from grueling farm life by visiting friends in the nearby city of Jalandhar, about fifteen miles away, which housed the district administration's headquarters. Village life lacked all the services and utilities we take for granted in modern life, such as running water, power, sanitation, and paved roads. Those services were available in Jalandhar, though.

In the winter of 1953–1954, Bauji took an extended trip, first to Jalandhar, followed by several weeks in the nation's capital, New Delhi, 240 miles to the south and a ten-hour train ride away. We lost touch with him completely when he was gone; there were no phones at the time. A letter arrived mid-January, saying he would return in a few more weeks.

***

January 27, 1954, is etched in my memory. Aunt Banti had arrived in the morning from Daroli Khurd to visit for a few days. She was Bauji's first cousin and was greatly beloved by our family. Early that day, Ranbir and I set about carrying out our daily chores. We cut green fodder with scythes in a nearby field until we had accumulated enough to form two large bundles. We positioned the bundles on top of our heads with the help of passersby and carried them home. They were much heavier than anticipated since the fodder was still wet with the morning dew. In our youthful foolhardiness, we never worried what harm would result from carrying such heavy loads on our heads, particularly to the long-term health of our spines. (My need for multiple back surgeries as an adult can attest to this.)

The approximately two-foot-long fodder still needed to be chopped into small bites before it could be served to the animals. We had an interesting contraption for that, something you could call state-of-the-art machinery at the time. The hand-operated chaff-cutter machine consisted of a large wheel, about three feet in diameter, with a handle on one end. The wheel had two curved spokes, with a sharp blade mounted on each spoke. The hub of the wheel was mounted horizontally on a train of gears. A set of two horizontal gears, spaced about one inch apart, rotated in opposite directions, pulling the long fodder in. The fodder advanced and was chopped into half-inch pieces by the blades on the wheel. Ranbir and I took turns rotating the wheel of the chaff-cutter, which was not an easy machine to operate. Decades later, I saw such machines driven by one-horsepower electric motors. Of course, we turned the wheel manually much slower than an electric motor would. But still, for a young man just a month shy of his eleventh birthday to generate even a fraction of a motor's output called for a very considerable exertion of muscle power.

The arduous part of the day was over. We mixed the chopped green fodder with an equal volume of chopped wheat chaff and fed the animals. As they chewed contentedly on their meal, I turned to the pleasant activities of the day.

In honor of Aunt Banti, my mother had prepared two dishes for lunch, a dish made from cauliflower and potatoes (*aaloo-gobhi*) and another made from mustard greens (*sarson da saag*), both favorites of mine. The *sarson da saag* goes especially well with *makki di roti*, the Punjabi version of corn breads, which she had taken care to make plenty of.

I was homeschooled, so after lunch on this day, I pulled out my algebra textbook, which was the same one used by the tenth grade in the neighboring high schools. Because my schooling followed an unstructured sequence, I was ahead of public school students of my age in some subjects and behind in others. Whereas I was only eleven at the time, the average age of a tenth-grade student was fifteen.

I particularly enjoyed solving equations involving three variables. I would skip the ones I couldn't solve on the first try and move on. Later in the afternoon, I would return to the intractable problems, which appeared much less complicated than they had the first time around.

I glanced at the newspaper, which had just been delivered

by the mailman. My only connection to the rest of the world was the daily English newspaper, *The Tribune*. The news was outdated by two days, but we were grateful for the window to the world that the newspaper offered us. Bauji read the news and often translated the highlights for us. In his absence, I would content myself by looking at the pictures and trying to read the headlines.

On this day, January 27, a picture of the foreign ministers of the United States (John Foster Dulles), Britain (Anthony Eden), France (Pierre Mendes France), and the Soviet Union (V. Molotov) appeared on the front page. The news item said something about the Berlin Conference, which went right over my head. A few days earlier, I had seen a picture of Mamie Eisenhower launching the first nuclear-powered submarine in Groton, Connecticut. I remembered it because of Mrs. Eisenhower, the First Lady. The names Dulles and Eisenhower—that was pretty much all I knew of America on that languid afternoon. But this was about to change.

My brother and I spotted Bauji on his bicycle about a quarter mile away in the late afternoon and ran to greet him. He flashed a broad smile as we approached him. In the rush to reach him first, Ranbir pushed me and I tumbled down.

Half an hour later, I was still smarting from Ranbir's shove in a corner of the front room. It had a bed, a worn-out chair, and a rickety three-legged table next to the bed. I sulked as I sat on the bed, my legs dangling. Bauji appeared in the doorway, holding a large, shiny object, which looked less like a book than a lovely photo album. He sat down on the bed beside me.

Bauji told me that he had brought me an atlas of America. He had stopped by the United States Information Service (USIS) building in New Delhi and picked up the atlas. He handed it to me and invited me to look at it. I eagerly opened it and got a rush just from the feel and quality of the paper it was printed on.

The atlas was unlike anything I had ever seen. The pages were bright white and did not stick together, unlike the newspapers, magazines, and books in India, which had coarse yellowing paper that made turning pages a chore. I turned the pages of the atlas rapidly and took in the scenes of America—the skyscrapers, people boating and skiing, shopping malls, and information on each state such as population, capital city, and important land and water features. There were its gleaming airports and multilane highways.

Bauji explained that there was an amazing world out there that he never got to experience because he needed to go to work young to support the family—but I could see it. I could have a better life in a place like America, and education was the key, he said. The immensity of the possibilities that Bauji described dawned on me then. I was touched that Bauji had made this special effort.

Bauji stood up, squeezed my shoulder, and left the room. I had forgotten my squabble with Ranbir in the twenty minutes Bauji and I spent together. I took to the atlas as a parched person reaches for a drink of water. For the next hour, the world stood still as I thumbed through it.

The atlas greeted me with a picture of President Dwight Eisenhower, a name I remembered well from a few days before below the picture of his wife. The president's smile was hypnotic. I wondered how such a powerful man could also be so friendly. I remembered from past issues of *The Tribune* some scowling pictures of other world leaders. Joseph Stalin with his bushy mustache had appeared several months earlier when he died in March 1953.

There were the colorful maps of the United States and of each of its forty-eight states and territories (Alaska and Hawaii not yet admitted as states until 1959). I was mesmerized by the images of apparently famous men carved into a mountain.

Bauji explained that this site was called Mount Rushmore National Memorial and contained images of four noted American presidents.

America seemed so big and so full of energy. That night, when my family went to bed, I stayed awake. I imagined myself walking the streets of Chicago and New York, surrounded by towering skyscrapers. As crickets chirped in the night, I feverishly dreamed of moving to America one day, away from the mud houses and narrow lanes of my village. I wanted to be a part of this distant, very powerful, and glamorous land.

I shared my thoughts with Bauji the next morning. He encouraged me to keep dreaming big. He explained what he meant by "education was the key" to the fulfillment of my dream. I couldn't go to America as a tourist because we had no money. As my first order of business, I would need to learn English and become very fluent in the language. I was just starting to read and write English, so I had a long way to go. I would need to study very hard in Indian universities and earn basic degrees. The most promising path to moving to America and leading a professional life there would be to apply to American universities for postgraduate education (what Americans refer to as graduate school) and compete with people worldwide to land a spot, hopefully with a scholarship.

How did Bauji know all this? He had spoken with the people at the USIS Center in New Delhi who made these suggestions. Bauji made it very clear that not only would the suggested path require dedication and hard work, but I would also need to have a taste for risk-taking.

***

The reader may well understand the lure of America that the atlas sparked in me. But why didn't I want to live in India and try to better my life there? The answer, in a nutshell, was the crushing poverty all around me. It wasn't just the hard life on the farm. In 1954, the standard of living across the country was abysmally low. India's prime minister, Jawaharlal Nehru, was so exasperated with the slums even in the country's capital that he once described Delhi as a vast overgrown village. The city near our village, Jalandhar, on which we depended for crucial services, was one such overgrown village. The cities differed in one respect from the villages, though—they had access to running water and power.

Without running water, the houses in the villages lacked flush toilets. People went into the fields to relieve themselves. It was always a challenge to find fields with tall crops, which might provide some privacy, especially in the few months after the crops were planted and after they were harvested. To this day, I hold flush toilets in deep admiration. Only those who grew up without such conveniences can appreciate my sense of wonder and gratitude that modern toilets do such a remarkable job with so little water per flush.

My family always had enough to eat, even though the diet wasn't consistently nutritious. It almost never included meat because we couldn't afford it. We had a fair supply of grains, lentils, and vegetables, as well as milk and butter. The lentils supplied some protein. Others in the village weren't as lucky. They lacked basic food supplies for parts of the year. Life in the towns and cities of Punjab, for the vast majority of inhabitants, wasn't any better. At least in the villages, people could raise milk animals such as water buffaloes to ensure some access to dairy products. And Punjab was considered one of the richer states of India; poverty was worse elsewhere.

Four weeks before the day Bauji gave me the atlas, heavy rains had caused our roof to leak profusely, rendering the winter cold even more miserable. We had no space heaters, let alone fireplaces or central heating. Water dripped on the foot of my bed. At midnight I roused Ranbir, my sister Surjit, and Bhabiji to help me move the bed to a drier spot. The next morning, I found my quilt thoroughly soaked. I had to wait two days for the rain to stop and the sun to come out so the quilt could dry. In the meantime, the only option was to keep using the wet quilt and shiver.

It took even longer for our courtyard to return to its hard surface, about a week after the rains subsided. The courtyard wasn't paved and its drainage to the shallow ditch lining the street outside was shoddy. About half an inch of rainwater collected there, forming a tiny pond with a very muddy floor. To access the street, I had to trudge through the mud and the water.

But we were not alone in this. During the rains, all paths leading out of the village turned into mud as well. Although my family was one of the four or five in the village that owned a bicycle., which we relied on to go four miles away to Adampur for supplies and medicine, bicycles became useless in such conditions.

***

That atlas brought me an awareness of a wonderful, thriving, far-off country and piqued my desire for its standard of living, its efficient organization, and its political system, which offered choices to its citizens. I received the atlas in 1954, at a time when India suffered from abject and dehumanizing poverty with few opportunities for young people like me.

The event firmly set a goal in my mind—to use the vehicle of education to facilitate immigration to the United States, to join the millions before me who had moved to America from all corners of the world to escape poverty. Taking off for a distant country with no support system wasn't for the weak of heart, however. Unbeknownst to me then, my genes included risk-taking in spades.

CHAPTER 2

A FAMILY OF RISK TAKERS

Whatever you can do, or dream you can, begin it.
Boldness has genius, power and magic in it.
- Johann Wolfgang von Goethe, "Faust: A Tragedy ('Eine Tragodie')," 1808

I was the last child among seven. My parents' oldest, a girl, died while still an infant of a sickness left untreated because of a lack of medical care. Their second child was a son, Sarwan, born in 1925. Their next three children were daughters: Parkash (born in 1931), Gurmit (born in 1934), and Surjit (born in 1939). The sixth was a son, Ranbir; he was born in 1940. And I was the last one to arrive; I was born in 1943 in our ancestral village, Daroli Khurd.

My paternal grandparents, Wariam Singh and Rali Kaur, had no formal schooling. My best guess is that they were born around 1880–1885. All their grandchildren called them Bhayaaji (Grandpa) and Maanji (Grandma). Their first child, my dad, was born in 1902. Another son, Parsa Singh, was born in 1915. My older siblings called him Chachaji. He died at the age of thirty-one; I was only three at the time and don't remember him. A daughter, Gurbachan Kaur, was born in

1919 and passed away in 1989. We called her Bhuaji and loved her dearly.

Bauji's formal education ended after he matriculated at the end of the tenth grade in 1920. After a two-year gig in Basra, he enlisted as a sepoy (private) in the British Indian Army. He climbed steadily through the ranks to the top noncommissioned rank of subedar. He was granted permission at the age of forty-two to take the series of examinations for earning an officer's commission. He passed and was commissioned as a lieutenant in the army in 1944. Two years later he rose to the rank of captain. Bauji's most consequential posting was his last, where he served as the station staff officer (SSO) at Fort William in Calcutta. He took early retirement in 1949 when he was forty-seven. My family settled for a few years in Daroli Khurd and relocated in 1952 to the nearby village, Dhandaur, where Bauji set out to develop a farm, which he rapidly mechanized. My older brother, Ranbir, and I worked with him on the farm. We were homeschooled, by Bauji, for four years (1952–1956) and then by a tutor for one year (1956–1957). Bauji sold off the farm equipment in 1958 to finance our education and the farm was turned over to tenants. He and Bhabiji lived in Dhandaur for the rest of his life. Bauji's health deteriorated over the next decade. He suffered from asthma and Parkinson's disease. He passed away at the age of seventy-one in 1974.

My mother was born in 1904 in a village six miles away from Daroli Khurd. Unlike Bauji, Bhabiji never received an education. All her life she was unable to read and write. In her younger days, she was a relatively tall (five feet, seven inches), beautiful woman. While Bauji had an enormous influence on me as I was growing up, Bhabiji's influence on me was limited, though she was an honest and decent person.

Bhabiji stayed in Dhandaur after my father died. I had sponsored my sister Parkash for immigration to the United

States after I became a US citizen in 1974. Parkash's family arrived in the US in 1977 and settled down in Queens Village in New York City. Two years later, Bhabiji left Dhandaur to come live with Parkash. She remained healthy till she had a stroke at the age of ninety-two. She passed away four years later, in 2000.

***

I grew up in a milieu where the family name had long been forgotten and was rarely used by anyone. This may have been partly due to the purposefulness with which the tenth guru of the Sikhs, the religious community in India that I came out of, emphasized the names Singh ("lion") and Kaur ("princess") for male and female followers of the religion, respectively. Guru Gobind Singh was keen to abolish casteism among his followers. He achieved that by eschewing the traditional family name, which packed a lot of information, such as caste and even the region a person came from. All his followers would henceforth be Singhs and Kaurs, preceded by their first name.

Sikhism is a monotheistic religion that originated in the Punjab region of the Indian subcontinent around the end of the fifteenth century. It is based on the spiritual teachings of Guru Nanak (1469–1539). Nine gurus succeeded Nanak.

The Muslim rulers in Delhi viewed Sikhism with suspicion, as just another variant of Hinduism. Tensions between the rulers and the Sikhs became palpable around the time of the fifth guru, Arjan Dev (1563–1606), who was executed on the orders of the Mughal emperor Jahangir after refusing to convert to Islam.

The founding Sikhs stood out as paragons of risk-taking. They took to arms under the leadership of the sixth guru, Har Gobind (1595–1644). The tenth guru, Gobind Singh (1666–

1708), was a warrior and a philosopher. Born Gobind Rai, he founded the Sikh warrior community called Khalsa in 1699. He introduced the five Ks—the five articles of faith that Khalsa Sikhs wear all the time. They are *kesh* (hair and beard), *kangha* (a wooden comb), *kara* (an iron bracelet), *kachha* (a cotton undergarment), and *kirpan* (an iron dagger to defend oneself).

He assumed the last name Singh for himself and commanded his followers to do the same. He fought the forces of the Mughal emperor Aurangzeb most of his life and was assassinated by agents of the emperor.

Over three centuries have elapsed since the founding of the Khalsa. The population of the Sikhs grew mightily over this time. We number about twenty-five million worldwide; 83 percent of us live in India and 76 percent of all Sikhs are concentrated in the northern Indian state of Punjab.

As the Sikh community grew, it was faced with two major issues. The first was naming. For every Sikh to be called Mr. Singh or Ms. Kaur just wouldn't do. There were just too many of us, and massive name confusion was arising by the middle of the twentieth century. We had to get back to using the family name. My father had never before used the name Minhas. Nor had I, all through the end of my schooling in India. I had to face the issue squarely when I applied to graduate schools in the United States and, later, for an Indian passport. I opted to use the family name. Mine was not a solitary instance. The last time I visited my village in India, in 2010, just about everybody was a Minhas now.

Guru Gobind Singh also wanted his followers to allow hair to grow naturally out of respect for the perfection of God's creation. Another reason for the guru's commandment may have been more strategic. He was disappointed when some of his followers, under grave threat of torture or death by the Mughal empire, had passed themselves off as non-Sikhs. The guru's commandment worked. The Khalsa would willingly face death rather than shave, cut their hair, or remove their turbans. Now that we had moved away from his naming conventions, what were we going to do with the commandment to not cut body hair?

In the twenty-first century, cutting hair and shaving faces appear to be the modus operandi for young Sikh men everywhere. So very often I see pictures of elderly bearded and turbaned Sikh men next to their clean-shaven children and grandchildren. However, the three core tenets of Sikhism—meditation upon and devotion to the Creator, truthful living, and service to humanity—remain unchanged for the community.

Perhaps a close parallel can be found in the Jewish faith. The Hasidim, a subsect among the ultra-Orthodox Jews, strongly discourage their males from shaving beards and expect men to wear black hats. Following a Biblical commandment not to shave the sides of one's face, male members of the Hasidim sport long, uncut sidelocks. Using the parallel of Judaism, I view clean-shaven Sikhs as the "Reformed Sikhs" and the unshaven, fully turbaned Sikhs as the "Ultra-Orthodox Sikhs."

As I have grown older, I have found my religious beliefs evolving, taking me far beyond the moniker of a reformed Sikh. I grew up with full exposure to my religion and was duly reverential of our Sikh gurus. The religion taught us the omnipresence of one God. As the bounds of my knowledge expanded while I matured, my faith in the presence of a single powerful being, who watched over us and called us to account, weakened progressively. It became clear to me that throughout history people had deified phenomena beyond their understanding, lumping such experiences into their versions of God. A rational observer today can explain a great deal of what had been hitherto unfathomable.

Natural phenomena, such as the 1918 flu pandemic, the

Ebola outbreak of 2014, and the coronavirus pandemic of 2020, would at one time have been explained as acts of God, sent by an angry creator to punish humans. Today we have scientific explanations of the origin of these epidemics. At the tail end of the nineteenth century, human understanding of the cosmos exploded, and we realized humbly that our planet was but one speck of dust in the universe and there was so much more out there than humanity on earth. The concept of God keeping watch over humanity seemed quaint. It no longer felt rational to believe in God. So, I turned into an atheist.

But I have continued to embrace Sikhism, from the viewpoint of belonging and knowing from whence I came. My infrequent visits to the Sikh temples, called *gurudwaras*, serve to connect me socially with the Sikh community, not to pray to God.

But the matter of the family name remains. How did we get the name "Minhas"?

***

The Minhas name is associated with Sikh, Hindu, and Muslim Rajputs. Sikh Minhas Rajputs mainly inhabit the Punjab state of India. Hindu Minhas Rajputs reside in the Indian states of Jammu and Kashmir, Himachal Pradesh, and Punjab. Muslim Minhas Rajputs mainly reside in Pakistani Punjab.

Our ancestral story is traced back to King Jambu Lochan (1320–1290 BC), who ruled areas covering parts of Himachal Pradesh, Jammu, and Kashmir. Tradition has it that one day the king came to the Tawi area to hunt and while he was lying in ambush for his prey, he saw a tiger and a goat drinking water from the same pond. The king founded the city of Jammu on the site. The name of one of Jambu Lochan's descendants, Malan Hans Dev, got transformed first to Manhas (Ma–n + ha-s) and then to Minhas.

The origin of the Muslim branch of the Minhas clan is traced to Bhagir Dev, a son of the raja of Jammu. In 1190, Bhagir Dev had gone hunting to the Dhanni area (present-day Chakwal in the Punjab state of Pakistan). He fell in love with a local Muslim Gujjar woman, converted to Islam, and married her. The Muslim branch of the Minhas clan is concentrated in Chakwal and nearby Jhelum, both about sixty miles southeast of Islamabad, the capital of Pakistan.

The Sikh Minhas clan, from which I come, started out in five villages in Punjab—Daroli Kalan, Daroli Khurd, Dhamunda, Padhiana, and Paldi—all of which were established around the year 1530 by two Minhas brothers, Mati Dev and Anshupal.

We Minhas folk revere the warrior saint Mati Dev. He walked away from his own wedding ceremony to defend a nearby village that was under attack by Muslim marauders. He lost his life but gained a high place in our hearts as our protector, the ultimate risk-taker.

***

My grandfather, Bhayaaji, had a penchant for risk-taking and sufficient drive to travel to Canada in his twenties. He left in 1906, leaving behind my grandmother and my dad. Bauji was four years old when his father took off for Canada. For the five years Bhayaaji was away, Bauji and his mother stayed with our grandma's parents in a nearby village named Padori.

Bhayaaji worked in western Canada's timber industry, both as a lumberjack and in the timber mills. His story is consistent with contemporary accounts, which painted the lives of Indian workers in Canada in the early 1900s as being extraordinarily rough. They were subjected to virulent racism at the hands of white Canadians. He was in the first major wave of Indian immigrants who came to British Columbia, the vast majority of whom were Sikhs. Many were former British soldiers, policemen, and others who had worked in different parts of the British Empire.

The British Columbians of the time were determined to keep the state white. The media's reporting on immigrant workers exacerbated the fires of racial hatred and white discrimination. Major news headlines portrayed the new immigrants as dirty and diseased criminals, a threat to women and children. Stores would refuse to sell goods to the Sikhs, and landlords would not rent houses to them. The Sikhs were rounded up and taken to the outskirts of cities, where they were forced to live in abandoned buildings. Bhayaaji called it quits after five years, when he had saved enough money.

A few years later, the Canadian government passed the draconian Continuous Passage Act. This was meant to get around the inconvenient rule that, as British subjects, Sikhs had the right to travel freely anywhere in the British Empire, of which Canada was a part. The act mandated that potential Indian immigrants had to travel to Canada directly from their place of birth by continuous passage. They couldn't stop on the way or change ships. But there was no steamship company operating a direct route from India to Canada at that time. The act stopped the migration of Indians to Canada.

A Sikh businessman, Gurdit Singh, decided to challenge the act by chartering a ship called the *Komagata Maru*. The ship set sail from Hong Kong on April 4, 1914. It carried 376 Indians, mostly Sikhs. However, they were never allowed to disembark in Canada. Two months after arriving on the shores of Vancouver, the *Komagata Maru* was escorted out of Canadian waters under the guns trained on them by a navy cruiser.

More than a hundred years after the *Komagata Maru* sailed into Vancouver, Prime Minister Justin Trudeau offered a full apology in the House of Commons for the government's decision to turn away the ship. "The passengers of the

Komagata Maru, like millions of immigrants to Canada since, were seeking refuge and better lives for their families. With so much to contribute to their new home, they chose Canada, and we failed them utterly," Trudeau said. "As a nation, we should never forget the prejudice suffered by the Sikh community at the hands of the Canadian government of the day. We should not and we will not."

Bhayaaji's younger brother, Tara Singh, never married. He had been a private in the British Indian Army in the early 1900s. Around that time, the government had been developing farming areas in the Sindh province (now a part of Pakistan). A new system of canals had been built to carry water from the Indus River for irrigation. Sindh had a sparse population though, and the authorities had been keen to get farmers from adjoining provinces to move there. Servicemen were encouraged with grants of land to settle down in the area on separation from the army. Tara Singh accepted a plot of one hundred acres of land.

Members of the family started moving to the allotted farm outside Nawab Shah in Sindh in the mid-1930s. The family in Sindh was anchored around Bauji's younger brother, Parsa Singh (Chachaji). Bauji's sister, Gurbachan Kaur (Bhuaji) and her husband, Sansar Singh Janjua, along with Chachaji and his family, formed the core of the family branch that settled on the farm in Sindh.

The farm in Sindh did very well under Chachaji's stewardship. Cotton was the principal crop raised on the farm. Bauji and his brother persuaded our grandparents to move to the farm in Sindh in the late 1930s. Over time, my grandparents developed deep emotional ties to the farm. When the British partitioned India on August 15, 1947, the province of Sindh was apportioned to Pakistan. Bauji, an avid student of current affairs, had anticipated the separation. Several months earlier, he had gone to Sindh and gathered everyone, and moved the family back to Daroli Khurd, which was in the part of Punjab state that would stay in India. My grandparents refused to leave, however. The farm in Sindh was their home now.

Both my grandparents were shot to death within weeks of the partition of the subcontinent.

They had believed the assurances of the founder of Pakistan, Muhammad Ali Jinnah, who had envisioned Pakistan as a secular republic where Hindus and Sikhs would live in peace with the Muslim majority. My grandparents' assassins coveted the farm. They may also have been driven by revenge since they had been displaced from the Indian Punjab. The sad story was carried to us by a couple of neighbors, who had hidden and watched the shooting and later made their way out of Pakistan.

Bhayaaji, a proud man, took a big risk when he set off for the distant land of Canada to better his life, and it panned out well. Not one to indefinitely accept racial humiliation, he didn't linger in Canada any longer than necessary. The other big risk he took, staying behind in Pakistan, clearly did not.

Bhayaaji, despite the gruesome manner of his death, was a source of strength to me as I set about taking risks of my own after I studied the US atlas. Two other members of my family, Sarwan and Bauji, motivated me, too.

***

My brother Sarwan's childhood alternated between growing up on the farm in Sindh under the oversight of our uncle, Parsa Singh, and living with Bauji and the rest of the nuclear family in the different locations where Bauji was posted in army service. Sarwan was already eighteen at the time I was born. Before I came along, both Parsa Singh and Bauji home-schooled Sarwan. But the process was complicated. At the farm, there were many interruptions due to the numerous chores that needed Sarwan's attention. His instruction was better organized when he lived with our parents. Bauji was able to provide supervision and lay out the schoolwork for the day before leaving for the office.

Bauji told me an interesting story about Sarwan's precociousness. At the time, our mother, Bhabiji, was staying with the other children at Daroli Khurd. Sarwan was staying with Bauji at his army post. Sarwan was on his own during the day as Bauji worked. Bauji had a collection of Shakespeare's plays in the original English. Sarwan and Bauji developed a routine with these plays. Sarwan would read a whole play in a single day. As he accompanied Bauji on an evening walk, Sarwan would recount the story of the entire play in his own words, in fluent English.

Bauji had gone out on a walk one evening, accompanied by a friend and Sarwan, along a street of the army cantonment lined with trees on both sides. The trees were grown, with strong limbs and a thick growth of leaves forming lovely canopies. Sarwan gave an account of the play he had studied during the day. Bauji's friend was astonished by Sarwan's grasp of the story. Soon after Sarwan finished providing them with his takeaway of the play, the two adults drifted into an engaging conversation on some other topic. Perhaps fifteen minutes passed before they became aware that Sarwan was no longer with them. He was only twelve years old, so they got very concerned. They called out his name loudly and started scouring the street for signs of his presence. Suddenly they were startled by a loud giggle. Sarwan had climbed a tree, high enough to be almost invisible from the ground, cloaked by the lush spread of leaves below him. This scholar of Shakespeare was still a boy, with tons of youthful energy and mischief.

In 1942, Sarwan sat for the matriculation examination in Karachi, the capital of Sindh province. Karachi was one of the foremost cities of British India. It was about 120 miles from our farm. The examination, which was conducted by the University of Karachi across the entire province of Sindh, marked the end of the first ten grades of school. Since Sarwan had never formally attended school, he was allowed to appear for this important examination as a "private" candidate. He passed with honors.

The education system in India was structured through most of the twentieth century to provide a major milestone at the end of ten grades of school, leading to matriculation. Formal education for most students ended at this point, at least in the first half of the century. Students desiring higher education would then enter an intermediate "college" and complete grades eleven and twelve. Upon completion of these two grades, they took standardized examinations. Those who passed these examinations were awarded the Faculty of Sciences (FSc) or Faculty of Arts (FA) certificates.

(Pilot Officer Sarwan Singh, at Ambala Station of the Indian Air Force, 1946)

Sarwan took a different path.

Six months after matriculating, he competed for admission to the Indian Military Academy (IMA) at Dehradun and was accepted for training at the end of 1942. He graduated from the academy after two and a half years of training. He was commissioned as a pilot officer (the equivalent of a second lieutenant in the army) in the Royal Indian Air Force in mid-1945.

The British rulers had been strongly opposed to the idea of commissioning Indian officers in the early 1900s. But their attitudes softened following the Indian military performance in World War I. They agreed to annually admit ten Indians to the Royal Military College, Sandhurst in England. After sustained pressure from Indian leaders, the British established the IMA, which began training in October 1932. Admission to the academy was very competitive. Only thirty-two candidates were accepted from all over India, to be trained for the three branches of the military—army, air force, and navy.

As I was only two and a half years old when Sarwan was commissioned as an officer, I can't quite remember what he looked like. My only impression of him is in the few pictures he left behind. I do have a memory of him during a visit he paid to our home in Daroli Khurd a few months before he graduated from the academy. The whole family was there at the time, with the exception of Bauji, who was away at his army post. Sarwan had washed his hair and let it down behind his back so it could dry. I was struck by how long his hair was. Years later, I was told that I made quite a stir in wanting to see the contents of his tall suitcase. I was small and couldn't see what was inside. He picked me up with a flourish and deposited me in the midst of his clothing so I could get a good look. I vaguely remember how loving he was with all the children.

Sarwan was scheduled to go on a two-month annual leave a year after he was commissioned, in mid-1946. His promotion to flying officer (equivalent to a full lieutenant in the army) was scheduled after he returned from leave. The whole family was living at the time with Bauji at his latest posting in Aurangabad, in southern India. Sarwan had spent only brief periods of time with the family in the preceding four years during some short visits, each lasting a couple of days. When the family learned that he planned to spend the vacation with us, everyone was delighted. Bhabiji prepared a special treat for Sarwan. It was a sweet dish called *pinni*. We kids had contributed to it too. We harvested almonds from the almond tree in the yard, and Bhabiji added them to the dish.

Sarwan had planned to take the train from his air force

base in Ambala, Punjab, to Aurangabad, a thirty-six-hour journey. One day before the date of departure, Bauji received a telegram. Sarwan had been killed when his plane crashed during a training flight. He was twenty-one at the time.

Investigations revealed that Sarwan was one of the brightest young pilot officers. His flying skills were admired by his fellow pilots and his superiors. What his colleagues knew, and his superiors didn't, was his penchant for extreme risk-taking and daredevilry. His fellow officers revealed that he used to engage in daring acrobatics with his plane, such as flying under telegraph wires.

Eyewitnesses to the fatal accident saw him engage in risky maneuvers. He would fly the plane straight up and then take it through a complete 360-degree flip. Another time he flew straight down, intending to carry out the same 360-degree flip in reverse. It wasn't clear if he was attempting to get as close to the ground as he could before turning around. People saw a fireball erupt in the engine when he attempted to pull up the plane. It straightened out from its dive, shuddered violently, and then headed nose-first straight into the ground.

In the span of a year, Sarwan had mastered aerial combat maneuvers very well. But he pushed himself and the plane, and this time, the plane failed him. Sarwan's zeal for risk-taking, though excessive, guided me in life. That his gamble failed him illustrates the very nature of risk. Things can go sideways. Abject failure is always a possibility.

***

Of all members of my family, I admired Bauji the most. I would argue that Bauji had one of the sharpest minds ever, even though during my long career, I have dealt directly with many people from the top rungs of big corporations and have had very sharp colleagues, plenty with advanced degrees. Often, while I struggled with complex concepts, his grasp of the same would be lightning quick. What made Bauji different was that his keen intelligence was leavened with human warmth. Knowledge can be accumulated and training can sharpen one's skills, but there is no substitute for natural intelligence.

The nearest high school where Bauji could attend for ninth and tenth grades was in Jalandhar. He stayed at a boarding house near the school. For the occasional trips home, he had to walk the fifteen miles; there were no buses and trains and he didn't own a bicycle.

In the crucial tenth grade, he suffered from a lingering eye infection for most of the year. He could not study for the all-important final examinations. He organized a study group where others would read the books and then the group would discuss the subject matter. He managed to place in high first division in the matriculation examination, ranking second in his class, without the benefit of reviewing his books with his own eyes.

He would have been a natural candidate for the intermediate college and then a four-year-degree college. Unfortunately, his family needed him as a wage earner. By this time Bhayaaji's savings had run dry. The family's land holdings in the village were meager, no more than a couple of acres. An opportunity arose soon after Bauji matriculated. If he could cobble together a recruiting fee of two hundred rupees, he would have a good shot at a job that would pay a monthly salary of two hundred rupees and would last two years. Two hundred rupees then was an impressive sum. He landed the job and promptly shipped out to the port city of Basra in Mesopotamia, today's Iraq.

At the end of his gig in Basra, Bauji returned and enlisted as a private in the army. Because of his academic bent and good facility with the English language, he was assigned clerical jobs. At every step of his army career, Bauji had to put up a struggle to be moved up to the next higher level. He performed so well that his British superiors made it very clear that they didn't want to lose him to a promotion.

Bauji found himself stymied at the age of forty-two in the highest noncommissioned rank of subedar. He had the ability and the intellect to be an officer. He put up a fierce struggle to persuade his British superiors to grant him permission to take the requisite tests, which were very exacting physically and academically. This permission was granted with considerable reluctance. Years later he told me the following story with relish.

One of the physical tests required him to jump over an obstacle with a rope. In the middle of the swing, the rope broke and my father landed on the hard ground with a thud. His examiner, a British officer, walked over.

"Are you dead yet?" asked the examiner with irritation and no sympathy.

"Not at all, sir. I am good to go for another swing," replied Bauji cheerfully, with a huge smile.

The examiner, chagrined, skulked away.

Bauji passed and was commissioned as a lieutenant. He was promoted to captain in 1946. Our family lived in a large bungalow in Jalandhar Cantonment. We were still there in the wake of India's partition in August 1947, when I was four years old. The neighboring area had burst into riots between Sikhs and Hindus on one side and Muslims on the other. Bauji was on a short assignment in another city at the time, but I could hear the explosions and the discharge of firearms from our bungalow.

Long friendships were torn asunder overnight with the partition of the Indian subcontinent. A Muslim army officer, a good family friend, was our neighbor. He would sometimes babysit me. My siblings and I thought nothing of walking over to his adjacent bungalow to play. I once ventured over there after the start of the riots. He was kind as before, but he urged me to return to our house. Bhabiji was distraught when she learned of my visit to the neighbor. She ordered me never to return to that "Muslim's house." That her feelings would undergo a sea change overnight shocked me deeply, even at that young age. I remember the man's affection and kindness, though I don't recall anything about his own family. Was he a bachelor officer? Did he have a premonition of the partition, the way Bauji did? Perhaps he had sent his family to a safer place ahead of the riots.

I have been described by the family as a gregarious child. I would take quickly to new acquaintances and was easily attached to friends of my parents. But this Muslim officer was special. I don't remember any specifics, but he was loving to us kids, just like our father. How could Bhabiji say such terrible things about the man we all loved? I remember crying as she heaped denunciation on Muslims in general and this one in particular. I had no answers, and Bauji wasn't there to assuage my hurt or to help me understand, as he usually did.

Bauji was in deep conversation with a visiting friend once. But I had something "important" to share with him. I was talkative and impatient as a child. I tugged at his chin and nudged his face toward me. His anger at the sudden interruption quickly dissolved as he and his friend realized the humor of a child physically turning his father's face to the urgent matter at hand. Both of them burst out laughing. I was surprised and a bit nonplussed. What could be so funny? Was it me?

Bauji was transferred to Jabalpur in Central India in late 1947, not long after the riots of partition. The family would accompany him, but Bauji was concerned about my sister Gurmit's education. Twelve at the time, Gurmit had shown academic promise, and a move would interrupt her schooling. Bauji believed so strongly in equal opportunity for education that he put her in a boarding school in Jalandhar. The fees for room and board were significant, but Bauji did not hesitate, despite the fact that this was at a time when women's education in India was an exception rather than the rule.

The stint in Jabalpur lasted eight months. He was transferred in May 1948 to Madras (today's Chennai), on the Bay of Bengal. There I had my introduction to the ocean when our family went to the beach. I was astonished by the immensity of the ocean; it spread as far as the eyes of a five-year-old could see. I saw the silhouettes of at least four ships over the horizon. Bauji told me the ships had made a long trip from faraway England and now they were headed to the harbor. When we went home, I tried to float the teaspoon in my teacup as an attempted demonstration of the ability of ships to float.

Alas, the spoon sank every time.

We also made a trip to the harbor. The harbor had been dredged and prepared for berthing ships relatively recently and was a novelty at the time. Before this, travelers boarded a tender, which ferried them to a ship anchored a few miles from the shore. This experience can be seen in the movie *The Man Who Knew Infinity*, when the mathematics prodigy Srinivasa Ramanujan left for England in March 1914.

My dad, Captain Chanan Singh, in Calcutta a few months before taking early retirement from the Indian Army, 1949

My family moved again in January 1949, when Bauji was appointed the SSO of Fort William in Calcutta (Kolkata). The fort was built by Robert Clive in 1781 on the eastern banks of the River Hooghly, the major distributary of the River Ganges, during the early years of the Bengal residency of British India.

It was named for King William

III of England. In front of the fort was the Maidan, which used to be a part of the fort and today is the largest urban park in Kolkata. The fort was immense, spreading over 170 acres. Today it houses the headquarters of the Indian Army's Eastern Command. It has provisions for accommodating ten thousand army personnel.

Although the British had technically departed India after the country's independence on August 15, 1947, several British officers stayed behind at the request of Indian leadership. Their experience was invaluable in completing the transfer of expertise to their Indian colleagues, both in the armed forces and in the Indian Civil Service. The transition was largely completed in two years.

One of Bauji's initiatives was to open up the fort to the general public in the form of guided tours. Visitors came in throngs, and the resulting goodwill for the army of a newly independent India was immense.

Bauji's office was only a ten-minute walk from where we lived, inside the fort. I recall going there one day. A very superior officer, an English brigadier general, was visiting. This wasn't a surprise, since Fort William housed a large part of the army's top brass. Bauji's office appeared huge to a five-year-old. But Bauji was not seated behind his desk as usual. He was standing up, chatting with the general, who was comfortably seated in the visitor's chair.

"Sir, this is my son, Sardul. He is almost six," said Bauji to the general.

"Delighted to meet you, young man. What do you do really well?" asked the general. I didn't comprehend, as I spoke only Punjabi.

"Sir, he can salute very well."

"Then go ahead, salute," commanded the general, looking intently at me. Bauji told me in Punjabi to salute the sahib. I saluted him smartly.

The Englishman was so pleased he promptly pulled out a rupee coin as a reward.

"No, sir, that won't be necessary. Your appreciation is reward enough," said Bauji. Addressing me in Punjabi, he said, "Beta, give the coin back to the sahib." *Beta* is a term of endearment, used by parents for children.

I harbored a pained expression as I reluctantly parted with the shiny coin.

Bauji served as an officer for only five years. In the waning days of British rule, the army had anticipated the need for home-grown leadership, drawn from Indian officers to fill the void left by departing British general officers. A commission had reviewed the records of promising officers from the lower ranks and drawn up a list for quick promotion to the rank of colonel. For many of these officers, the recommendation meant skipping several ranks. My father had been included in this list.

However, after India gained independence, the list was ignored by the new top brass. Bauji considered the army leadership's lack of follow-up unfair and challenged it. He laid it on the line: "Either respect the recommendations of the commission or let me retire." The army let him retire. My family returned to our village in Punjab.

I saw Gurmit, the sister we had left behind, after two years. At our reunion, the first thing she did was gather me in her arms and twirl me around joyously. Of all my siblings, I have felt most closely connected with Gurmit.

After Bauji's retirement in 1949, we lived in our ancestral village, Daroli Khurd, for about three years. He established a new farm in a nearby village, Dhandaur. Dhandaur had been populated exclusively by Muslims and had emptied out after India's partition, as its inhabitants left for Pakistan. The houses were constructed of mud. They leaked profusely when it rained.

I got deeply involved with the farm operations, even though I was only ten when Bauji started the farm. He acquired a Ferguson tractor. By today's standards, it was a puny machine, rated only at twenty-six horsepower. But at the time it was quite the wonder within a radius of thirty or so miles. Several farming implements followed in short order: a single-furrow and a double-furrow plow, a nine-furrow tiller, a weeder, a seed drill for planting wheat, and a trailer for hauling large loads. My feet were not long enough to push the clutch and the brake all the way down, so I would stand up from the seat to extend my reach. I was soon able to take out the tractor and plow a whole field by myself.

As Bauji was establishing the farming operations, one incident left a deep impression on me. A marauding bull got loose. It was destroying crops. There was, and remains, a deep cultural and religious reluctance in India to hurt cows, oxen, and bulls, even among non-Hindus—but still an angry farmer took a hatchet and cut one of the animal's legs deeply. A crowd trailed the limping bull as blood gushed from the open wound. Someone was sent to fetch Bauji; they figured he would know what to do. But when he saw the animal's wound, all color drained from Bauji's face. So shocked was he by the severity of the wound that he fainted. People quickly transferred him to a cot and someone administered a shot of whiskey, which revived him. He and others prepared a bandage and applied it to the bull's wound. They arranged to restrain the bull in the same spot for a few days. They fed him and kept a close eye on him. The bull's wound healed and he was released. My memory is vague about whether he went back to destroying crops.

Why did Bauji faint at the sight of the bull's wound? This was the first time I saw him react with such intense emotion. He normally sought to keep his emotions in check and maintain a placid temperament. But he held a deep sensitivity to suffering, of humans and animals alike. He felt the animal's pain and anguish and was overcome by it.

Bauji fell ill in the fall of 1954 and had to sit out the crucial wheat planting season, September and October. These activities fell on the shoulders of Ranbir and me. I was eleven and my brother fourteen. The two of us planted wheat on close to forty acres of land. As Bauji recuperated, I would read to him from the many English books that populated his library. Then I would discuss the contents with him, in English and in Punjabi. That winter was very fruitful for my studies, as I made significant progress in learning the English language.

I attribute the special zeal with which I approached my studies to that American atlas I received in January 1954. The goal of immigrating to America had been seeded by the atlas, and learning English was an important first step. The qualities of self-confidence and hard work that I acquired on the farm, in no small part thanks to the independence of my labor, helped me realize that goal. I credit my dad for teaching me to dream big. He would ask, "Why not you?"

My homeschooling through the first ten grades also nurtured my ambition. Ready access to Bauji's library inculcated in me the love of reading. His collection had such classics as Victor Hugo's *Les Misérables* and Thomas Hardy's *Tess of the d'Urbervilles*. I first read them at the age of twelve and read them again a year later. What a difference a year would make in comprehension! My approach to learning mathematics was to make it enjoyable and challenging. When I ran into an intractable problem, I would continue on to the next. When I returned to it a few days later, the exercise was no longer so unmanageable. The sheer joy of solving difficult math problems was indescribable. Mathematics has continued to be a joy all my life.

***

It was a point of pride for Bauji that he managed to educate all three of his sons—Sarwan, Ranbir, and myself—privately at home. All of us grew up on farms and mixed our learning with hard farming activities. Self-confidence, respect for the dignity of labor, and love of learning emerged in us alongside the practical things we were taught.

Risk-taking was going to be an important prerequisite for fulfilling my dream of immigrating to America one day. My grandfather Bhayaaji and my brother Sarwan had it in abundance. So did my dad. His taking off for Mesopotamia at the age of eighteen, laying it on the line with his army superiors twice—winning promotion to commissioned officer and later resigning in the wake of the unfulfilled recommendation of the military commission—and, most important of all, taking on the task of his sons' education in his unique way, all called for an enormous appetite for taking risks.

CHAPTER 3

UNIVERSITY BOUND

Before everything else, getting ready is the secret of success.
 - Henry Ford, "My Life and Work," 1922

That homeschooling in the village would lead me to university was not a given. There were huge gaps in my education by the time I was twelve. I could spare only meager time for studies thanks to the farming chores. I had more time to study in the winter after the main crop of wheat had been planted in October. But the household chores, including tending to the livestock, always beckoned.

My studies had been mostly centered around mathematics. My study of English was disorganized and lacked a firm understanding of grammar. My knowledge of history and geography was spotty. I had not studied any sciences to date, such as chemistry and physics. My knowledge of the Hindi and Punjabi languages and literature was rudimentary. Bauji chose the same route for Ranbir and me as he had for Sarwan: we would appear for matriculation examination as private candidates. But he recognized the need for formal training if we were to be successful.

Bauji rented a house in the summer of 1956 in a neighboring city, Hoshiarpur, about fifteen miles from Dhandaur. At the time, this city was an important education center. After India's partition in 1947, Government College, Hoshiarpur had been upgraded to house the fledgling Panjab University, the Indian part of the much older University of Punjab in Lahore, which was now in Pakistan. The college was renamed Panjab University College. It reverted to the original name in the early 1960s after all departments had moved to Chandigarh, where the university had a brand-new campus.

Ranbir and I left the farm that summer for Hoshiarpur and focused on our studies exclusively for the first time ever. Our parents stayed in the village. Gurmit would start her final year in the three-year BSc (Honors) chemistry program that fall. She had been staying in the women's dormitories, but she moved into the rented house with Ranbir and me. The house was in a relatively new development known as Railway Mandi on the city's outskirts, close to the railway station. Bauji found an excellent tutor for us, Mela Ram.

Neither Ranbir nor I had ever sat for a formal examination. It fell to Mela Ram to assess our strengths and weaknesses and prepare us for the matriculation examination. We had vast areas of subject matter to master. It didn't help that we were encountering much of it for the first time. Mela Ram put us through a grueling program of studies in the next nine months. He had us do science experiments in the labs of a nearby high school, though we had never set foot in a school lab before.

The nine-month period, from June 1956 through March 1957, was one of immense work. Mela Ram would tutor us for ninety minutes a day, six days a week. He would assign us punishing amounts of homework, due the following day. In hindsight, what amazes me is how it never occurred to me that I was being driven mercilessly. I embraced all the work I had to do because I didn't know any different. Perhaps my age—I was thirteen years old for most of the tutoring—helped cushion the blow of hard work. All I remember is the sense of excitement and wonder with all the new material that Mela Ram guided us through.

One Saturday during the summer of 1956, Bauji was visiting from the village. Gurmit seemed to be in awe as she described how hard we were working. We sat at a long table inside one room, with the windows open. On particularly hot days and evenings, we would move the table to the open area of the second floor. We had no fans. We would sweat profusely and work right through. The table lamp would attract an army of moths, some of which missed their target and landed in our flowing hair (as we wouldn't be wearing turbans indoors). We were a mess. Gurmit wondered how we could keep working, unbothered by the extreme discomfort. But it never occurred to me not to complete the homework. In the back of my mind lurked the notion that I didn't want to let Bauji down. He had made a huge sacrifice. He lost our help on the farm. And setting up a new household in the city was expensive.

Bauji had made a mighty effort in our absence to keep the farm going, but his poor health made it impossible to continue. He sold off the farm machinery in 1958 to finance our education. He let portions of our farm out to tenants, which would guarantee cash flow for the next several years.

Ranbir and I took the matriculation examination in March 1957. The upshot of all the hard work of the previous nine months was a happy one; both of us passed in the first division. My brother and I were now at the same level of formal schooling. I had turned fourteen and he was sixteen at the time of our matriculation. I was two years younger than most of my fellow students when we enrolled as full-time students in the FSc nonmedical program at Panjab University College in August 1957.

The FSc program was equivalent to the final two years in an American high school. I had a concentration of mathematics, chemistry, physics, and English, with the Hindi language elected as an optional subject. The material was rigorous. Ranbir and I sat for the final FSc examination in the spring of 1959. Both of us placed in the first division and earned high enough marks to be accepted to Panjab University, Chandigarh.

In the meantime, our sister Gurmit had completed her chemistry studies and earned her MSc (Honors) degree in chemistry. She married a freshly minted chemistry PhD, Sarjit Singh Sandhu, in the summer of 1959.

I had two key challenges during those two years at Panjab University College—adapting to a regular school schedule and learning social skills. All those years on the farm made me self-sufficient in many ways, but they deprived me of the opportunities to develop the skill set to get along and bond with fellow students. This process of acquiring social skills started at Panjab University College and continued through the rest of my life.

(Me, at Panjab University College, Hoshiarpur, December 1958)

In my early life, the absence of kids my own age left a void that I have never quite been able to fill. Kids learn to strike up a tone of easy camaraderie with their peers as if through osmosis, but my tool kit wasn't overflowing with social skills and street smarts.

CHAPTER 4

PANJAB UNIVERSITY

A university should be a place of light, of liberty, and of learning.
- Benjamin Disraeli, "Speech, House of Commons," March 11, 1873

As I was casting around for a university major in June 1959, my new brother-in-law, Sarjit Singh Sandhu, suggested that I consider chemical engineering. Until that point, I had never heard of chemical engineering. I had only the vaguest notion of other engineering fields, such as electrical, civil, and mechanical.

Sandhu's recommendation should not come as a surprise. I had performed exceptionally well in mathematics in the matriculation and FSc examinations, earning an almost-perfect score in each. I had done well in chemistry, too. The natural bias of Gurmit and Sarjit toward chemistry and my love of mathematics clearly (to them) pointed the way toward chemical engineering.

The closest institute offering a chemical engineering major at the time was Panjab University, located in Chandigarh, then a modern city about six hours by bus from my home. The school was very new; I would be in the second batch of students admitted to the program.

In August 1959, I boarded a rickety bus at Adampur Doaba, three miles from my village. The bus would take me to Jalandhar, where I would board a slightly more comfortable bus for Chandigarh.

***

If anyone can claim to be the father of Panjab University, it was Amar Chand Joshi. Joshi was the vice chancellor, equivalent to a university president in America. The meticulously modern campus of Panjab University is credited to the able planning and farsightedness of the chief architect of the university, Pierre Jeanneret, but Joshi examined all the plans in great detail.

Joshi was awarded the doctor of science (ScD) degree in 1937 by Punjab University (also called the University of Punjab). He held the vice chancellorship of the university from 1957 through 1965. Joshi was a dynamic educational leader. His most creative period followed his departure from Panjab University in July 1965 to become the education advisor to India's Central Planning Commission. During the two-year period at the Planning Commission, he undertook a keen study of the educational problems of the country and made recommendations, which had a considerable impact on the teaching of science in Indian universities.

The campus was humming with construction in my first year there. The only department building to have been completed when I arrived was the massive white building that primarily housed the chemical engineering department; about one-third of it housed the pharmacy department. The administrative offices at the front of the building, where our department head and his staff worked, were particularly fetching.

About a decade later, the entire front wing was taken over by the office of the vice chancellor.

(During a visit in 2010, I discovered that the front wing had been partitioned off from the rest of the building; the latter continued to house the chemical engineering department. But the facilities had degraded terribly. The stone steps of the grand staircase were chipped so badly that they were dangerous to climb. The white building that I knew had turned gray. The main hallways were very poorly lit and appeared not to have been painted in a long time. The department head's office in the rear of the building had cracked windowpanes and chipped and threadbare furniture.)

(Department of Chemical Engineering, Panjab University, Chandigarh, circa 1963)

Joshi established a close collaboration with the Illinois Institute of Technology, Chicago (IITC) to jump-start the newly formed chemical engineering department. Professor Ralph Peck from IITC headed the department in the beginning and laid the foundation of the curriculum. Joshi had arranged for the delivery of the major equipment from the United States under the PL-480 aid program, administered by the Office of Food for Peace. The office was created when President Dwight Eisenhower signed the Agricultural Trade Development and Assistance Act in July 1954, commonly known as Public Law (PL) 480.

Joshi and Peck did a great job with procurement. The

machine shop had the latest lathes and metalworking machinery. The electrical engineering lab had an assortment of transformers and synchronous and induction motors. The mechanical engineering lab had massive power hammers, wood saws, and an elaborate foundry section. The unit operations lab had the most modern equipment at the time, including a complex piping system for fluid flow studies, a spray dryer, a multiple effect evaporator, crushing and grinding equipment, and the equipment to study unsteady-state heat transfer.

Peck was very polite with students and teachers alike. He strove hard to learn Indian customs. Even though I was a lowly freshman—all right, there were only two classes in the department at the time, so perhaps that designation wasn't as meaningful—I would make an effort to speak with him as often as I could. I wanted to understand what Americans were like, since the goal of immigrating to America was always in the back of my mind. But Peck was very hard to understand. I wished he would slow down while speaking. I learned that he had grown up in the Canadian province of Ontario and had moved to the United States during his academic career.

Peck once showed me how to use a slide rule. I had just purchased one, with the brand name Aristo Studio. I had mastered the use of log tables at Panjab University College, Hoshiarpur for performing numerical calculations. Moving to a slide rule was a major step up. We didn't dream of Texas Instruments (TI) calculators at the time, let alone desktop and laptop computers.

One of my classmates, Kapil Dev Sharma, observed my interaction with Peck closely. He was jealous and tried to make fun of me by noting that "you crept so close to Peck that you almost disappeared in his armpit." I ignored his accusations of brown-nosing.

I learned some interesting things about Peck fifty-five

years later from my graduate school thesis advisor, Peter Skelland. On the strength of some of Skelland's publications, while he worked for Procter & Gamble in the UK, Peck sent him an offer for an assistant professor position at IITC in 1962. Skelland had gotten an assurance from another professor that he would be given several weeks to get his bearings before he would be expected to assume a full teaching load.

So Skelland flew into Chicago, and Peck met him at O'Hare Airport. The following conversation ensued.

"Everyone in the department is so excited to have you, Peter. They can't wait to get to meet you."

"I have heard so many good things about the IITC and am looking to be a part of it. Thanks for picking me up, Ralph."

"We have an orientation program set up in the morning. Your full teaching schedule is ready and the students are eagerly awaiting your lectures. They start the following morning."

Skelland was stunned. He felt like he was asked to change a tire on a moving car. It took him four months to acquire some sense of normality.

I was sad to hear of Peck's death from cancer at the age of seventy-one in 1982.

Peck hired a brilliant academic, Bimalendu Ghosh, to succeed him as the department chair. Ghosh had an excellent pedigree—he had earned a doctorate in chemical engineering at Carnegie Institute of Technology in Pittsburgh. Ghosh was an excellent teacher. I took several courses with him, including industrial stoichiometry, thermodynamics, engineering economics, and chemical plant design. I enjoyed his lectures; they were bright and witty, and he could cut right to the heart of an issue. One negative mark against Ghosh was his disinterest in chemical engineering research—in his long tenure of over twenty years as the department head, he didn't set up graduate-level research. At the time, India needed universities that would excel in both teaching and research. At least in the field of chemical engineering, Panjab University remained known only as a teaching university.

I caught an interesting glimpse of a different side of Ghosh several years later, in 1964, when I was studying for my master's degree at the Indian Institute of Technology (IIT), Kharagpur. IIT hosted the annual meeting of the Indian Institute of Chemical Engineers, and Ghosh was to present a short paper on "unsteady state drying and a proposal for follow-up studies." We met up for coffee.

"How are things in Chandigarh? How is the department doing?" I asked.

"We have established a master's degree program. Things are going well."

"I saw the synopsis of your paper for tomorrow's session. It proposes follow-up research. Glad you are moving the department into research."

"Well, not quite. I put something together to justify this trip," admitted Ghosh with a wink.

Until that moment, I had never doubted Ghosh's integrity, though my image of him changed in an instant.

Another faculty member, Dr. Kaul, was hired as a reader, which is equivalent to an associate professor at an American school, after he claimed to be a PhD in mechanical engineering from a British university. Joshi had met him on a visit to the UK and made the offer without conducting a thorough check of his credentials. The man had never earned a PhD. Kaul was a handsome, young Kashmiri man. He seemed to have struck up a good friendship with Ralph Peck and dated Peck's daughter as well.

Kaul lasted about a year. I took a couple of first-year courses from him. He was lost with the subject matter and was unable to answer even elementary questions, such as the correct resolution of mechanical stresses in a structural frame.

Word got around that the man was a fraud. He left the department toward the end of my first year.

Among the good faculty at Panjab University, of which there were many, Principal Vidya Chandar stands out. He had retired from the prestigious position of principal at Government College, Ludhiana, and had started teaching many areas of mathematics at our department to fill in during a critical faculty shortage. He would often regale students with stories from Lahore, where he had taught before the partition of India. Not only were his lectures interesting and fun, but he interacted with us with a gentle and humane touch.

While Chandar did an excellent job teaching all the introductory mathematics in the first two years, we suffered from a lack of rigorous instruction in applied chemical engineering mathematics. The faculty just didn't have anyone with advanced degrees in chemical engineering with a sound foundation in applied mathematics. As a result, I later had to take extra math courses in graduate school at the University of Notre Dame.

P. S. Lele was another good faculty hire. Lele had earned his PhD in chemical engineering from the prestigious Banaras Hindu University (BHU). He had the advantage of having worked alongside Octave Levenspiel, the groundbreaking chemical engineering professor, while on a post-doc fellowship at IITC. Lele brought back ideas and concepts that were still very nascent in the field, ideas incorporated into a well-regarded book Levenspiel would publish a few years later.

The students who took an elective course with Lele, including me, were indeed fortunate. Along with three fellow students, I published a paper under Lele's guidance, in our senior year, in the prestigious *Chemical Age of India* journal. This was a rare accomplishment at the time. I was told three years later, when I started at Notre Dame, that this publication was one reason my application to graduate school stood out.

I was fortunate to have had another good teacher, K. S. N. Raju. He taught me to pay attention to the fundamentals of chemical engineering. I credit him for my acquisition of a solid academic base while I was an undergraduate. That base served me very well when tackling the challenges of graduate school. Mr. Raju (yes, he lacked a PhD at the time but would acquire one later) was not flashy. He was a pleasant, quiet man, not at all eager to carve out his own little fiefdom in the department, as some professors were. I learned the value of humility from him. At challenging periods in my career, Raju's face would flash in my mind's eye. The memory would help me take a calm, detached look at whatever problem I was facing.

My connection with Raju had a sad epilogue. Forty-seven years after I last saw him, I visited India in 2010. I wrote up my impressions in an Indian newspaper, *The Hindu*. Raju saw my piece and contacted me. Within a few months he learned he had cancer, to which he succumbed a few months later. We had started building a friendship, but our time was short.

Ghosh's powerful intellect, Lele's visionary approach, and Raju's humility and focus on fundamentals shaped my growth as a chemical engineer. It dawned on me that the challenge to a chemical engineer was not as much in solving a problem as in formulating it first and having a clear understanding of all the constraints and the assumptions that were needed to arrive at a solution. I learned at Panjab University of the awesome responsibility placed on the shoulders of the practicing chemical engineer. A great many people rely on the chemical engineer's analysis of a problem and assessment of risks. Facts mattered. Integrity mattered.

I have talked of the strengths I was able to acquire, thanks to the good luck of having some very good professors. The relative youth of the chemical engineering department necessitated experimentation by the leadership in the selection of courses to be offered. In my estimation, the department overdid the survey courses, such as introductions to civil, mechanical, and electrical engineering. Too much emphasis was placed on engineering drawing. The latter could easily have been cut by three-quarters without harming our training as chemical engineers. In hindsight, all these courses could have been substantially shortened, to make room for increased emphasis on applied mathematics and organic chemistry. More rigorous training in both would have obviated my need for catch-up work later on, in graduate school and during my career.

***

From the outset, I hated engineering drawing. I had trouble conceptualizing shapes in three dimensions. Our teacher, J. N. Bhatnagar, made things worse. He had some favorite students. With the others, he was dismissive, and even cruel and insulting. I and one other student failed this subject at the end of the first academic year. We would get a chance to retake the examination in October. The official term was "given a compartment." The results of all other courses taken that year were to be withheld until I cleared the compartment. It was a double frustration, flunking one subject and not knowing how I had performed in the rest.

That exam was a crushing disappointment. I had never failed an examination before. My mindset placed me among the top students. From early on, I had been conditioned to excel. And here I was, humbled by engineering drawing. I had been brandished with the scarlet letter *F*. I burned with humiliation.

I had no choice but to pick myself up off the floor and apply myself rigorously. I made an effort to genuinely understand the spatial concepts which had eluded me the previous year. The preparation had to go on even as I carried the full load of my sophomore year, which had started in August 1960.

It was as if a light had been switched on in my mind. All of a sudden, I could think in three dimensions. I got a very good grade in engineering drawing the second time around, the equivalent of an A. But the more gratifying news was the release of the results for the entire first year. I had placed second in the class of thirty. My classmates and the faculty discovered new respect for me. The stain of getting the compartment didn't quite wash away, but the sting of failure was eased. It may have been my first real lesson in resilience.

The overall result for the four years was tallied by including 20 percent of the marks earned in each of the freshman and sophomore years and 100 percent of the marks earned in each of the junior and senior years. In my senior year, I topped the class. The composite result for the entire four years also had me ranking second in the class of thirty.

At least five students in my batch had finished two years of the equivalent of a community college before starting at Chandigarh. For them, our freshman year was mostly a repeat of what they had already been through. The rest of us saw it as an unfair advantage. The top ranker in our four-year program was among that group of five.

My academic performance can't be viewed in isolation. As I focused on my studies, I had to struggle mightily to fit in with my fellow students. My tenure at Panjab University was the first time in my life when I studied and lived with classmates. My inability to read other people created severe stress, especially in the first year. I didn't quite know how to react to the normal verbal sparring between young people. When they sensed my discomfort, they would double down with teasing, sometimes laced with cruelty. During a period in the middle of my freshman year, I would time my visits to the dining hall to avoid running into my classmates.

There was no easy way out for me. I had to understand the

basic fact that verbal jousting between young people was a way of life. Once I internalized the new discovery that others weren't inherently evil, I was able to relax bit by bit. In my second year I felt comfortable enough to start sharing an occasional joke. Does it mean I became adept at banter and repartee? I improved but I can't say it was easy for me. Could I walk into a room and own it? Not so much.

I am proud of my capacity for resilience. I dealt with a very serious deficiency in my emotional tool kit, which, if uncorrected had the potential to severely hurt my academic performance. I can see how it could have derailed my efforts to achieve my goal of immigrating to America.

It turned out I wasn't the only one in the class with sights set on leaving India for greener pastures. Fourteen out of my class of thirty emigrated within a few years of graduating from Panjab University. Eleven of us ended up in America. Two went to Canada, and another went to Australia.

In the last two decades, I reconnected with some of my former classmates now living in North America. I got to know some better, including Kashmiri Lal Gupta, Mohinder Singh Ahluwalia, Kanwal Krishan Kalia, Jagdish Lal Malhotra, and Hardev Singh Koonar. All had done well, except one.

Remember Kapil Dev Sharma, the fellow who was jealous of me for speaking with Professor Peck? Apart from that single incident, we got along well. He immigrated to the United States right after graduation from Panjab University. After earning a master's degree, he started his professional career at Monsanto Corporation. I lost track of him at this point. I learned of Sharma's life trajectory after I retired. He had gotten hooked on gambling, which destroyed his career. He lost his house to pay gambling debts. His wife and kids kicked him out of their lives. He hovered close to the gambling dens of Reno and Las Vegas for the rest of his life. He died destitute in 2018.

Sharma's life illustrated that not all immigration stories work out with a happy ending. But for me, it was a risk worth taking.

* * *

Whatever happened to my brother, Ranbir? After all, I did mention that both of us were accepted for admission to the chemical engineering department at Panjab University.

Ranbir was there alongside me for all four years. We had built a certain close bond on the farm. It wasn't too demonstrative. We always had adjacent rooms in the dormitory. Ranbir was very introverted. He gave advice quietly when I sought it. He managed the money—tuition fees, room and board, and pocket money. We used the pocket money sparingly, perhaps on a movie once in a while, or on an extremely infrequent occasion to go for tea at a local shop on the campus. Bauji was satisfied with how Ranbir managed our money.

But we led more or less separate lives. We made different sets of friends. Sometimes I would learn from my friends and classmates what Ranbir was doing.

Ranbir's reputation for very high intelligence and a willingness to help others spread quickly. I remember the countless times classmates made a beeline to Ranbir's room for help with difficult classwork. One such occasion stands out in my mind.

We were juniors. A sophomore who lived on the same floor needed help with an advanced mathematics problem. Like everyone else, he went to Ranbir for help. Ranbir had been away from that course for a year by then, but it mattered little. Not only was he able to recall the solution in perfect detail, but he never once referred to a book or his old notes. This sophomore was astonished. Talkative by nature, he went around to all who would listen, singing praises of Ranbir's genius.

One vast difference between us was our understanding of engineering drawing. While I clearly had great trouble with spatial concepts, Ranbir was utterly at home with them. He was the favorite of the lecturer, Mr. Bhatnagar. He scored top marks in first-year drawing, and he helped me greatly as I prepared for the makeup examination four months later. At the end of our four years at university, when I was ranked second in the class, Ranbir came out at number three.

After graduating, Ranbir stayed in the department as a junior lecturer from 1963 to 1965. He also enrolled in the two-year master's degree program, offered by the same faculty who taught us in the undergraduate years.

A few years later, as I was getting ready to immigrate to America, I was disturbed by what I was learning about Ranbir. His tenure as a junior lecturer had been rocky, though he was still in his teaching position at Chandigarh when I left for the United States. Unfortunately, he didn't have a good rapport with most of the faculty, which is a kinder way to say they had fractious relations. He was turned off by what he saw as their unimpressive intellect and resented the unethical behavior of some. He had started viewing his colleagues as aligned against him. He fired off a complaint to the vice chancellor against the "habitual late arrival" of his fellow professors. The vice chancellor was flabbergasted. Ranbir was tagged as unstable.

He had by then completed all the course requirements for his master's degree. For him to collect his degree, all that remained was the formality of completing a form and turning it in. When he was visiting with our parents in the village, Bauji sensed his hostility toward his colleagues. Ranbir hinted that he had no desire to collect a degree from an institution that would staff the department with such "incompetent" and "disreputable" faculty. Bauji urged him to mail the signed form. Ranbir promised he would, but he never did. He blew two years' work just to make a futile gesture.

CHAPTER 5

IIT

Here in the place of Hijli Detention Camp stands the monument of India, representing India's urges, India's future in the making.
  - Jawaharlal Nehru, "First Convocation Address of IIT, Kharagpur," 1956

For the finals of two senior-year lab courses at Punjab University, we had an external examiner, Moca Narasinga Rao. Dr. Rao was the head of the chemical engineering department at India's foremost technical school at the time, the Indian Institute of Technology, Kharagpur. He must have liked my performance. He requested our department head, Dr. Ghosh, to have me apply for the master of technology (MTech) program at Kharagpur. I followed up and was accepted for the two-year program. Kharagpur was 1,500 miles east of my home in Punjab.

The journey from Jalandhar to Calcutta and then to Kharagpur in August 1963 was long, and it was my first long travel by train. It began at the train station in Jalandhar, fifteen miles from my village. I changed trains in Delhi for the thousand-mile journey across the northern plains of India.

After twenty-four hours the train pulled into the Howrah Terminus, the cavernous train station built across the Hooghly River from Kolkata. I boarded another train heading southwest to Kharagpur Junction, which was also a major train station.

Train platforms in India have many purposes. They are places to eat, to sleep, to pray, to shoo away dogs. And to wait. I found these platforms packed with people, luggage, boxes, parcels, and stray dogs. There were people with shocking disabilities, begging for alms. For a twenty-year-old, these scenes were very raw.

The train I boarded in Delhi for Howrah was already packed with people, tired, hot, and stinky. I rushed along the platform to find a third-class carriage with some space. Most Indians traveled third class at the time. These carriages were fitted with wooden benches with no seat separation. The upper-class carriages—first and second class—were marginally more comfortable, with separate seats, though none had air conditioning. People seemed stuffed in. Organized chaos prevailed as the platform dwellers swarmed the train, the seeming mayhem of boarding broken by the aching goodbyes on the platform. Alas, I was alone. No goodbyes for me.

As the day dawned, the train hurtled along somewhere in central Uttar Pradesh, India's most populous state. I saw an attractive lady, with two teenage daughters in tow, board at one stop. A Sikh gentleman in his late thirties and an older man, wearing the traditional dhoti (a loose piece of cloth wrapped around the waist) instead of pants, boarded at another stop. My fellow Sikh confided in me that he was on his way to the funeral of his brother-in-law, who had been shot dead by enemies. He seemed remarkably composed for one traveling under such circumstances. Even the bizarre seemed ordinary on the train.

By eleven a.m. a spirited card game was underway in our

carriage. I don't play cards so I observed. The mother was busy with her two hyperactive daughters, especially the older one, who seemed to be about fifteen. That girl could talk. The mother hushed her a few times, but the girl continued without losing a beat.

Suddenly, I realized with alarm that the dhoti-wearer's threadbare underpants were showing. He was sitting awkwardly and his underpants barely provided him any modesty. He was directly in the line of vision of the mother, who had determinedly turned her face away. I was uncomfortable telling the man, so I whispered into my Sikh friend's ear. He sternly told the man to fix his dhoti. The man blushed a deep crimson, rearranged his clothing, and pretended to study the outside scenery from the window of the speeding train. The card game petered out rapidly.

Much more would happen in the twenty-four-hour trip. Kind strangers pestered me for personal information and rewarded me with every type of food they were carrying. There were old parents, couples, and extended families. There were babies who wailed and a studious young man who read all through the night. I was jealous of his ability to remove himself from all the mayhem around him.

***

All students admitted to the MTech program got free tuition, as well as a stipend of 250 rupees per month. The amount was generous; it paid for room and board and still left a fair amount for spending money. I indulged myself with the purchase of a spanking new bicycle. A bicycle was necessary on the sprawling campus of the IIT. The stipend induced jealousy among the undergraduate students. When we lined up at the cashier's window every month to collect the money, they would refer to us as a bunch of pensioners.

Admission to the undergraduate programs at the IIT was hypercompetitive. For the lucky few who got in, the institutes were very expensive, constituting a considerable drain on their parents' resources. Here we were, only one to four years older, and had everything paid for. The younger students didn't want to acknowledge, it seemed, that we too had come through very stiff competition and that we had already paid our dues in our respective undergraduate schools.

The chemical engineering department at IIT Kharagpur was established in 1951. The first graduate program, with specialization in combustion engineering and fuel economy, was offered in 1952. The graduate program had since expanded to include two other areas for specialization toward the master's degree—chemical plant design and fabrication, which is the program I had been accepted into, and petroleum engineering. The department also had a doctoral program.

Besides me, there were seven other students in the chemical plant design and fabrication program. Each one of us was from among the top two rankers from universities across India. My colleagues came from Jadavpur University in Calcutta (West Bengal), Harcourt Butler Technical Institute at Kanpur (Uttar Pradesh), Delhi Polytechnic in Delhi (the nation's capital), Laxminarayan Institute of Technology in Nagpur (Maharashtra), Alagappa Chettiar College of Engineering and Technology in Karaikudi (Tamil Nadu), Andhra University in Hyderabad (Telangana), and last, but not least, from IIT Kharagpur itself. The eight of us represented just about all sections of India. Getting to know students from all other parts of India, with widely varying languages and cultures, was breathtakingly exciting for me.

All postgraduate students, as we were called, were housed in a set of dormitories named the Acharya J. C. Bose Residence Hall. Bose Hall was truly a microcosm of India. I was one of the very few Sikhs there. The Sikhs at IIT were conspicuous for our uncut hair, unshaven whiskers, and turbans. It was a new experience for me to come across people from outside my own Punjabi/Sikh culture. One grows up fast in such a milieu.

(From left to right, Ashok Biswas, Avinash Gupta, me, J. Rajan, and three unknown students outside the Chemical Engineering Department at IIT Kharagpur, 1964)

A Punjabi such as myself understood little of the Assamese or Bengali spoken by the students from the eastern states, and was utterly bewildered when a group of students from the south would break into Malayalam, Tamil, Kannada, or Telugu. Nor could I make any sense when the folk from the western states would switch to Marathi or Gujarati. English, a putatively foreign language to India, was the common language among us.

Most residents of Bose Hall constituted the crème de la crème of their respective parts of India. I tried to use it as an opportunity to learn about the country outside Punjab, such as their customs and religious observances. More importantly, my conversations and interactions with them revealed how all of us shared the idea of Indian nationhood.

Punjab, my home state, lay on the direct route of invaders from Afghanistan and beyond as they eyed the riches of the rulers in Delhi. Punjabis developed a marshal tradition since they were the first layer of India's defense. The word *Punjab* means the land of five rivers—Beas, Chenab, Jhelum, Ravi, and Sutlej. Its fertile crest of land, blessed with plenty of water, naturally gave rise to our farming tradition. My ancestors embraced both traits: they were soldiers and they were farmers.

The southern states, such as Tamil Nadu, Karnataka, and Kerala, were protected by geography from the military warfare of the north. The Vindhya Range of mountains constituted an impenetrable barrier between the north and the south. These southern states had the luxury of focusing on developing Hindu culture and an educational tradition.

Indians didn't even have a single language to unite us. Yet, through the millennia, the concept of Indian nationhood has prevailed; perhaps we are bound together by shared religion and philosophy. I greatly enjoyed learning about our differences and our commonalities.

***

IIT standards were rigorous, and I needed to catch up quickly. The quarter system was a painful surprise. Three months was too short a time to get deep into a subject. At the other extreme was the full-year system we had at Panjab University. An enormous amount of a subject was covered in nine months. Reviewing the entire course content at the end of nine months for the critical final examination was stressful and encouraged memorizing rather than fully understanding the material. The semester system of allotting four and a half months to a course, which I would experience at graduate school in America, seemed to be just right.

My performance in two courses in the first quarter—machine design and fabrication techniques—was disastrous. I had trouble making the adjustment from the leisurely pace I was used to at Panjab University to the very intense pace of the quarterly system at IIT. The course material unspooled very rapidly, and the reality didn't hit me until toward the end of the quarter that I had not been paying sufficient attention. I just could not coast based on the strength of my performance in undergraduate school. Nor could I afford to be distracted by the desire to understand the different cultures of India.

My poor performance in the first quarter was a terrible shock. It earned me a stern rebuke from the department head, Rao. I made a determined effort in the second quarter to pay close attention to the lectures and the subject material. I was able to reverse my nosedive of the first quarter and went on to earn straight As during the rest of my studies at the IIT. A lesson I learned at the end of that first year was that I didn't suffer from a lack of ability or intelligence in comparison with my colleagues from other parts of India. It was my lack of attention that caused the problem.

Besides Rao, the faculty included two full professors, several associate professors, and a few junior members. Rao was clearly the star of the department. He was a bright bulb and the rest of the faculty was in his shadow. But for all his brilliance and star power, Rao had unappealing sides to his personality. He was a bully. Once I saw him chew out N. C. Roy, a senior member of the faculty, in front of students. Roy was so devastated that he left for home immediately after the chastisement and wouldn't return to work for two days.

I took a nuclear engineering course from B. V. Dzampov, a visiting professor from the Moscow Power Institute. I completed a special project under Dzampov's guidance on the design of a 25-megawatt nuclear reactor using the old Calder Hall technology. The design used carbon dioxide gas as the coolant for the reactor core and graphite moderators.

It was through Dzampov that I came across a very unpleasant fellow in the mechanical engineering department.

Sometime in April 1964, my colleague Qaisar Raza and I had an appointment to see Dzampov. We went to his office at the appointed time but he wasn't there. Dzampov was a full professor and had a spacious office. His large desk had his executive chair on one side and two regular chairs across the desk for visitors.

India was, and is, a status-conscious country. Raza and I would normally have waited outside the office, so I can't quite explain the attack of bravado that led us to wait inside the office. I topped the foolhardy action by seating myself in Dzampov's chair behind the desk, as Raza slipped into the one facing it.

After we had waited for a few minutes, we saw a man whizzing past. Suddenly, he whirled back. He looked loaded for bear. We would learn later that he was Professor Makkadum.

"Who are you people?" he shouted at us.

"We're Professor Dzampov's students from the chemical engineering department. We're waiting to see him," I stammered. He was staring hard at me.

"Who gave you permission to sit in the professor's chair?" he sputtered in rage, which seemed to be building by the second. His face was contorted, quickly changing color from red to purple. We were terrified.

"Very sorry, sir," I blurted. Both of us were out of our chairs by this time. We were inching toward the door, which Makkadum was blocking.

"You people have no manners. Write down your names on a sheet of paper. I shall report you to Professor Rao." We did as we were told and the man left. Dzampov showed up in another fifteen minutes. We were too embarrassed to tell him what had happened. He could tell that we were shaken, though. He seemed to think that his tardiness had upset us. We didn't try very hard to disabuse him of the notion.

Makkadum did indeed call Rao, who wisely ignored the complaint.

Within a few days, the news of our encounter spread all over the campus. Another story was making the rounds a few weeks later. Dzampov was late to the office one day. Makkadum, Dzampov's senior in the hierarchy, confronted him, tapped his watch, and called him on it.

"Mr. Dzampov, you are late. It is unacceptable."

"Oh, sorry about that."

But Makkadum wasn't finished. He got angrier by the second, just as Raza and I had observed.

"You people, coming from Russia to teach us. You think you are better than us?"

Dzampov did indeed teach us well. I learned a great deal about nuclear reactors in his course. Unfortunately, he didn't think much of appointments. The man was always late. Maybe Makkadum had a point.

***

At the end of the first academic year at the IIT, we were required to undergo two months of industrial training. I elected to receive my training in June and July 1964 at Rohtas Industries Limited in Dalmianagar, in the state of Bihar. It was a huge chemical industry complex.

My second academic year, August 1964 through May 1965, was focused on a research project. I elected to work with N. C. Roy, the same unfortunate fellow who had been yelled at by Rao in public. A colleague on this project was Ashok Biswas, who would continue on it to earn his PhD.

Ours was the first batch in the IIT system that would take two years to finish the requirements of the MTech degree; before my batch, the requirements for the degree were met in one year. The appendage of the second year for a research project was pretty much an experiment. I am proud of what I accomplished in nine months. I built the entire experimental setup and developed the theoretical foundation for the research project. My master's thesis earned me an A. What Biswas had to do for his PhD, after I left, was to gather the actual experimental data and analyze it for conclusions.

I used a significant part of the second year to plan the future. The most rational path to achieving my dream of immigrating to the United States would be to seek admission *and* full financial support toward a PhD degree at an American graduate school. But I didn't view a PhD just as a mere tool to reach my ultimate goal. I enjoyed exploring the frontiers of chemical engineering. I wanted to immerse myself in advanced chemical engineering before venturing out into either academia or industry. I applied to several top-notch universities, such as Columbia, MIT, Princeton, Purdue, the University of Illinois at Urbana, the University of Wisconsin, and the University of California at Berkeley. The reputation of the University of Notre Dame was a little lower at the time.

But for one grievous mistake, I might have landed in the absolute top rung of American schools. I was granted admission to graduate school by most of them, based on my strong academic record at Panjab University and IIT Kharagpur. But I needed a full assistantship, which would pay for my tuition and cover all my living expenses. I didn't realize the importance American schools attached to the results of the Graduate Record Examination (GRE). The American consulate in Calcutta had a section that interacted with students who were exploring graduate studies in America through events and presentations. They took the show to the key universities in northeast India. I had my first meeting with the consulate personnel at a presentation at the IIT. I followed up with a couple of visits to events held at the consulate. When the subject of the GRE came up, I heard that the GRE tested innate knowledge and that one couldn't quite prepare for it as you would for a regular school test.

At this point, I had been removed from the textbook material for about a year. I didn't review any of it and took the GRE in Calcutta in February 1965. As I said, I made a grievous mistake. My test scores were low. To their credit, the faculty at the University of Notre Dame elected to give more weight to my academic record and offered me a teaching assistantship, anyway.

I learned later on from some colleagues that they had ignored the advice they received at the consulate and took pains to review the textbooks of their specialization before taking the test. They scored high.

At the end of the day, I didn't do too badly. The graduate chemical engineering program at Notre Dame was very good. The faculty included several professors of international repute. The head of the department, Julius Banchero, was the coauthor of a textbook that was used worldwide. Another professor, Ernest Thiele, was a pioneer in the field. Thiele's name was synonymous with chemical engineering; we often ran into theories and methodologies that bore his name.

James Carberry was already developing an international reputation at the time. Textbooks authored by Carberry on chemical reaction engineering and by my own thesis advisor, Peter Skelland, on mass transfer would be published while I was still at Notre Dame. They were considered seminal and would be used around the world for decades.

***

Perhaps my acceptance among the upper echelons of American institutions and landing at Notre Dame speaks to the quality of education at the IIT. When I was at Kharagpur, there were five Indian Institutes of Technology—at Delhi,

Bombay, Madras, Kharagpur, and Kanpur, the last in the northern state of Uttar Pradesh. Since then, the list has expanded to sixteen.

Lesley Stahl of CBS News reported on the IITs in March 2003. After observing that the biggest import from India to the United States was manpower, she stated that most of them came from the IITs, which she called some "super technical universities": "The best and the brainiest among the immigrants from India seem to share a common credential: they are graduates of the Indian Institutes of Technology, better known as IITs."

The top ranks of US and Indian companies and academia and of the Indian government are liberally populated by alumni from the IIT system. Raghuram Rajan is one of the success stories among the IIT alumni. He graduated from IIT Delhi with a degree in electrical engineering. He is the Distinguished Service Professor of Finance at the University of Chicago. Between 2003 and 2006, he served as the chief economist at the International Monetary Fund (IMF). Importantly, Dr. Rajan was the governor of the Reserve Bank of India, a position akin to the Federal Reserve Bank's chairperson from 2013 to 2016.

I owe a deep debt of gratitude to the Indian state for educating me. During my four years at Chandigarh, my parents had to absorb the cost of only my room and board. While these were by no means insubstantial, they paled in contrast to the real cost of education—the facilities, the faculty, and so on. My two years at IIT were paid for in full by the Indian state, including room and board.

India made a critical decision after gaining independence from Britain to offer free college education to all students who could compete successfully. Most Indian colleges and universities accept students based on their performance in the country's equivalent of US high schools. The IITs are an exception; they have a very tough national-level entrance examination, called the Joint Entrance Examination (JEE). So fierce is the competition to get into the IITs that a cottage industry of coaching schools has sprung up to prepare students for the JEE.

***

During my six years of engineering education in India, I was able to visit Bauji only sporadically. The two-month undergraduate summer breaks allowed some opportunity to reconnect. He encouraged Ranbir and me to do the physical chores on the farm so we would not lose touch with the idea of manual labor. The livestock, which had been thinned a bit, needed our attention.

By the time I graduated from IIT, Bauji's health had declined. The left side of his body had weakened considerably, and he was prone to falls if he wasn't careful. He was still fully mobile, though. At the end of the summer of 1965, I said my goodbye to Bhabiji in Dhandaur. Bauji and I left the village for Chandigarh a few days before my departure for the United States. We stayed at Gurmit's residence there, which was off the campus of Panjab University. Ranbir had his own place on campus.

On a hot morning on August 28, 1965, Ranbir, Gurmit, Bauji, and I set out in rickshaws for the Chandigarh bus station. There was no waiting room like what you would see at a typical Greyhound bus station in the United States. We jostled for space in the crowded station. Bauji had a brave, bright smile. Ranbir was his usual quiet, withdrawn self. Gurmit's emotion was right there on the surface of her face. When the bus pulled into its allotted space, people rushed to find a decent seat. I said goodbye to my family and boarded the bus. I was lucky to find a window seat at the rear of the bus.

During the six-hour bus ride, my mood turned pensive. Bauji had trouble standing up straight when he said goodbye to me. Yet he smiled broadly to cheer me up. Clearly, he didn't want me to see him sad. I was also worried about Ranbir. He seemed to trust no one anymore. I felt helpless as the bus sped toward New Delhi.

I had in hand my Indian passport, my US student visa, and my airline ticket. I had borrowed $600 from a relative, the price of the one-way flight to Chicago. My immediate family was too poor to have that kind of money. I was all set to fly to the United States. But a war intervened.

***

The war didn't quite come as a surprise. Since partition in 1947, India and Pakistan had locked horns on several issues. The overriding issue was the state of Kashmir, over which the countries had already fought a war in 1948. Other border disputes erupted occasionally. On April 8, 1965, the two countries had come to blows over a barren region in the state of Gujarat, called the Rann of Kutch. The skirmishes flared up and were temporarily brought to a halt under the mediation of the British. Initial successes in these skirmishes, however, emboldened the ruler of Pakistan, Ayub Khan, to plan a covert infiltration into Kashmir. Hostilities started on August 5 when Pakistani forces dressed as Kashmiri locals infiltrated Kashmir to precipitate an insurgency against Indian rule. The Indian Army crossed the cease-fire line on August 15 and opened with a retaliatory response.

At the time I arrived in New Delhi, on August 28, the talk of a declared war was in the air. My travel agent informed me the next morning that the international flight on which I was scheduled to depart in the early morning of August 30 had been canceled. On August 31, he determined that I would be better off looking for an international flight out of Bombay and booked me on a flight to Bombay departing that afternoon. The airline that operated the canceled international flight arranged for a hotel room for me there.

The clouds of war had darkened over the subcontinent even since I boarded the bus in Chandigarh three days before. On September 1, my second day in Bombay, Pakistan launched a major counterattack in Jammu, the Indian territory adjacent to Kashmir, and India reacted by having its air force launch air raids into Pakistan, which quickly responded in kind. India declared war before the end of the day. Air raid sirens were going off in Bombay night and day while I observed the total blackout of the city during my two nights there. It was a very surreal experience as I stared into the pitch darkness of night from my hotel room, not knowing if we would come under air attack at any time.

Bombay escaped aerial warfare. I was able to secure a seat on one of the very few international flights still operating. We took off into the darkened skies on the night of September 2. I could barely see the outline of the city below. My emotions were in a jumble as the plane flew out over the Arabian Sea. I felt wistful about leaving India at a time of crisis. But the determination I had made years ago in my village, when my dad brought me the American atlas, kept coming to the fore. I was on the right path and wouldn't look back.

The raging war that I left behind ended in a stalemate and ended up resolving nothing. Under growing international pressure, both countries accepted a cease-fire on September 22. The two countries would go to war again in 1971. Pakistan would lose its eastern wing, which would emerge as the new country of Bangladesh.

***

How does one prepare oneself to go live among people of a

different race? British colonialism had left behind a poisonous residue in India. Two centuries of subjugation had imbued us Indians with a complex mix of feelings regarding white folk. I was only four years old at the time of independence. The previous racial attitudes that flowed seamlessly into people of my generation were contradictory. We felt rage and humiliation at how the white colonialists had treated Indians. But several characteristics of the British we had come to admire, such as their advances in science. The discoverers who marched across our textbooks were Brits, other Europeans, and Americans. Since Indians had not been in charge for two centuries, we didn't quite have the self-confidence we needed as we bade goodbye to the departing Brits. It would take more than a generation to squeeze the feelings of inadequacy out of the fibers of our souls.

What I had read about America set it apart from Britain. President Franklin Roosevelt had greatly angered Winston Churchill with his insistence that the latter move toward granting full independence to India. Churchill had no intention of keeping any promises he made to Roosevelt in exchange for the massive American help he needed in waging World War II. If Churchill had not lost to Clement Attlee in the post-war election, India might have had to wait for independence a good deal longer.

Complicating the picture was American slavery and the long history of Jim Crow laws in the South following the Civil War. Indians avidly followed the news from America in the early 1960s, as the South seemed to explode with civil rights marches and the resultant police brutality. We read of how Bull Connor had directed the use of fire hoses and police attack dogs against the Freedom Riders on May 11, 1961, in Birmingham, Alabama. We saw pictures of Governor George Wallace defiantly standing in the schoolhouse door as he tried to prevent black students Vivian Malone and James Hood from enrolling at the University of Alabama on June 11, 1963.

Since I was heading to a northern region of America, I convinced myself, as a defensive measure, that the people of the South were different from the rest of America. I reassured myself that I wouldn't face unpleasant experiences in the Midwest as a result of my skin pigmentation. I made a conscious decision to give Americans the benefit of doubt and approach them on an equal footing. It was a risky assumption that all people I came in contact with would be decent human beings and would harbor no racist attitudes.

In hindsight, it turned out to be a smart decision. It allowed me sufficient space to build self-confidence and the opportunity to meet many wonderful people without having to pick my way through damaging racial clutter.

CHAPTER 6

GOLDEN DOME

Whatever you value, be committed to it and let nothing distract you from this goal.
The uncommitted life, like Plato's unexamined life, is not worth living.
  - Father Theodore Hesburgh, "The Hesburgh Papers," 1979

After stepping out of O'Hare Airport in Chicago, I took a cab to the Illinois Institute of Technology, Chicago; it was located in the Bronzeville section of the city. I was astonished by the speed and the smooth flow of cars on the highway. The speed also terrified me. Soon the cab was carousing through the city's tall buildings. I could see skyscrapers at a distance. As the cab pulled into the South Side of Chicago, I noticed an abrupt change; the majority of the people were black, and the buildings appeared to be in poor repair. Finally, the cab rolled up to IITC, an oasis, as it were, in the midst of the relative poverty of the South Side.

I paid off the cabbie and was left with $20, ready to start my life in America. Mohinder Ahluwalia, a former classmate in Chandigarh, had arrived at IITC a week ahead of me and was pretty much settled at this time. I stayed in Mohinder's dorm for two nights as I prepared for my bus trip to Indiana, even though he already had a roommate and it was a bit crowded. Mohinder lent me some cash to tide me over till my arrival in South Bend, the seat of the University of Notre Dame.

I had considered cutting my hair and shaving while I was still in India, but I feared offending my family. Instead, I cut my hair and shaved off my whiskers on my second day in Chicago. I never regretted my decision, nor was I ever upbraided for it by my family.

The actual process of saying goodbye to the turban and the whiskers turned out to be rather comical. After a good night's sleep, I showed up at the barbershop with Mohinder at the appointed time. The barber had never cut two-foot-long hair that had been rolled into a bun at the top of the head. He managed that task, but he would not give me a shave since the appointment was only for a haircut. Mohinder and I instead shaved my face in his dorm. When Mohinder's roommate returned a few hours later, he blurted out that I had looked "mean" the previous night, but not anymore. This was my first close contact with a white American, a friendly young man from downstate Illinois.

I boarded a bus for South Bend the following day, September 4, 1965, a Saturday, excited by the prospect of starting life in the United States. As I took my seat on the Greyhound bus, I was struck by how comfortable it was. The seat was soft but I didn't sink into it. The legroom was ample, good enough for someone much taller than me. The window next to me had a shade, and I could adjust the interior light to my liking. My mind flashed back to the buses I had ridden all my life in India. I called them rickety for a reason. They bounced on the potholes in the road, not getting much help from the rudimentary suspension system of the bus. The bench seats lacked a separation. They were hard and provided quite a challenge to one's spine. The Indian highways, which we called trunk roads, were only two lanes wide and were shared by buses, tractor trailers, bullock carts, bicyclists, and the occasional pedestrian. I never saw a bus go faster than forty miles per hour. Now I was enjoying a quiet bus ride to South Bend in a comfortable seat at speeds approaching seventy miles per hour, especially after hitting the Indiana Toll Road.

The stark differences between India and the United States were evident everywhere I looked. I was reminded of it by the caliber of the dorms in India and the one in Chicago I had just left. It was in the quality of food served in the Indian dorms compared to what I sampled in Mohinder's dining hall in Chicago. The differences weighed on me.

Why was India so poor and America so rich? Were Americans inherently more intelligent and capable? I wasn't equipped at the time with the knowledge and judgment needed to answer these questions. But the sense of embarrassment, even shame, was gnawing at me. I tried to calm myself with the thought that it was all right to come to America to better my life, since America was the country of immigrants. Countless others had done what I was doing. I should feel no embarrassment.

Immigrants walk around with a scar left by their crossing into a new country, an invisible mark of the exile that became their condition when they uprooted. Their children grow up without grandparents, without a reservoir of collective family memory passed down through generations. I was more fortunate than many others. Many members of my family—brother, sisters, cousins—would immigrate to North America in the decades following my arrival in 1965. But the scar of exile remains firmly etched on me. My children and grandchildren have grown up without that collective family memory of my village, my language, and the culture that constituted me.

An announcement from the driver interrupted my thoughts: "Ladies and gentlemen, look straight ahead, to the right. You will see the golden dome of the University of Notre Dame." Sure enough, the beautiful dome was clearly visible from the toll road. Two images of Notre Dame have stayed with me throughout my life—that golden dome and the magnificent visage of the university library, later named the Theodore M. Hesburgh Library after its illustrious president who led the university from 1952 to 1987.

The bus reached South Bend in the late afternoon. I took a taxi to the Notre Dame campus. All I had on me was the letter of the offer of the teaching assistantship from Dr. Julius Banchero, the head of the chemical engineering department. It provided no instructions on where to go and whom to seek on arrival. Neither the cab driver nor I had the slightest notion of where to alight or who to contact.

He inquired at the campus gate for instructions. He was told of a group of freshmen who had just arrived with no clear idea of where to go. They had gathered a couple of hundred yards down the road on the campus. We drove on and spotted the cluster of about twenty young men. The cabbie eagerly unloaded me, collected his fare, and took off.

Word must have spread because within fifteen minutes an assistant dean showed up with a few cars in tow. He loaded us into the cars and led the caravan to the Students' Infirmary. All the beds were unoccupied, and the infirmary would be our home for the next three to five days. The nun in charge made it clear that all of us were expected to find housing within the week and would remind us several times a day.

One young man in the group, Fred, introduced himself to the rest of us. He would have been a freshman, like most of the others in the group, but he seemed very mature for his age. Fred was an American whose family lived in Mexico. He had the unique advantage of being a foreign student with the ease of someone operating on home turf. Our acquaintance turned into friendship. He was helpful as I started making the calls to landlords for a room.

The pressure to find my own lodgings started immediately. I had very little money left from what Mohinder had loaned me. Fortunately, I had a full week before classes started for the fall semester. I was stressed as I walked into the chemical engineering department on Monday morning, September 6. Dr. Banchero, the department head, and his assistant, Helen Deranek, were very welcoming. They arranged an advance payment.

On-campus housing for students was tight and was open only to undergraduates; graduate students had to fend for themselves. I met another graduate student that Monday. Jorge Guzman had just driven up from his home in Mexico City. He had this lovely sports car, a Mustang. We were able to rent an apartment together in South Bend, and he graciously offered to let me ride with him to and from school.

I took all my meals on campus—breakfast and lunch at the "Student Huddle" (later renamed the Huddle Mart) and dinner at the South Dining Hall. Early dining hours in America came as a big culture shock. I was accustomed to dining no earlier than eight p.m. in India; the South Dining Hall would open for dinner at four thirty p.m.

My teaching assistantship covered my tuition and paid me $2,100 for the nine-month academic year. This sum easily covered all my living expenses and allowed me to save some money too. The following summer, I was able to pay back the money I had borrowed to buy my airline ticket. Besides that, I was able to purchase a used car, a 1960 Ford Fairlane, for $200. It served me well for the remaining two and a half years at Notre Dame.

***

When I met with Banchero on September 6, he asked me to return two days later so he could review my academic past. I showed up at the appointed time.

The chemical engineering department was housed in a decrepit building. It had previously housed the chemistry department, which moved into an adjacent new, air-conditioned building. The two buildings were connected, so we would often take a shortcut through the new building on the way to the Student Huddle.

"Good morning, Sardul," Helen greeted me with a wide smile. She was still working on the pronunciation of my name. I would later help her with the soft "d." She led me into Banchero's office, which was decidedly *not* ostentatious. A desk, his chair facing the door, and two chairs for visitors made up the bulk of the furnishings. There were also two bookshelves lining the rear wall. Prominently displayed on his desk was a big picture of his wife and two daughters.

After the initial pleasantries, Banchero started the discussion.

"Sardul, I am struck by one difference you have with the other new students."

"Sir?" I tried to catch a drift of where he was going.

"You are the only one with a master's degree. May I see your transcript?"

I excused myself to go to my desk, fished out the transcript, and headed back to his office. He took a quick look and seemed to make up his mind.

"I think there is no point in your having to repeat the courses you already took. How about helping me grade class assignments on one of the graduate courses I shall be teaching?"

"That would be very nice, sir."

I was delighted. He was giving me a teaching assistant (TA) assignment for a graduate-level course, Advanced Thermodynamics. His expression of faith in me was gratifying. The semester started the following Monday, September 13. I carried a full load of coursework in addition to the TA duties grading for Banchero.

All went well with my course load and the TA duties for the first eight weeks. Then a near-disaster happened.

Not owning an automobile limited my social activities, such as going to bars and participating in mixers at St. Mary's College, the women's college located across US Route 31 from the Notre Dame campus. However, Jorge and I decided to go to a pre-Thanksgiving event organized by the International Students Organization (ISO), of which both of us were members.

There I met a coed from St. Mary's College, a beautiful girl from Colombia. We were drawn to each other. I had little experience dating or dealing with women, and my infatuation scared her away, which goaded me to redouble my efforts. The end result was, as expected, a disastrous letdown. I rode an emotional roller coaster for two weeks and took my eyes off the ball, especially my TA duties. Students' homework went ungraded for many days.

Banchero had no tolerance for slackers. One morning as I was checking my mailbox, which was across from his office, he darted out and pierced me with his cold gaze. "Your TA work is unacceptable. You better fix it fast." As quickly as he had emerged, he retreated to his office.

I was stunned. I had gone a full cycle with Banchero, from warmth to harsh reprimand. The reality dawned on me. He had the power to toss me out of the teaching assistantship and even out of Notre Dame. I needed to get my act together, and fast.

The reprimand chased away my infatuation with the Colombian girl. I told Jorge that I would not go anywhere other than to school and back to the apartment till I got out of the awful mess I was in.

As I focused on my job, I discovered an interesting thing. Besides grading the papers, I found myself writing notes on them, questioning assumptions, suggesting alternative pathways. For the first time that semester, I started enjoying the TA work for Banchero.

I got the reprieve from Banchero in the same spot, four weeks later. He was a big, hulking man who moved with surprising agility. One moment I was alone sorting through my mail and the next moment, Banchero had his hand gently patting my shoulder.

"You are doing a great job grading papers."

"Thank you, sir," I stammered.

"Students are complaining that you are a tough grader. But that suits me fine. Keep up the good work." And then he vanished into his office.

I was elated. On the way back to my desk, I may have shouted some unintelligible hurrahs in the corridor, which left my colleagues frowning quizzically. The first semester was ending and Banchero's approval helped me attack my finals with special vigor. I was proud of the outcome of my first semester at Notre Dame.

***

At the time I applied, I was only vaguely aware that Notre Dame was a Catholic school. The full reality dawned on me after I arrived. Priests and nuns seemed to be omnipresent on campus, which was quite a culture shock to me.

I was approached by a priest as I made my way to the South Dining Hall on one blustery, cold evening.

"I was very sorry to learn of Dr. Bhabha's death. I had the privilege of knowing him," said the priest.

"Oh, thanks, Father," I blurted out. The priest sped up

toward the cafeteria, leaving me behind in a fog of confusion.

One of the leading lights of the Indian nuclear physics establishment, Homi Jehangir Bhabha, was the founding director of the Tata Institute of Fundamental Research and of the Atomic Energy Establishment, Trombay. Dr. Bhabha had died in a plane crash near Mont Blanc, Switzerland, on January 24, 1966, on his way to attend a meeting of the International Atomic Energy Agency's Scientific Advisory Committee. But I didn't even know of the accident that took Bhabha's life.

I slowed down so that a nun behind me would catch up with me.

"Excuse me, Sister. Did you see that priest who was just talking to me?"

"Yes, I did."

"Forgive me. Do you know who he is?"

"He is Father Hesburgh," said the nun with an amused twinkle in her eye.

This is how I met the famous Theodore M. Hesburgh, the president of the university, the only time I would speak to him before my graduation.

As the first academic year was nearing its end, I started looking around for a thesis advisor with an assured source of funding for research. My teaching assistantship would end in June 1966. One of the professors I briefly talked to was James Kohn.

Kohn and I developed a mutual dislike early on. I could never figure out the source of his unhappiness with me. It could have been as simple as my bearing, how I spoke, or how I approached him. He had taught us advanced heat transfer in my first year. I did not mind being called upon to stand up in class and write equations on the blackboard. What I resented was the sense that he expected me to flounder. Once, he predicted the end result of a problem. I challenged his conclusion, which upset him. His voice grew thick with anger as he worked out the solution step-by-step. It didn't help his mood that I turned out to be correct. As we came out of the class, my colleagues congratulated me on being right.

But it was an ephemeral victory. I had made a powerful enemy in the department. The result of my talk with him concerning my need for a thesis advisor was foreordained. He went out of his way to stress how he really wasn't that well known professionally and that others, such as Banchero and Peter Skelland, were far better known internationally. I did not push. I talked to him because I was expected to speak with the faculty members. I did not relish the idea of working for the man.

My initial judgment of Kohn was not off the mark. He had little tolerance for dissent. Many years later, I ran into him at a meeting of the American Institute of Chemical Engineers. I was astonished at how he told me personal stories. What happened to the wall of animosity that I could not pierce when I was at Notre Dame? I learned that his only son had loudly opposed the war in Vietnam. Kohn was so incensed with his son's "lack of patriotism" that he kicked him out of the house for good. As he relayed the story, he was sad but showed not the slightest doubt that the punishment of his son was just.

I continued my interviews with the faculty. The memory of my meeting with Peter Skelland remains vivid. I was finishing his second advanced fluid dynamics course. I had earned an A from him the previous semester and would go on to earn another A in the second semester. I had not had any interactions with him outside class, but I could sense from our limited contact that he liked me.

We connected while he collected his mail in front of Banchero's office. He greeted me with a big smile and invited me to follow him to his office on the third floor. He was energetic and seemed to be in a perpetual hurry. As he bounded up the stairs, he cleared two with each step. I tried to keep up with him.

Skelland had earned a PhD from the University of Birmingham and had worked as a researcher at Procter and Gamble, UK. He was recruited by Ralph Peck (the same Peck who showed me how to use a slide rule at Panjab University) to join the faculty at the Illinois Institute of Technology, Chicago, in 1962.

(Peter Skelland, my thesis advisor; Source—Georgia Institute of Technology)

I followed Skelland into his spacious office on the third floor. His large desk was surprisingly bereft of any papers, nor did it have any family pictures or mementos. I had met his wife, Peggy, a beautiful English lady. His office gave no hint of the man, or of people who may have been important to him. The office was impersonal.

He settled into his chair and gave a bright smile. Skelland was handsome to a fault. His silver mane of hair was impressively thick. He was approaching forty at the time and was acutely aware of his good looks. I had heard whispers from fellow students of his infamous "wandering eye." The picture above was taken when he was close to seventy, still very much the debonair gentleman.

"Sardul, are you looking for a thesis advisor?"

"Yes, sir. I am trying to learn about the research interests of various professors. I hope also to learn of their activities in the chemical engineering profession."

"Well, I am close to finishing the book *Non-Newtonian Fluids and Heat Transfer*. You may have seen Helen typing the manuscript downstairs."

"Yes, Helen has been busy typing it. Is that the area of your research?"

"No, my immediate focus is liquid-liquid extraction. One of my graduate students at IITC, Bob Wellek, published good work in this area. My plan is to continue exploring the subject."

"Sir, is the work going on in the department right now?"

"No. I have applied to the National Science Foundation for a grant. In fact, let me look." Skelland rifled through drawers and pulled out a thick typed document. "I shall have Helen make a copy of my NSF application for you."

I thanked Skelland and took my leave. I reconnected with him in late May 1966 to check on the status of the grant. He was in high spirits.

"The grant was approved just last week. Are you still interested in working on this project?"

"Sir, very much so."

"I shall have Helen fill out the paperwork. You will start on the research assistantship when your teaching assistantship ends."

I was incredibly lucky indeed. I had no financial aid lined up after the TA job ended in mid-June. The arrival of the NSF grant was fortuitous. Not only that, but it also paid better than the TA position, with no more grading of papers. The research assistantship (RA) supported me during the rest of my stay at Notre Dame, through February 1969.

During my search for a thesis advisor, the name James Carberry would have been at the top of the list. But Carberry was on a sabbatical at the University of Cambridge during my first year at Notre Dame. He returned in September 1966. I took a course from him in chemical reaction engineering. Midway through it, he assigned the class an interesting problem, which involved the catalytic oxidation of sulfur dioxide to sulfur trioxide, a critical building block in the manufacture of sulfuric acid.

Carberry liked how I approached the problem. One day

after class he asked to speak with me. We climbed the stairs and walked over to his office on the third floor. His office had an unkempt look. He had returned from the UK very recently and was still getting settled. His desk looked well organized, though. A picture of his two daughters was prominently displayed on it.

"Sardul, would you like to look a bit deeper into the oxidation problem?"

"What would you like me to do, Sir?" I said tentatively. I did not want to take on a huge project. I was already on the RA financed by Skelland's NSF grant. I was reluctant to make a big commitment to Carberry.

"If you set up a mathematical model of what is going on in the reactor, we can look at the various design sensitivities."

"How long will it take?" I was still hesitant.

"It is an open-ended exercise. You can fit the work into your schedule. I think there is a good chance we can publish the results in one of the reputable publications."

That was the hook I needed. Over the next month I worked wildly. I developed a mathematical model of the oxidation reactor. But the analytical solution was impossible. It could only be solved numerically. The model involved a set of simultaneous first-order ordinary linear differential equations. I solved the equations using the fourth-order Runge-Kutta technique on Notre Dame's 1107 Univac computer.

In the late 1960s, the computer code had to be punched into cards. Programming and working with computers were new to me and an experience I found exhilarating. Carberry and I gathered the results of the simulation and wrote up two papers. He credited me as the senior author of both. The larger, and more substantial, paper appeared in the June 1969 issue of *British Chemical Engineering*. The second paper appeared, also in 1969, in the *Journal of Catalysis*. These were important publications; I received comments and questions from researchers in the field for years.

Carberry went on to author the classic textbook *Chemical and Catalytic Reaction Engineering*, which was published in hardback in 1976 and brought out in paperback in 2001. The book elevated him to star status in our profession.

***

All candidates for the doctoral degree must pass the critically important PhD candidacy examination. My first two academic years, including the intervening summer, had been dedicated to taking graduate-level courses. The candidacy examination was offered in June every year. I decided to take it in June 1967.

The bar was set remarkably high for clearing the candidacy examination. The historic pass rate had been nearly 50 percent. It was not very different from the testing rigor and the low success rate of would-be lawyers who take the bar exam in New York and California. For example, the overall pass rate for first-time takers of the New York bar exam between 2010 and 2020 hovered in the 40 percent to 60 percent range.

Just like the bar examination, there were no limits on the subject matter in the candidacy examination. The candidates could expect to be tested on anything in the broad field of chemical engineering, ranging from the core to the various affiliated areas. The examination was given over twelve hours, in four sessions of three hours each, spread over two consecutive days.

I started preparing for it at the start of the second semester, in early February 1967. Old textbooks came out. I reviewed material I had not looked at in years. I made up for my lack of preparation for the GRE examination by taking no chances with the PhD candidacy examination.

Time flew as I immersed myself in preparation for the big

(With fellow graduate students, fall 1967)

examination. Six graduate students had signed up for it. A couple of days after the examination, a few senior members of the faculty had a long meeting to review the results. They met in a professor's office across from the large room that housed the graduate students. From my desk I could hear muffled sounds from the important meeting. Professors would occasionally dart out for supporting information to help make the final decision. At one point, I saw Skelland head out to his office and return with some files. I learned later that he dug up my course records to bolster my position.

The meeting ended mid-afternoon. James Kohn had been assigned the task of announcing the results, but he did not seek us out. He parked himself in the small room across from Banchero's office that usually served as the backup room for Mrs. Deranek. All six of us went to him to get our results. He wore a scowl. Kohn appeared chagrined that I had been successful. He prefaced the good news with "you didn't quite cover yourself with glory." He just could not conceal his animus. He did not congratulate me. But I had passed. Three of us had, maintaining the historical 50 percent pass rate. One of the failed candidates had Kohn as his thesis advisor, which may have partly explained his foul mood.

I was then free to focus on my research. Skelland had defined the larger framework of the research project in his grant application to the NSF. His style was to offer broad direction. He did not get into the weeds himself. The entire research project, including writing my dissertation, took a year and a half.

(Me, outside the Department of Chemical Engineering, May 1968)

Banchero and Skelland set up a research committee for my PhD project. I distributed copies of my dissertation and reached out to each committee member to schedule the defense of my thesis. On February 23, 1969, I would be turning twenty-six. I consciously selected a date a couple of days before my birthday so I would have the bragging rights to be called a "doctor" at the age of twenty-five. In retrospect, my obsession with age was silly. Regardless, I defended my thesis successfully. The chairperson of the committee, the head of the mechanical engineering department, approached me with a big smile. "Congratulations, Dr. Minhas." I was thrilled.

I collected my degree at the commencement ceremony in June 1969. Daniel Patrick Moynihan was the keynote speaker. He was the White House Urban Affairs Advisor to President Richard Nixon at the time. He would go on to serve as the United States ambassador to India from February 1973 to January 1975 and the United States senator for the state of New York between 1977 and 2001.

I had my second and final interaction with Father Theodore Hesburgh in the receiving line. After I shook hands with Moynihan, Father Hesburgh was next.

"Congratulations, Dr. Minhas. How many years?"

"Three and a half, Father. Thank you so much."

"That is an excellent time. Nice," said Father Hesburgh, making my day.

I adapted my PhD dissertation into a research paper, which Skelland and I sent to the *AIChE Journal* (AIChE stands for the American Institute of Chemical Engineers). The journal was the most prestigious publication in our profession at the time and had an acceptance rate of around 30 percent. It was a matter of great pride for me when the journal accepted our submission with a few minor changes. It was published in the November 1971 issue.

Now that I had finished my PhD program, I had a fair basis for comparing the educational system in India with that in the United States. My thoughts are best captured in a paper I published after I retired ("Innovation—A Strategic Advantage," *The Broad Mind*, Takshashila Institute, March 21, 2014). It identified the educational system as a critical factor affecting innovation. I had noticed that the American system involved a great deal of vigorous exchange between students and teachers. The system in India relied strictly on one-way communication, from teacher to student. What I learned in my student years still holds true. Innovation thrives in the United States; all you need to do is look at the internet or your iPhone. Countries like India and China rely a good deal more on industriousness and less on innovation.

***

I met Vitauts (Bill) Bankovics during my first week at Notre Dame. Bill's workstation was close to mine. He made a special effort to connect with me. Bill's parents had immigrated to the United States from Latvia (a part of the Soviet Union for much of the twentieth century) and settled in Oklahoma. Bill had earned his bachelor's degree in chemical engineering from the Colorado School of Mines. His plans for doctoral studies at Notre Dame appeared a bit unsettled at the time because his preferred thesis advisor, James Carberry, was away for a year on sabbatical at the University of Cambridge. Through Bill, I met Alex Varn-Warnas, a graduate student in the physics department. Alex's parents had emigrated from Lithuania, another former Soviet Republic.

Bill, Alex, and I would sometimes go out to dinner in South Bend. Alex's car came in handy. In November 1965, just two months after I arrived in the United States, the three of us visited a family restaurant. We ordered drinks and relaxed after a busy day. The bench seats were soft and comfortable. Alex got up, fished a dime out of his pocket, and fed the jukebox. Soon we were entertained by Dean Martin as "That's Amore" wafted across the dining booths. So did the thick cigarette smoke from other diners. The waitress returned to collect our dinner orders.

"What are the choices for fried chicken?" I asked.

"Sir, you can have a half fried chicken," replied the waitress with an encouraging smile. She might've sensed my unease and sought to make me feel comfortable. But I was flummoxed by her answer.

"Can I please have a fully fried chicken instead?" I said, sounding desperate.

The waitress did a double take and looked at my colleagues, and all three broke into peals of laughter.

"The chicken we serve you will be *fully* fried, sir," assured the waitress gently.

Bill and Alex did not let me forget this incident for the better part of a year.

What was it that nurtured our friendship? Our common immigrant experience may have been a strong factor. Bill was a young boy when his parents immigrated, and he had lost his accent. But Alex had a very thick accent. I once accompanied Alex to his parents' home in Chicago. His parents were very decent, salt-of-the-earth kind of people. I found my shared immigrant experience with Bill and Alex a powerful bridge to white America—they were immigrants *and* white Americans.

Bill was a conservative Republican who had voted for Barry Goldwater in 1964. He admitted that his political philosophy may have been inspired by his virulent dislike of the Soviet system, from which his family were refugees.

(From left to right: Kyo Ho Lee, me, Robert Loboda, and Bill Bankovics, spring 1966)

True to his politics, Bill preached personal responsibility. Yet Bill was the most giving person I have ever known. He took the time to encourage and cheer me when I was down. He insisted I get snow boots before the first snow in November. He convinced me to buy them after he shared the story of another foreign student a year before, one from Pakistan, who elected not to protect himself with snow boots and cracked his head when he slipped on ice.

Unfortunately, Bill did not stick around for a PhD, his original goal. After three years in graduate school, he was frustrated with the lack of progress on his doctoral dissertation. He elected to collect a master's degree and left in the spring of 1967 for a job with Eastman Kodak in Rochester, New York.

I received my introduction to American politics from Bill. Our discussions helped me cement my own liberal Democratic political beliefs.

Another aspect of formulating my political opinions was the huge outburst of protest against the Vietnam War, coinciding with my tenure at Notre Dame. I was electrified by Bobby Kennedy's announcement of his anti-war candidacy for president on March 16, 1968. I was equally thrilled when Lyndon Johnson withdrew from the contest two weeks later, on March 31, 1968.

The Indiana presidential primary was a critical test for the candidacies of Bobby Kennedy, Eugene McCarthy, and Hubert Humphrey. For my circle of friends, the choice lay between the two anti-war candidates—Kennedy and McCarthy. Humphrey carried the torch for Johnson, justifying the war when it lacked rationale.

I had strongly turned against the Vietnam War in my two and a half years at Notre Dame. I supported Kennedy's candidacy and signed up as a campaign worker in South Bend. My fellow students and I went door-to-door, advocating Bobby's side to people willing to talk to us.

The memory of Kennedy's visit to Notre Dame on April 4, 1968, still remains fresh. His motorcade on campus was mobbed by wildly cheering students. Perhaps the emotion had its roots in students' memory of his brother, Jack. At least a couple of times Bobby was in danger of being pulled down from the car. Some students were reluctant to let go of him as he shook hands from the moving car.

Later in the day, Kennedy met his campaign workers at a private residence in South Bend. As I shook his hand, I was struck by the intensity of his deep blue eyes. He gave me his full attention as he shook my hand and thanked me for helping him.

Kennedy's day ended on a cold, rainy street corner in Indianapolis, where he informed a throng that Martin Luther King had been assassinated an hour earlier in Memphis, Tennessee.

Just three months later, on June 5, 1968, Bobby Kennedy lay mortally wounded on the floor of the kitchen of the Ambassador Hotel in Los Angeles and died in a hospital early the next morning. I was glued to the TV as Kennedy's coffin was transported by a private funeral train, after the mass in St. Patrick's Cathedral in New York City, to Washington, DC, to be buried in Arlington National Cemetery on June 8. My support of Bobby's campaign was based on two hopes. One, if he became president, the implementation of the Civil Rights Act of 1964 would continue forcefully. Two, he would extricate America from the morass of Vietnam, which would go a long way in uniting the country. Bobby's death shattered my dreams.

Not everyone at Notre Dame shared my nascent political views, though I did learn a great deal about American life from some of them. Bill Davidshofer, who started graduate school for political science at Notre Dame a couple of years before I came, was of German stock from Iowa. He was fascinated with the concept of power, at the individual and national levels. He admired the philosopher Nietzsche. His doctoral dissertation was originally focused on the inner workings of the early days of the Soviet Communist Party. Realizing that this approach was too ambitious and open-ended, he changed his research to the French Left about the time I finished at Notre Dame. He taught at just one place after earning his PhD, the University of Maine in Presque Isle.

Where Bill was voluble, Tommy Hindson was a bit introverted. He too was a political science graduate student. Tommy and I shared adjoining

(Tommy Hindson, Bill Davidshofer, and me, 1967)

rental rooms in a house in South Bend for over a year. Tommy grew up in Philadelphia. Interestingly, his late father had been a chemical engineer. He had me over twice to his mother's house in Philadelphia when I later lived in New York City. His family was most kind to me. Tommy too taught at a single place after earning his PhD, at Texas State University in San Marcos.

***

Prior to coming to America, my dating experience had been limited to one single experience in Calcutta. During one of the visits to the American consulate in Calcutta, I met a young lady, Haimanti, who lived with her older sister. We could converse only in English because I didn't speak Bengali. We hit it off and she invited me to lunch at her sister's place. We took in an afternoon movie. She was my first date ever. I was twenty-two and had never taken a girl out. All through the day, I had an out-of-body experience watching myself date a girl. It looked surreal. Nothing came of it, though. I took the train to Kharagpur at the end of the day and that was that.

Within three months of my arrival in South Bend, the holiday season rolled around. I got invited to several holiday parties. Many of them were through the auspices of the ISO, which was open to native-born Americans as well. Both Bill Bankovics and I had enrolled as members. The ISO offered me a great opportunity to meet people from all over. For instance, the holiday parties involved many South Bend families and local students who attended other schools, such as the South Bend campus of Indiana University. A couple in Chicago, Patrick and Patricia Crowley, had close connections with the University of Notre Dame. They would invite several of us from the ISO to their home in Chicago for a pre-Christmas party, as well as a New Year's Eve party. I attended both every year starting in 1965.

One local party was held at the exceptionally large home of a couple in South Bend. The husband was a successful lawyer. The wife, mother of three children, was a very pretty lady in her mid- to late thirties. As I recall, the party music was supplied by a record player. The home was festooned with lovely Christmas decorations, anchored by a tall, very beautifully decorated tree. Alcoholic beverages served to lighten the mood as the evening progressed.

I found myself in conversation with Katie, a beautiful redhead, perhaps a couple of years younger than me. I was nervous, not quite knowing what to say and how to carry the conversation.

"You speak English well," said Katie reassuringly, after I expressed misgivings about my command of the language.

"Thanks. These couples on the floor, they are dancing so well," I marveled.

"Sardul, do you want to dance?" Katie took hold of my hand and started to get up. I felt shell-shocked. I had never danced in my life.

"I can't," I stammered. I must have looked like a deer in the headlights. Katie eased back into her seat. She said a few words to put me at ease, but the earlier magic between us was gone. She soon excused herself.

(Me in January 1966)

Our hostess had observed the brief episode. After Katie had moved to another corner of the room, she came over.

"You may not know, but you are a handsome young man. Katie isn't the only girl tonight who is attracted to you." I know she was trying to boost my self-confidence. She may also have meant the compliment. You, the reader, be the judge of that.

I was thrilled to be complimented by a beautiful woman. My ego was certainly boosted. It strengthened my resolve to date. Not owning a car hampered my fledgling dating life, however.

After I bought the Ford Fairlane in the summer of 1966, I started dating in earnest. Girls from South Bend would come to the Notre Dame campus in the quest to meet the "Notre Dame guys." The Student Huddle was a popular social place. That is where I met Carol, a freshman at the local Indiana University campus. Now that I had a set of wheels, I could go out to my heart's content. I dated Carol for most of the summer, until her father got a job in Chicago and the family moved.

Through the remainder of my time at Notre Dame, I dated moderately. Perhaps the longest relationship was during my third year at school with Linda. I used to drive out to a popular cafeteria-style restaurant in South Bend for dinner. Linda had a part-time job there, which involved multiple duties. Sometimes she would be the cashier; other times she would clear tables. I said hello the first time I saw her. When I was about to leave, she came over and requested a ride home. I joked later about how she picked me up that day. We went out regularly in the summer of 1968 and continued seeing each other till a couple of months before I finished graduate school, when we ended our relationship amicably.

All the girls I dated in school were white girls. This pattern would continue the rest of my early life, and even the girl I met and married several years later is white. In this era—the mid-sixties and the seventies—there were very few Indian immigrants to the United States. The local Indian communities wherever I lived were exceedingly small. The pool of datable Indian girls was non-existent.

As a brown person, by and large, I was untouched by racism in my years at Notre Dame. For long periods of time, I functioned without any awareness of being different—a testimonial to the open-heartedness and sense of fairness of Americans. One incident of overt racism does come to mind.

Some early mornings my colleagues and I would end up at a South Bend diner after a night of bar hopping. (Apparently, Professor Carberry also had a vigorous social life, as we would sometimes run into him at this diner.) One night, the counter was crowded. I stepped away from my friends and approached a couple of men at the counter who looked to be in their sixties.

"Excuse me. Are you going to be done soon?" I inquired.

"Keep your shirt on, brownie," was the gruff answer from one annoyed diner.

I was taken aback. Since I had arrived in the United States, nobody had spoken to me this way, so brusquely and with such undisguised racism. I could not think of an appropriate response and rejoined my friends.

Thankfully, this was an isolated incident. In my assessment of my years in graduate school, America had treated me fairly and generously. Without the teaching and research assistantships, I could never have fulfilled my dream of immigrating to the United States. It is true that I earned them on merit. But the University of Notre Dame did not have to go looking abroad; there was enough home-grown talent. It was a calculated effort to bring in talent from other countries and seed the domestic talent pool. It was also by design that the school accepted applications from the non-white world. Its policy promoted diversity in the school and in the country at large.

At Notre Dame, I met people from all over the world. Like me, they came to America and became part of the American dream. We all contributed abundantly to our adopted homeland.

***

Many companies came to the campus to recruit every year. They included the giants of industry—DuPont, Dow Chemical, Union Carbide, Procter & Gamble, Boeing. In January 1968, I decided it was a good idea to start signing up for these interviews.

My immediate goal was to land a job at a reputable company. Did I want to work for an engineering and construction company? Or would I rather work for a much larger manufacturing company, one that would, in effect, use the resources of the former? What were the rungs for advancement? Did I aspire to head research and development (R&D) at a reputable manufacturing company, such as DuPont? Did I want to aspire to something even higher, such as general management, and what assignments early on in my career would help me get there? I didn't know enough to answer these questions.

I hit it off with three companies: Scientific Design Company, located in New York City, and two New Jersey companies, Esso Research and Engineering Company and Allied Chemical Corporation. Esso went through name changes later, first to Exxon and then ExxonMobil. I was invited to visit their home offices for extensive job interviews.

Such job interviews typically have someone, usually another professional, assigned to shepherd a candidate around. At Scientific Design, the person assigned as my host was David Koch. Koch took me to lunch at a famed eatery, La Brasserie, in Midtown Manhattan. I was greatly impressed by the ambiance of this restaurant. I made one slip. I referred to the restaurant later on as "The Brassiere," which drew a quick chuckle and correction from Koch.

Does the name David Koch sound familiar? Indeed, this was the same David Koch who went on to become the ninth-wealthiest person in the world as of 2014. *Forbes* magazine estimated his net worth in August 2017 at $48 billion.

Koch had earned a master's degree in chemical engineering from the Massachusetts Institute of Technology in 1963.

He was a college basketball star; his record at MIT for the most points scored in a single game held for forty-six years. His father, Fred Koch, founded Koch Industries. Fred had four children, all boys. He had insisted that all of them study chemical engineering. Three complied. The eldest, Frederick R. Koch, earned an MFA degree at Harvard College and went on to become an art collector and restorer of historic places. The Koch patriarch was none too pleased with Frederick's lifestyle, including, it was whispered, his sexual orientation.

My interviews at Scientific Design Company and Esso Research and Engineering went off well, resulting in a job offer from each. I was impressed by the quality of the people I interviewed with at Scientific Design; most of them held PhD degrees in chemical engineering. The Esso people were good too, but did not stand out as much. I accepted the offer from Scientific Design, with an annual salary of $16,000. In hindsight, going with Esso would have been a smarter choice in terms of the future potential for advancement, but I had also been dazzled by the glamor of New York City, thanks in no small measure to what David Koch had shown me.

As I caught the New York flight from South Bend in the last week of February 1969, I was elated at the prospect of starting my career at a prestigious engineering and construction company. Though I was excited by the vision of living in one of the great cities of the world, I was still apprehensive about all that I didn't know outside the world of academia.

CHAPTER 7

BIG APPLE

The essence of faith is the knowledge that all flows and everything must change.
 - Thomas Wolfe, You Can't Go Home Again, 1940

I was guided by the thought that change is the only certainty as I started my career with Scientific Design Company. I was scheduled to report for work on Monday, March 3, 1969.

The company had booked me into the Commodore Hotel. I could walk the ten blocks to my office at Two Park Avenue. The hotel had been a city landmark since it opened on January 28, 1919. It had been named after "Commodore" Cornelius Vanderbilt. Such was Vanderbilt's energy in his trade on Staten Island, New York, that captains nearby took to calling him "the Commodore" in jest. The hotel boasted many famous guests, including Albert Einstein, who stayed at the hotel for a few weeks in April 1921. He was touring the East Coast to promote the creation of Hebrew University in Jerusalem.

During my two-week stay at the Commodore, I used my time away from work to search for an apartment. I got invaluable help from an Israeli colleague, Raphael, who had earned an MS degree in chemical engineering at MIT and became a good friend. He helped me understand the general layout of Manhattan and guided me to the areas I should focus on for finding an apartment.

At the very outset of the search, Raphael drew a map of Manhattan on a napkin. Until then I had not realized that Manhattan was a long, relatively thin island running north to south. He pointed out the sections of the city, such as the Upper East and West Side, Midtown, the Murray Hill neighborhood, the East Village, and Greenwich Village. I was astonished by the location and size of Central Park, which I was to visit many times, sometimes with Raphael.

Raphael helped me understand that the two villages, bounded by Fourteenth Street on the north, were the epicenter of the counterculture movement. The Upper East Side was favored by young professionals. The Upper West Side was popular at the time with artists, bohemians, writers, and the like. Midtown appeared to house the upper crust of New York. The campus of Columbia University stretched along a fifteen-block area north of 110th Street, bounded by the Hudson River on the west.

I settled on a rent-controlled one-bedroom apartment on the Upper West Side, just off Broadway on Ninety-First Street. The thirty-minute subway commute to my office was reasonable. Columbia University wasn't far. The Hudson River was only three blocks to the west. The milieu of the Upper West Side appealed to me. But I earned an ugly introduction to a seamier side of New York City in the process of renting the apartment.

My landlord, Jerry, was an aggressive, obnoxious businessman. I had located this apartment through an advertisement in the *New York Times*. There was a shortage of apartments in the city, a chronic problem at the time, so I was eager to snag it. It was within three blocks of the subway stop, and the controlled rent would be $171 a month. But Jerry blithely added, on top of the one month's rent as security deposit, yet another month's rent as the fee for the rental agent. It was outrageous, and there was no use arguing with him. He was a bully. He invited me to go find another place if his terms were unacceptable. I caved.

(On a Circle Line boat cruise around Manhattan, summer 1969. Photo by Raphael. The bespectacled young man in the foreground was among a group of tourists from Sweden.)

***

Scientific Design Company was a technology development leader in the chemical and petrochemical industries between 1950 and 1980. It was founded by Ralph Landau, a legendary chemical engineer who had earned an ScD at MIT in 1941. Its research, development, and design activities led to the grant of 1,400 patents, and its technologies were practiced in three hundred plants worldwide.

The parent company was reorganized in 1963 as Halcon International, which would have several subsidiaries. Halcon Development Company would carry out R&D. Scientific Design Company would carry out the design and construction activities. Halcon Chemical Company would be the manufacturing subsidiary. The company was headquartered at Two Park Avenue, between Thirty-Second and Thirty-Third Streets, in lower Manhattan.

Scientific Design Company took the entire seventh floor of the building. Halcon International was housed on the eighth floor, where Landau and his top lieutenants had offices. Halcon Development Company took most of the fifteenth floor. I found myself riding the elevator to the fifteenth floor often because it housed the mainframe computer. I also had extensive interactions with the development people on the fifteenth floor.

A sizable chunk of the Halcon Development Company's workforce held advanced chemical engineering degrees from MIT, primarily doctorates. The contingent at Scientific Design mostly held master's degrees in chemical engineering, with a few PhDs sprinkled here and there.

One of my interviewers, when I visited from South Bend, was Monroe Malow. Holder of an ScD in chemical engineering, he was a senior manager at Scientific Design. He impressed me greatly with his demeanor and knowledge. In my second week, I requested to see him. At the scheduled time, I walked from my cubicle to his office. His door was closed.

"Dr. Malow will be with you right away," said Stephanie, his blonde secretary. "Something urgent came up." I lingered near her desk and made small talk, a pleasant way to while away a few minutes. After a ten-minute wait, Malow emerged from his office with a broad smile.

"Sorry to keep you waiting, Sardul. Welcome to the company."

Malow's office wasn't spacious but it looked functional. His degree from MIT was displayed on one wall. For a busy manager, the desk wasn't too cluttered, though it did feature a picture of his wife. I could see the adjacent building on Park Avenue through the office window.

Malow confided that he remembered our discussion during my job interview, "which impressed me," he said. He explained how process design was the heart of chemical engineering. It was the ideal place to start one's career in the profession. Process design was where all the results of R&D came together, and the engineer would then turn them into the design of chemical equipment. It was the critical building block from ideas into real chemical plants.

Malow's exhortations hit the mark. I set out to learn all I could from the experienced engineers on the floor. David Koch, whose cubicle was across mine, was one of them. He went out of his way to be helpful as I endeavored to learn the fine points of process engineering. Koch returned to his family business a year later.

The tools available to engineers at the time were primitive when viewed through the lens of the electronic advances of the twenty-first century. I still used my slide rule for some calculations. We had calculators to perform basic functions such as addition, subtraction, multiplication, and division. Scientific calculators such as the HP-35 wouldn't appear on the market for another three years. We relied heavily on the mainframe computer, an IBM 360.

Process design was laboriously slow. The company had developed programs for the design of complex chemical equipment such as distillation columns. The turnaround time on the mainframe computer for a single run could be a couple of days. The design of a multicomponent distillation column, which can be completed today using the latest personal computers in a matter of hours, took a week or longer.

Notwithstanding these limitations, the power of process engineering rapidly dawned on me. I was fascinated by the innumerable opportunities afforded to the process designer to be creative. I learned to optimize the size of process equipment, which would, in turn reduce the overall capital investment for a project. The designer could also reduce the operating costs, which would strongly impact the profitability of the chemical plant and cash flow throughout its operating life.

My first assignment was with a team of engineers (Koch was also on the team) designing a new plant to manufacture maleic anhydride, an important intermediate for the production of fiberglass-reinforced resins, which are used in construction products such as countertops, tubs, and sinks, as well as pleasure boats and automobiles. Our client company was Monsanto.

***

I took to exploring the city energetically. My friend Raphael was helpful with tips regarding the popular bars, but sometimes I would go out on my own and take a chance with new places.

I unwittingly walked into a historic event within my first few months in the city. I had gone to Greenwich Village on Saturday, June 28, 1969. Raphael had told me of the lively music and bar scene in the village, and I was eager to check it out. Unbeknownst to me, police had raided Stonewall Inn in the Village earlier that morning. The inn and its bar were hangouts for gay people and drag queens. What followed the raid is referred to as the Stonewall riots, which broke out that same day and continued for the rest of the summer.

I found myself in the midst of an enormous crowd of young people, mostly men but some women, too. What astonished me was the exhibition of same-sex affection in public. I observed men kissing other men. The poet Allen Ginsberg, himself gay, described that evening: "You know, the guys there were so beautiful—they've lost that wounded look that fags all had ten years ago." The scenes are seared into my memory.

I was so mesmerized by the goings-on around me that it didn't occur to me that I was in the wrong crowd, since I had set out to discover the straight party scene in the Village, and that I could be in danger. The heavy police presence I could see throughout the crowd could have provoked violence. After perhaps an hour, I had the good sense to ease out of the crowd and head for the nearest subway home.

In all fairness, the New York Police Department since then has shown the capacity for introspection and rectitude. Nearly fifty years after the raid at the Stonewall Inn, New York's police commissioner apologized for what his department did. "The actions and the laws were discriminatory and oppressive," Commissioner James O'Neill said during a June 7, 2019, briefing at police headquarters. "And for that, I apologize."

This misadventure in Greenwich Village was but a small window into the much broader cultural and social scene that I discovered and learned to enjoy. I particularly loved outings to Central Park on weekends.

That such an oasis of calm could exist in the midst of the hyper-noisy city was a marvel. This area of Manhattan, from Fifty-Ninth Street to 110th Street between Fifth Avenue and Central Park West, had been set aside by the New York State Legislature on July 21, 1853, as a "public place." Besides offering New Yorkers a reprieve from the pressures of extreme urban life, the park serves another very useful purpose. Its thousands of trees and the 843 acres of trails, lawns, gardens, and ponds act as a natural air conditioning unit for the urban "heat island" that Manhattan turns into on the hottest days of July and August.

I loved walks through the Shakespeare Garden, even though it looked neglected and was a bit overgrown; it would be cleaned up by volunteers a couple of years after I left the city. I enjoyed the impromptu music. There would be a lone musician in one location and a group of musicians playing a variety of instruments in another. Watching and interacting with other visitors to the park gave me great joy. Some came from afar, others lived in the city.

My social life occasionally extended to the beaches of Long Island. During my second spring in the city, in 1970, I answered an advertisement in the *Village Voice*, which led to my renting a weekend share, along with about ten other people, in a boardwalk house. The house was in the Davis Park hamlet of Fire Island. I would take a Long Island Rail Road (LIRR) train from Manhattan and disembark at Patchogue. A twenty-minute ride on a ferry would take me to my destination on Fire Island.

The summer of 1970 was memorable. Our house was mixed-gender, though the ratio may have slightly favored the men. However, we avoided dating people from the same house, which ensured a generally congenial atmosphere through the three months we spent together. Fire Island had a tradition called "Sixish," which consisted of mixing and dancing at the beach. (Actually, people would gather closer to seven p.m.) One such evening I was in deep conversation with a girl when I heard a greeting from behind me. It was Brian Ozero, one of the managers at Scientific Design and my boss on several projects. Ozero whipped past me with a beautiful young lady on each arm and proceeded to dance. It was hard to reconcile my image of a dignified boss in the office with the carefree swinger at the beach.

I dated many young women when I lived in Manhattan, but got close to only a few. One of them—I'll call her Margie—was an exception. I dated her for several months. But her life was complicated. Though she was my age, she had already been married twice. She lived life with a certain degree of abandon, which was exhilarating to me in the beginning. But I craved stability in the long run.

I got to know David Koch socially. I remember the night when he came to a party in my apartment, accompanied by a date. Koch was a confirmed bachelor for a long time. He played the field, dating such luminaries as the actress Ali MacGraw. He would marry much later, at the age of fifty-six.

Koch was a full-fledged libertarian, opposed to most

government regulation. He opposed rent control, unbothered that thousands upon thousands of New Yorkers would lose their apartments altogether if the rents were allowed to rise in a free market—myself included.

My original apartment was on the ground floor and bordered a narrow alley. It was narrow and long—called a "railroad apartment." I didn't realize it then, but I was to learn later how unsafe it was.

(Me in my upstairs apartment, April 1971, photographed by Margie)

The apartment got burglarized about a year after I moved in. The thieves had entered through the window overlooking the alley. I lost most things of value. To add insult to injury, the thieves drank from one of the Coke bottles in the fridge. They carefully left it on my dining table, still one-quarter full. It appeared to be some kind of message, perhaps one of impunity.

I replenished my wardrobe after the burglary. I was able to buy theft insurance, thanks to a colleague at work, who connected me with his carrier. I regained peace of mind.

The thieves struck again. Just ten days after the first burglary, they cleaned me out once more. The insurance company paid up and promptly dropped me. So much for that peace of mind.

I had a bright yellow shirt that I wasn't very fond of. Nor, it seems, were the burglars. That was the only garment they left behind each time. Not only did they rob me twice, but they clearly let me know their opinion of my fashion sense. That hurt. I related the story to Brian Ozero at work, looking for sympathy. The man almost fell off his chair laughing.

Mercifully, an apartment on the second floor became vacant soon, and I grabbed it.

***

Halcon Chemical partnered with Atlantic Richfield Company (Arco) in 1967 in a fifty-fifty venture to form Oxirane Corporation. They manufactured propylene oxide, an important building block for producing polyurethane plastics. Polyurethane foam is used in upholstery fabrics in commercial and domestic furniture and in insulation panels in the construction sector. The plastic is also injection-molded to form components for various markets—agriculture, automotive, industrial, and so on.

One particular success story of Halcon Development Company was its landmark process for manufacturing propylene oxide. The company licensed the process to numerous players around the world, and Oxirane built two of its own plants at Bayport in Texas, referred to as Bayport I and Bayport II. I was a part of the team of process engineers that designed the second plant.

In the summer of 1971, there was a small explosion in Bayport I, located southeast of Houston, almost ten miles straight east from Johnson Space Center. No life was lost, but it caused considerable damage. After the repairs were made and the plant started up again, management decided to install round-the-clock coverage by four process engineers, two each from Scientific Design and Arco. The move was intended to be temporary, to last four months.

Our vice president of engineering, Manfred Gans, went around the hallway in his usual hurried style one day. He poked his head into my cubicle, pointed at me, and said "you." Before I could catch up with him, he hurried to a nearby cubicle and went through the same motions at one of my colleagues, Morris Gelb. We soon learned that we had been selected for the Bayport I assignment.

I was thrilled. This was a wonderful vote of faith in my capabilities. The assignment would last from September 1971 until January 1972. It was an opportunity for growth, both professionally and personally. It was great to get out into a real chemical plant and see the fruit of our design efforts. During my assignment, I made some recommendations, which were accepted by the plant management.

Before I left New York, I had all sorts of misgivings about Texans. I had this vague idea that overt racism was more prevalent in Texas than in the Northeast. The reality was very different. I found the people I interacted with, both in the plant and outside work, hospitable and quite willing to engage. However, there was a red line that I quickly became aware of. Texans didn't take kindly to criticism as a group. They were well aware of the mocking stories about them that made the rounds in other parts of the country.

I found an apartment in Seabrook, off Clear Lake, barely two miles from the space center. The four months in Texas turned out to be a very happy period of my life. I made friends at the plant, both in the blue-collar and professional ranks. A senior shift operator, Mac, invited me to his home. I became good friends with a plant chemical engineer, Michael Spuhler. He introduced me to his wife Rhoda and his young children, John and Stephanie. We have kept up our friendship through the decades.

I also met Jack, an electrical engineer, who was on assignment to the space center. Jack was of Irish American lineage; his parents still lived in the Bronx. Jack was a sailor. Once I sailed with him to Galveston, my first time on a sailboat.

Jack would casually introduce me to others sharing the lunch table in the NASA cafeteria. One guy and I shared a pleasant conversation over lunch. After he left, Jack told me this guy was an astronaut, undergoing rigorous training at the space center.

"Why didn't you say so when we were introduced?" I complained.

"Because then you would be star-struck." Jack's logic was impeccable.

The icing on the cake during my stay in Texas was the lovely Texan women I got to meet. They were more open and direct than the women I knew in New York. The closest I ever came to losing my heart, before meeting the woman I would marry, was to this young blonde Texan named Ann. I was astonished by her command of accents. I almost fell off my chair when I heard Ann mimic my Indian accent. It was so weird listening to how I actually sounded. It was uncanny. She would tease me and it worked.

I did not allow my relationship with Ann to blossom further because she was married at the time. While I was developing feelings for her, would her commitment to me not wane over time? If I could sweep her off her feet sufficiently to make her consider leaving her husband, how could I be sure of the steadfastness of her feelings for me? She could always come across someone more charming and better looking one day.

***

By the time I returned to New York in January 1972, I had started looking into ways of broadening my skills. I had become a pretty good process engineer, and the Texas assignment familiarized me with the plant environment. I became aware of an opening for a research engineer at Halcon Development's facilities in Little Ferry, New Jersey. After I expressed my interest, I was offered the position.

I transferred to Little Ferry in March 1972. I plunged into

a new process the company was researching for the production of ethylene glycol, which promised huge cost savings over the existing manufacturing process. Ethylene glycol is an important precursor for polyester fibers as well as for many antifreeze formulations. With the help of technicians, I piloted several parts of the new process. I learned firsthand how the basic data for developing new processes was gathered. I also acquired the gut feel of how processes actually functioned by observing their behavior in the pilot-sized equipment. This important insight helped me later in my career while troubleshooting problems in full-sized manufacturing plants.

I lived in an apartment in Maywood, a suburb of Hackensack. I acquired two new skills while I lived there, outside of my work experiences. I signed up for a month-long swimming course at the Hackensack YMCA. Though I couldn't swim when I started, I emerged four weeks later fairly competent in performing breast and back strokes. I could also swim the butterfly and side strokes. For the first time in my life, I was able to wade deeper into the ocean at the beach and enjoy the waters.

I also signed up for tennis lessons, offered by a middle-aged gentleman who had played at the lower rungs of professional tennis in his youth. He taught the class the basics of tennis. Ever since, I can step onto a tennis court with some confidence.

As I approached the end of my first year in Little Ferry, I took stock of my professional development. I had developed a good understanding of process engineering research. The hands-on experience I received had been invaluable. The awareness dawned on me, something I missed while interviewing at Notre Dame, that career prospects at engineering companies are constrained by the very nature of the business they are engaged in. They always work for a manufacturing company, referred to in industry parlance as the "owner." The owner makes the key decisions on capital investment and selection of personnel. It is the owner who gets to make the call between alternative options considered for design.

(With my new Ford Capri, in the spring of 1972)

Large manufacturing companies have a vast range of functions, of which research, development, and engineering are but a small part. Manufacturing plants, marketing, sales, purchasing, and industrial safety offer a glimpse of the vast universe beyond engineering. I mentioned earlier that turning down the offer from Esso Research and Engineering was a mistake. That realization sank in as I was completing my first year in Little Ferry.

I decided to actively seek a job at a manufacturing (also referred to as "operating") company. I found an advertisement for senior process engineers by Stauffer Chemical Company. The location for these positions was Dobbs Ferry in Westchester County, roughly twenty miles north of Manhattan. The location was ideal for me. Manhattan would be within easy reach if I were to live within commuting distance of Dobbs Ferry.

I answered the advertisement. I was impressed by the caliber of people who interviewed me. Stauffer extended an attractive offer, which I accepted. When I tendered my resignation, John Hogan, Halcon International's vice president of human resources, called me in. He told me that I was well regarded in the company and even showed me a job evaluation where my manager had identified me as a potential process manager. He urged me to stay, which I found very gratifying. But I had made up my mind to leave.

I started my new job at Stauffer in June 1973.

***

I had arrived from India in 1965 on a student F1 visa. A few days before departing for New York, I reported to the local office of the Immigration and Naturalization Service in South Bend and obtained permission to work. Within a month of starting with Scientific Design, the company sponsored me for immigration. My green card arrived in September 1969. At that point I was free to travel abroad, and I took the opportunity to visit my family.

(With Ranbir in Fredericton, Canada, July 1972)

When my brother, Ranbir, saw me off at the Chandigarh bus station in August 1965, he was teaching in the chemical engineering department at Panjab University. He left within months for teaching positions at the Pilani Institute of Technology in Rajasthan and then at the Indian Institute of Technology, Delhi.

He had an arranged marriage to a pretty and very smart girl, Kuldip, from a village not very far from our own. He and Kuldip moved to Fredericton, New Brunswick, in Canada in September 1968. Ranbir had been awarded an assistantship to work toward a master's degree.

I flew to Fredericton in October 1969. I was impressed by my sister-in-law. Despite having an arranged marriage, they clearly shared mutual affection and love. After receiving his master's degree in chemical engineering in 1970, Ranbir switched to computer science. I drove to Fredericton in July 1972. He was wrapping up work on the master's degree in computer science at the time. I noticed something worrisome, though. He seemed to have developed a lot of friction with members of the Indian community in Fredericton, at least the ones I got to meet. Judging by the comments he made to Kuldip, he distrusted the motives of most of them.

Just a few months later, Ranbir and Kuldip moved to Toronto, where Ranbir had accepted an offer of an assistantship at the University of Toronto to work toward a PhD in computer science. I visited them again in Toronto in early 1973. He was very distant in his interactions with me. He had never been demonstrative with his feelings, but in Fredericton, we could at least have a conversation. Now he was less trusting and less willing to engage.

Ranbir wasn't the only family member I was able to see after I received my green card. I first returned to India in October 1970 after an absence of five years. Bauji's health had deteriorated badly. He was rapidly losing motor control on his left side. His asthma had gotten worse. But the joy Bauji and my mother, Bhabiji, felt when seeing me was palpable. I took Bauji for evaluation by a few specialists, but none was optimistic about arresting the pace of his Parkinson's disease.

I was torn by a torrent of emotions. I felt guilty every time I flew back to New York. Bauji's suffering tore at me. But what was I supposed to do? Have him move to the United States with me? The physicians I took him to see in Punjab were very well known in the field. What was the guarantee he would get better health care in America? The flip side of a decision to bring him to America would be the total disruption of my life. I wasn't ready for that. And yet, the struggle between guilt and resentment continued after I returned home to the United States.

I developed a case of severe migraine headaches after I returned to New York. They would strike in the middle of the night while I was asleep, and the pain was unbearable. I happened to come across a psychiatrist who had recently emigrated from India. He worked at Columbia University as an associate professor.

"Are you married?" asked the professor.

"No, despite my parents' strenuous efforts during my visit home last month."

"Are your parents all right, health-wise?"

"No. My dad is very ill, but I had to leave him behind."

"I shall give you a prescription for tranquilizers. I think that will fix your migraines."

The tranquilizers worked immediately. The good doctor had diagnosed my malady correctly. I was suffering from severe emotional trauma.

***

In his book *Solitude: A Return to the Self* (2015), Anthony Storr ruminated about how people look at marriage as the ultimate source of happiness. He opined that if people did not invest the idea of marriage with unbridled happiness, "fewer marriages would end in tears."

I had been conditioned to the Western way of finding a mate—unhurried and looking for a connection in a natural setting. Such attempts while I was in India were anything but.

I returned to India again in December 1972. My parents were very serious about finding me a *suitable* girl to marry. The girl should be from a Sikh family. If not that, she should at the very least be a Punjabi girl. Of course, she should be well educated, fluent in the English language, and so on.

I agreed with Storr's views in my bachelor days. I just didn't see marriage as the panacea of all that I desired and

(With my sisters Parkash (left) and Gurmit near Dhandaur on my India visit, December 1972)

worked for. Why then did I go along with my parents' plans and agree to explore potential matches? Guilt. I hadn't really done much to bring joy and comfort to Bauji, and this was clearly important to him. I may even have convinced myself that if I met the right girl, I would take the plunge.

Colonel Parmar, an active-duty officer in the Indian Army, came from the village of Kalra, just a couple of miles away from my ancestral village of Daroli Khurd. Parmar's brother-in-law—we shall call him Tarsem—was a farmer in an adjoining village. Tarsem approached us about Parmar's daughter, "Pammi," who was studying for her bachelor's degree in Bombay. He was pretty sure that the young lady was at the time visiting her parents in Mhow in the central Indian state of Madhya Pradesh, where Parmar was posted. Tarsem wrote Parmar a letter saying that he and I would be coming to visit. While cell phones are ubiquitous in today's India, even landlines were rare in the early 1970s.

Tarsem set out for Mhow by train the next day; it would take him two days to arrive. I opted to fly instead and managed to get there ahead of him. Tarsem's letter had reached Parmar before my arrival. Parmar met me at the airport, and we collected Tarsem from the train station.

"Sardul is visiting from America. We thought it would be great for him and Pammi to meet," said Tarsem, after getting settled in the car.

Parmar looked sheepish. "Actually, Pammi is in Bombay. She had to cut short her visit."

Air travel was expensive then, especially for those on Indian incomes. There was no way I could expect Parmar to fly the young lady back home so she could meet me. Chagrined by the poor planning, I was not too enthusiastic about flying on to Bombay to see her. Logistically, a meeting in Bombay would have required the presence of Pammi's parents too. Perhaps they couldn't afford the air travel. Either way, the idea of meeting in Bombay wasn't broached.

But Tarsem and I were already in Mhow, and the Parmars were gracious hosts. I stayed with them for two nights. Parmar showed me around. The name of the city is an acronym for Military Headquarters of War. It was, and is, an important base of the Indian Army. Parmar gave me a tour of the base and introduced me to some of his brother officers.

We parted with the vague understanding of staying in touch. We all knew that the absence of his daughter pretty much killed the endeavor. I reproached myself for embarking on a distant meeting such as this without receiving verification of the basic elements of the plan.

Another Parmar was a well-to-do businessman in Jalandhar. A middleman, Jaswant Singh Parmar, proposed the businessman's daughter—we shall call her Asha—as a potential match. I planned to take an old acquaintance, Swaran Singh Parmar, with me to the meeting with Asha and her parents. Parmar is a common family name in Punjab.

Swaran was my contemporary. While I studied chemical engineering at Chandigarh, he had studied chemistry. He then earned a PhD from one of the universities in Punjab. He also came from the same village, Panchhat, where my mother had grown up.

Asha's father had a financing business, primarily for the purchase of trucks and other heavy-duty vehicles. He was reputed to be rich. The family lived in a nice house in Jalandhar City. The middleman, Jaswant, was a business partner of

Asha's father. I had committed to Jaswant on the date of the meeting.

Swaran and I drove to Jalandhar that day from my parents' house. But I was conflicted about going to meet this young lady and had pretty much decided to back out. I had business at the local bank anyway and needed to do some shopping as well. But as I hung around in the vicinity of the bank, I was stunned by the sudden appearance of Jaswant. It is as if he had been monitoring my movements all morning.

"Are you ready to go see Asha?" he inquired with a wide smile.

"Ah, yes," I stammered, angry that he had waylaid me.

"We were all set to go there, Uncle," said the ever-alert Swaran.

The terms "uncle" and "aunt" are freely used in India as marks of respect toward older people. We followed Jaswant's car to Asha's house.

The visit lasted perhaps forty-five minutes. Asha was a good-looking young woman. She lived in a well-furnished house. Swaran, who was already married, was bowled over by Asha's looks. I left Asha's family with the understanding that we would reconnect soon afterward.

My thoughts about Asha were complicated. I needed to resolve the basic question; did I really want an arranged marriage? If the answer was yes, Asha would have made perfect sense as my future partner. But the answer in my mind was a firm no.

Swaran had no idea of the issue that I had been wrestling with, nor did he know the conclusion I had reached. He appeared convinced that I was going to say yes to marrying Asha.

He excused himself for the rest of the day and met up with me the next morning. He claimed to have made inquiries about the young woman. Supposedly, the gossip mill had it that "her character wasn't good." Driven by a petty motive, jealousy, he had no problem slandering Asha just so I wouldn't get to marry someone "so pretty."

After that, word spread rapidly that I wasn't interested in finding a wife, at least in Punjab. The number of queries dropped off. As I flew back to New York, I knew that the woman I would one day marry would be someone I knew and loved. There would not be an arranged marriage.

CHAPTER 8

WESTCHESTER

The only way to do great work is to love what you do. If you haven't found it yet, keep looking. Don't settle.
- Steve Jobs, "Commencement Address, Stanford University," June 12, 2005

The job change from Scientific Design to Stauffer Chemical Company landed me in a much bigger pond.

Stauffer was founded in 1886 in San Francisco as a partnership between two young Europeans—a German, John Stauffer, and a Frenchman, Christian de Guigne. It developed a strong position in commodity chemicals such as sulfur, potash, and phosphorus, and became a significant manufacturer of herbicides and insecticides. Around the time I joined the company, it was the country's third largest producer of phosphorus, behind the FMC Corporation and Monsanto.

Stauffer had a strong R&D capability, along with a thriving central engineering department. Each had a western component, located in Richmond, California, and an eastern component, based in Dobbs Ferry, New York. The two engineering groups, along with a licensing engineering group, reported to a vice president, Dave Roberts, who was located in the corporate offices in Westport, Connecticut. The two R&D groups reported to another vice president in Westport. All technical groups came together under Harold Mickley, executive vice president.

Leonard Wender, manager of the Chemical Engineering Department, had hired me. Five sections reported to him—Process Design, Process Development, Process Systems, Environmental Group, and Materials Science. I would be joining the Process Design Section, reporting to the section head, Dr. Duke Lay.

Soon after joining the team, I requested a meeting with Wender, which he happily granted. My goal was to understand the larger organizational structure, the critical projects on Wender's plate, and how I could help. Of course, I had already had a similar discussion with Lay, my direct boss, who had encouraged me to speak with Wender.

The meeting with Wender went well. He described the operations in Dobbs Ferry, in Richmond (California), and in the Westport headquarters. What he said next inspired me very much. He told me that he had been impressed with my set of skills, which combined strengths in process engineering and process research. He expected the latter to come in handy as I interacted with the Research Division. I was thrilled. It felt good to be visible to someone at Wender's level.

It wasn't only his praise that influenced me. From the beginning, I was impressed by the quality of questions Wender asked me during the interview. I was just as impressed by his decency and the respect he showed me. In the following years, our interactions revealed him to be a man of integrity.

One day the phone rang, and I answered.

"Hello, Sardul. This is Len Wender."

I had been working on the design of a complex piece of process equipment in my office. I pushed away the clutter of paper near the phone as I tried to focus on Len's call.

"Good morning, Len."

"LeCashman stopped by. He couldn't say enough good things about one of your memos. I thought you would like to know," said Wender.

John LeCashman was the executive assistant to Mickley. Praise from LeCashman was a big deal. This was classic Wender, who supported me in good times and bad.

While I assume this call came from his office, I saw Wender use a pay phone many times to make personal phone calls. He would bring his own supply of quarters to feed into the phone. He could have made these calls from his office. He could close his office door and ensure privacy while he talked. But he sacrificed privacy in the interest of personal integrity. He just wouldn't make personal calls on the company's dime. His honesty was appealing.

***

I rented a one-bedroom apartment on the outskirts of White Plains, bordering Hartsdale, in Westchester County. White Plains was the county seat and the commercial hub of Westchester. The apartment was far more spacious than the ones I had rented in Manhattan and in New Jersey. It felt good to live in a very nice apartment building, which was named Tompkins Manor. I also enjoyed having an assigned parking spot, not a common feature of NYC apartments.

Within a few weeks of starting at Stauffer, I made a lifelong friend. Bob Rickman, an electrical engineer, was a contract employee who worked through an agency. I was drawn to Bob's calm demeanor, though I would often be startled by his sharp sense of humor. Thanks to his encouragement, I joined Westchester Ski Club, which rented a house in Vermont every winter.

I had tried to learn to ski when I lived in Manhattan. I would go with friends to the ski resort at Hunter Mountain in New York state. Though I had learned the rudiments of skiing, the best I could do then was negotiate a beginner's slope.

I spent ten days of vacation during the winter of 1973–1974 at the club's ski house in Vermont. I took formal ski lessons and skied zealously every day at one of the two resorts—Killington and Ramshead. The upshot was that by the end of the vacation, I had gotten a lot better at skiing, even starting to ski down expert slopes.

I dated several girls I met through the Ski Club and on the ski slopes. One exception was a young lady I met at a cultural festival in 1974 at the Metropolitan Museum of Art in Manhattan. The festival featured dances from different cultures. I remember going to at least two—the Morocco and India pavilions. The beautiful, talented dancer in the Indian pavilion performed a couple of solo numbers. She had taken care to dress properly in a sari and adorn her forehead with the red dot, called a bindi. However, something was off to me. Her skin was white.

I introduced myself while the crowd dispersed at the end of her performance. Her name was Ratilekha. She was quite willing to exchange contact information. Ratilekha's father, a white American, had married a woman from the Indian state of Kashmir. I don't know when she moved to the United States, but after moving here, she had made a determined effort to stay an Indian in form and spirit. While living in Manhattan, she wore her sari everywhere.

We dated over a four-month period. After two months, I took her to a reception in Manhattan that had been arranged in honor of Triloki Nath Kaul, India's ambassador to the United States. Kaul previously served as India's ambassador to the Soviet Union, China, and the UK. He also served in the top career position in the Indian Ministry of External Affairs as

Indian Foreign Secretary from 1967 to 1972. Although dressed in Indian clothing, Ratilekha stood out among the Indian women at the reception because of her light skin. But she handled herself with aplomb.

Ratilekha was very private about her life before I met her. I never found out if she had any living relatives in the United States. She was staying at a woman's boardinghouse in Manhattan at the time we dated. She once made a comment regarding my professional career, suggesting that I was in a rat race to acquire titles and wealth. The comment didn't sit well with me. Why did she enthusiastically agree to keep dating me if that was how she saw me? I took steps to end the relationship.

The mystery was solved a few months after we stopped dating. I called to see how she was doing. I learned that she had moved into the local Hare Krishna Ashram and became a *sannyasin*, a term for females who enter the life stage of renunciation within the Hindu philosophy. Sannyasa is traditionally undertaken by men and women in the very late years of their life. It amounts to the renunciation of worldly and materialistic pursuits and dedication of one's life to spiritual pursuits. Ratilekha was in her late twenties or early thirties, though. Her decision came as a shock, but at least it explained her judgment of my career aspirations.

***

My first assignment at Stauffer was to design several new processes for implementation at Stauffer's insecticide plant in Mount Pleasant, Tennessee. The small town of Mount Pleasant was sixty miles southwest of Nashville. When I traveled to the plant, I would stay overnight in either Nashville or Columbia. The latter, ten miles northeast, was the county seat of Maury County, in which the plant was located.

The Mount Pleasant plant stank to high heaven. I wasn't forewarned, however. I found out for myself as soon as I left the main road between Columbia and Mount Pleasant during my first visit to the plant. As I drove the winding one-mile-long road to the Stauffer plant, the extreme stench of rotten eggs invaded my nostrils. During the first day in the plant, my clothes, my shoes, and my hair were saturated with the smell.

My nose rapidly became immune to the stink, though, and because of that I made the terrible assumption, at the end of the second day, that I could drive straight from the plant to the Nashville airport and board my flight home. I noticed people giving me strange looks at the airport and hastening to get away from me. The truth dawned on me. I quickly purchased a spray deodorant from one of the airport shops and applied copious amounts all over. I would never make that mistake again. In the future, I would return to my hotel room, shower, and change into a fresh set of clothing before checking out and heading to the airport.

The company had used an old batch process for decades to manufacture the powerful and potent group of insecticides, collectively known as Parathion. Stauffer's R&D groups had developed a new, continuous process that promised higher yields, lower costs, and, importantly, smaller processing inventories of the toxic intermediates.

Process inventories had a direct bearing on safety. The batch process was carried out in large reactors, some as big as 1,000 gallons. If something were to go wrong—a leak, a runaway reaction causing an explosion, a bad batch that had to be disposed of as waste—during the processing of a batch, the potential harm to plant personnel and to the plant environment was significant. A continuous process could be carried out in a series of much smaller reactors. Thousand-gallon reactors could be replaced with hundred-gallon reactors. The resultant danger from defective processing would be significantly less.

The higher yields meant lower consumption of raw materials for producing a certain amount of the final product and hence a reduced manufacturing cost. There was the added benefit of producing smaller quantities of byproducts, resulting in lower costs of disposal. The overall impact of replacing the ongoing batch processing with the new continuous process would be reduced manufacturing costs and greater safety. My team of process engineers—of which I was the lead—was charged with engineering the findings of R&D into a workable manufacturing facility. One challenge of the assignment was to shoehorn the new processing train into the existing manufacturing plant, taking care to use as much existing equipment as feasible.

The insecticides, Parathions, were used on cotton, rice, and fruit trees. They were highly toxic. The standard of workplace safety and emissions in the 1970s was far laxer than what became acceptable even two decades later. The plant produced a significant amount of organic byproduct waste streams, as well as a sizable polluted aqueous discharge. Shocking as it may seem today, the organic waste was pumped deep underground in "deep wells," where it would inevitably escape into water aquifers. The practice, tolerated at the time, was banned several decades later by the Environmental Protection Agency (EPA). Today, Parathion is banned in twenty-three countries, and the World Health Organization has called for a global ban. In Germany, Parathion is called *Schwiegermuttergift*, loosely translated as "mother-in-law poison."

Anyhow, the products, as well as the manufacturing processes—both the old batch and the new continuous processes—met the regulatory requirements of the time. My assignment brought me into direct contact with a great many other disciplines—R&D, of course, but also representatives of the manufacturing plant, people from the business division in the corporate offices, engineering, and construction companies we hired to carry out the detailed engineering on the project, and the representatives of the many equipment vendors that came calling.

As we developed the detailed process design for the new facility, all the above groups had stakes in the outcome and needed to be invited in at an early stage. It was a huge educational and growth experience for me. It taught me how to work with a multitude of interests. The key person in the Research Division was Larry Humphrey, a smart chemical engineer in its Process Development Group. Humphrey was the guy who had actually piloted different parts of the continuous process. Since he had observed firsthand how the process worked, he knew its quirks and limitations.

I would hold large process engineering meetings to review the details of our process design. We would go over the process flow diagrams (PFDs) line by line. The PFDs captured our entire process design effort. They included every step of the new process in great detail, including the design details of the new equipment.

The contingent from research alone was half a dozen people. It included Humphrey, his boss Harold Sorstokke, and bosses higher up in the chain of management. The people in Process Systems attended; they were the folk to whom we handed over the output from Process Design. They developed the details of piping and instrumentation. We would also have an attendee or two from the Project Management Group. Representatives of other disciplines were invited as needed.

I ran into a big problem during these meetings. Humphrey was quiet and reserved. He didn't intervene in ongoing discussions, even when they clearly dealt with process development. People assumed he was on board as they made decisions and drew up the agenda for the next meeting. Just to make sure that we had addressed everyone's concerns, I would specifically invite Humphrey's input. He would proceed to quietly tell a story that differed markedly from what everybody, including his own bosses, had just concluded. People would get upset at the wasted time, but Humphrey always kept his cool. Nothing seemed to bother him.

I soon learned to seek out Humphrey's views at every critical juncture in the meetings. I could not afford to assume that he would speak up on his own. Humphrey taught me a valuable lesson in how to plan and run meetings.

By today's standards, the engineering tools we used in the mid-1970s were primitive indeed. We had no desktop computers, and the mainframe computers were painfully slow. It would take the better part of a week to schedule a meeting. The secretary would send out a meeting notice, await feedback by mail, and then send out the final meeting notice, also by mail—an entire exercise completed today on scheduling software in a couple of hours. Following a meeting, one person would be deputized to write the minutes and send out yet another memo.

Also working on implementing the continuous intermediates process at the Mount Pleasant plant was Donald "Don" Schaller. He was my counterpart from the Process Systems Group, so we worked closely during the three and a half years I was in the Engineering Department. He particularly impressed me with his smarts, personality, and talent. We became good friends. We had a similar career trajectory and had joined Stauffer within a month of each other. Don was bright, astute, and very methodical. He had a razor-sharp sense of humor and did not suffer fools gladly.

Sometimes Don and I socialized outside work. He once invited me to dinner. He and his wife were aware that I would bring a date. But they did not expect me to show up with someone like Ratilekha, the dancer. There she was, dressed in a sari like an Indian lady, looking stunning. Don's first reaction on seeing her—his jaw dropped—was precious.

Our friendship was lifelong. There were long periods of time during which we lost touch, but we would always reconnect and pick up where we had left off.

***

I decided to take a European vacation in the summer of 1974. A Eurail Pass cost me $250 and would allow me to travel first class by train all over Europe. I started out in Scandinavian countries. In each city, I visited the historic sites and signed up for tours given by English-speaking guides. I was careful to set aside a part of the day when I could just roam around the city on my own and strike up conversations with people.

It was impressive how vast numbers of people in Scandinavia spoke particularly good English. After a stay in Copenhagen, the train took me across the Swedish Kattegatt strait over to Malmö in Sweden. I went to a summer concert there featuring a variety of artists. Many sang Swedish songs. Quite a few of them also sang songs from America in English. In Malmö, later in Stockholm, and then in Gothenburg, I met people who were outgoing and friendly.

People were just as welcoming when I crossed over to Norway. All streets in Oslo seemed to point to the harbor. I got a kick out of the tour guide explaining why the streets were so wide and straight: "so that cannons could be fired at enemy ships in the harbor." Like any good tourist, I went to Vigeland Park. Its powerful sculptures of nude people are often called "the Gems of Oslo." I was astonished to learn that all sculptures were the work of a single artist, Gustav Vigeland.

The city of Bergen was idyllic. I didn't know that it had once been the capital of Norway for about a hundred years. I shall never forget the stunning fjords.

I made short stops in Frankfurt and Paris on the way to London. Later in my career, business would take me to Europe frequently and I was able to see all these cities again. But the memories of that first vacation are special.

On my arrival in London, I received the grievous news that my dad, Bauji, had passed. I made a week-long dash to India so that I could offer strength to my mother, Bhabiji, and my sisters, Parkash and Gurmit. I didn't know then that my biggest loss would be the void in myself. I sat in Bauji's room alone, looked at the bed to which he had been confined during my last visit, and wept. The conversations we had shared echoed from the walls of his room. I could see him, talk to him, and laugh with him during my two previous visits. His letters would always give me a rush of excitement. All that was gone.

Before leaving my parents' home for the return trip, I took care to pack some books that had been neglected for a while—*Dr. Dev* and *Pinjar* by Amrita Pritam and *Train to Pakistan* and *I Shall Not Hear the Nightingale* by Khushwant Singh. Both Bauji and I were particularly fond of Singh, who in the mid-1970s was the editor of *The Illustrated Weekly of India*, published in Bombay (later renamed Mumbai). While in the United States, I had managed to get an occasional copy of the weekly to keep up to date with events in India.

I returned to the United States after Bauji's death with a heavy heart and willed myself to focus on my job. One upcoming event would lighten that weight. I passed the oral examination for citizenship and received my naturalization certificate at an uplifting ceremony in July 1974 in a courthouse in White Plains.

The joy I felt at achieving citizenship was marred, temporarily, by an ugly incident in White Plains. During the nine years since my original arrival in America, I had been essentially untouched by racism, but for that single incident in the diner in South Bend. I had functioned without any awareness of being different, thanks to the open-heartedness and sense of fairness of the white Americans whose world I inhabited.

I was at a popular nightspot in White Plains with some friends in late October 1974, probably the only non-white person there. A white guy next to me at the bar and I started making small talk. He was pleasant enough at the start. He mentioned some people from India he worked with. We had been talking for about fifteen minutes when a pretty young woman stopped at the bar and ordered a drink.

The guy had been drinking hard and was a bit unsteady by this point. He made some comment to the woman, which turned her off. She turned her back to him and now faced me. I said hello and we launched into a five-minute conversation, which resulted in her sharing her phone number with me.

After she left, I sensed the man had turned hostile.

"Why did you come to America?" he demanded.

"Why do you want to know?" I was no longer in a polite mood, either.

"You Indians never, ever, go back to your country. The Indians I know at work are always saying they would go back. But they never do."

"My country is the United States. I am a citizen. Why should I leave?"

"I don't give a shit. You guys don't belong here," he shouted.

Within ten minutes, he had insulted some other people too and was tossed out by the bar's security. But that was no comfort to me. I was seething at how he treated me. After so many years of living in America and after finally becoming an American citizen, I had been on the receiving end of an act of virulent racism.

Despite the rough experience in the bar, I didn't lose sight of what still needed to be done. I filed an application in 1975 to sponsor my sister Parkash and her husband for immigration to the United States.

***

I was aware that racial and ethnic conflicts were not limited to America. After all, who would know such conflict better than a Punjabi, whose homeland was split between Pakistan and India when he was just a child? When I planned my next vacation to India, to start in December 1976 and end in the new year, that trip would include transit through Pakistan to the Wagha border, where I would cross over to India.

It was virtually impossible for the citizens of India to visit Pakistan, and vice versa, on account of the toxic relations between the two countries ever since British India was partitioned in 1947. Fortuitously, I was now an American citizen. I could travel to Pakistan on my US passport. I made a quick check before departing. American passport holders did not need a visa to enter either Pakistan or India.

I had planned on flying into the Western Pakistan city of Karachi and catching a domestic flight to Lahore. I would sightsee for a day or two in Lahore, then cross into India by train at the Wagha border.

When I alighted at the Karachi airport, I made the assumption that my checked baggage would be automatically placed on the flight to Lahore. In fact, passengers were expected to clear all baggage through Pakistani customs at the Karachi airport, and personally check it in for domestic flights. I waited for two days in Lahore, most of the time at the airport, for the baggage to arrive. The airline promised me that its agents in Karachi would look for my baggage and place it on the "next" flight to Lahore. It didn't happen.

During the wait, some interesting things happened. The airport would empty out pretty quickly after flights arrived and departed. However, on my second morning there, I was startled by a huge number of people flooding into the airport. All of a sudden, the entire lounge area in the arrival section was jampacked. One airport worker told me that the crowds had been bused in from neighboring villages to greet Zulfikar

Ali Bhutto, the prime minister of Pakistan.

Soon enough, Bhutto's flight from the nation's capital, Islamabad, landed, and he walked into the arrivals building. The official greeting party was big, led by the governor of the Pakistani state of Punjab, the country's largest. The greeters included the state's chief minister too, the real power in the state. I pushed close to the rope line and got a very close view of Bhutto. He walked within a few feet of where I stood. He was slightly stooped as he walked, engrossed in an animated conversation with the chief minister. The same day, the local English newspaper had a black-bordered front-page greeting for the prime minister. An equivalent in America would have been a similar front-page above-the-fold greeting in bold ink by the *Los Angeles Times* if President Jimmy Carter were to visit California. I was stunned by the level of sycophancy in Pakistan.

Seven months after I saw Bhutto at the Lahore airport, he was deposed in a coup by the country's Chief of Army Staff, General Muhammad Zia-ul-Haq. Zia imprisoned Bhutto on trumped-up charges and hanged him two years later.

In the thirty-year life of Pakistan since its birth in 1947, it was ruled by the army for fifteen years. For the first ten-year stint of civilian rule, from 1947 through 1957, the army had stayed in the background but exercised absolute control through its civilian proxies. Bhutto had provided Pakistan relatively free civilian rule for four years before the army struck and took back control.

Two days' fruitless wait at the Lahore airport was enough. I flew back to Karachi to retrieve my luggage. So much for sightseeing in Lahore. The incompetence of the airport authorities in Karachi was astonishing. After my initial departure for Lahore, my bag lay unattended in the arrival area for a day. Then someone from the airline recovered it, walked it past customs, and stored it in a corner of the airline's office. The people who were responding to my telexes from Lahore didn't have the sense to place my bag on a flight. I took custody of the bag and booked another flight for Lahore.

As I waited in the departure lounge at Karachi airport, I spotted a Sikh gentleman. Fully turbaned Sikhs were a rarity in Pakistan, since most, if not all, Sikh families had departed for India after the partition. I walked up to him and greeted him with the traditional Sikh greeting of "Sat Sri Akal" (God is true and supreme). He looked up with suspicion. To him, this clean-shaven man looked like every other Pakistani. But he relaxed soon after I introduced myself.

He told me he lived in Bombay, where he edited a magazine.

"Which magazine, if you don't mind my asking?"

"*The Illustrated Weekly of India.*"

"Oh, my goodness. Are you Khushwant Singh?" I was now talking excitedly. My voice rose. People turned to look. I got ahold of myself, apologized, and told him how I had read many of his books. He asked me about my life and we had a good conversation. He said he was on his way to Islamabad to attend a literary conference.

Despite this welcome distraction, I soon caught my flight to Lahore. Now I could resume my original plan: take the train to the Wagha border and cross over to India. But I was in for a big shock. The Indian authorities told me that my US passport allowed me to enter India visa-free only if I entered by air.

As a native-born Indian, it felt weird to be detained overnight by Indian security forces and shipped back to Lahore the next morning. The Indians were polite, however. They knew my background and treated me as one of their own, with one difference. Officially, I couldn't enter, and the security personnel had to follow the rules.

A young Swiss man and his girlfriend, originally from the

Philippines, were my fellow overnight detainees. As their unofficial interpreter, I helped ease their way into eating the Indian meal the guards had cooked for us. I would imagine that most overnight detainees at Wagha were people from countries outside the Indian subcontinent, with a large proportion of Westerners. But the cook seemed to be blissfully indifferent to the reality that he was cooking for people whose tastes ran milder than the highly spiced Punjabi food he prepared for us. For me, the food was a treat. For my fellow detainees, not so much. I had brought a bottle of B&B (Benedictine and Brandy, one of the oldest premixed cocktails) from New York as a gift for my brother-in-law Sarjit Singh Sandhu. I decided to put it to better use that night with the young couple detained with me, and we had a rather pleasant evening.

Back in Lahore the next day, I prepared to fly to Islamabad to get a visa from the Indian embassy. The visa application required a couple of photographs. I sought out a local photo studio. The owner and his colleagues were businesslike at first. When I revealed that I was an Indian, they turned most gracious. It was a confirmation for me that the enmity between India and Pakistan was fueled by politicians as a vehicle for their own ambitions. The two countries' people continued to see each other as one, just as they were before the partition.

After the photograph was taken, we sat outside the studio. Friends of the studio owner and the owners of nearby shops joined shortly. Tea and a vast assortment of sweets were ordered. One person wondered aloud about my Punjabi accent and correctly placed it as from the Doaba region—the geographical area centered around Jalandhar, my home city—of Indian Punjab. The welcome these Pakistanis extended to me—someone from the Indian side of Punjab—was most touching.

This encounter, so far from home, reminded me of a relationship back in the United States. I was good friends with a fellow employee at Stauffer, Nasim Hassan, who came from Lahore. I had ascribed our friendship to the common yearning for their countries of birth felt by those who left for America, and how we could see from a distance the vast similarities between the people of Pakistan and India. That I would get a similar reaction right there in Pakistan was very gratifying.

My passage through Pakistan continued to be full of surprises. The flight into Islamabad arrived late in the day, and I asked the cabbie to take me to the Intercontinental Hotel. In the middle of all the mad rush and back and forth I had been through, I wanted to treat myself to a couple of nights of rest in a luxury hotel. Imagine my chagrin when told that the hotel was full.

I walked out dejectedly. Who did I spot in a group of people engaged in an animated conversation? Why, Khushwant Singh himself. He was speaking with India's ambassador to Pakistan, K. Shankar Bajpai. I walked up and said hello to Singh. His eyes lit up with recognition.

"You are still here? You told me you were going straight to Wagha from Lahore," asked my puzzled new friend.

I explained to him the whole mess with the visa. Singh turned to the ambassador, introduced us, and explained my visa problem.

"Be sure to tell them at the embassy tomorrow that you met me," advised the ambassador.

Dropping his name definitely helped, but it was still a long day at the embassy. While waiting for my visa to come through, I ventured out to the shops and restaurants in the vicinity of the embassy. I struck up conversations with the locals. As I walked on a big untended lot of land just across from the embassy, I was accosted by a group of three Pakistani men. They insisted on knowing my name and the "real" purpose of my visit.

At first, I didn't take them seriously, but they quickly turned hostile to the point of threatening me with arrest. I was stunned. They were plainclothes members of the Pakistani security forces who maintained a close vigil on the goings-on at the embassy of their mortal enemy country, India. I showed them my American passport and they retreated, but not before warning me that my movements would be closely watched. I was saddened by the contrast between the welcome accorded to me two nights earlier by Pakistani civilians and that offered by the harsh face of the government of Pakistan.

With the Indian visa stamped on my American passport, I flew back to Lahore for the third time and boarded the train once again for the Wagha border. Most of the travelers in my compartment were Afghans who had never seen a railway train before entering Pakistan. They stood out from the other passengers by both their language and their very light complexions. One lady in the group, in her mid-thirties, had bright blue eyes and light, silken skin. I don't know that she could sense the impact her looks had on me. She smiled sweetly every time I looked her way. But she seemed to understand neither English nor the local language of the train riders, Punjabi.

Some Afghan men did have a rudimentary knowledge of English. I learned they were heading to New Delhi to meet up with family and friends. On learning of my Indian origin, their anxious faces broke into big smiles. I was reminded of the degree of friendship and warmth Afghans feel for the people of India. Afghanistan and India had enjoyed warm relations after the British left the subcontinent, both officially and at the people-to-people level. They may feel an added kinship because both India and Afghanistan have had hostile relations with Pakistan.

After all my misadventures in Pakistan, my trip to India

was smooth. When I arrived at our village, Dhandaur, I could see that Bhabiji, my mother, had been under enormous strain. I was late arriving in India by four days. Her mind had gone back to the 1947 riots when Muslims and Sikhs were killing each other. In her mind, I had been at the mercy of those "barbarians." During those four days, when she had no news of me, she prayed feverishly in the village Gurdwara (Sikh temple) for my safety. I tried to reassure her by telling her of the lovely welcome I had received in Lahore. She remained doubtful.

Parkash, her husband Joginder, and their four sons had been living with Bhabiji in Dhandaur since the last few years of Bauji's life. Parkash had opted to move to my parents' house from her home, at considerable self-sacrifice, to be of help to our parents. She had stayed with Bhabiji during the nearly three years since Bauji died to keep company with our aging mother. Joginder had retired from the army and Parkash saw no future for her family in India. She was anxious to move to America. I assured her that I had filed for her sponsorship within a year of acquiring my citizenship in 1974.

My sister Gurmit, her husband Sarjit, and their family lived on the campus of Guru Nanak Dev University in Amritsar, a city about twenty miles from the Wagha border. Sarjit

(Gurmit, Bhabiji, and myself, with Gurmit's daughter Sumeet in front—Chandigarh, India, January 1977)

was the dean of science and head of the chemistry department. Gurmit was a lecturer in the department. She requested me to sponsor her and Sarjit for immigration to the United States, which I agreed to do on my return.

Gurmit took a few days off from work and we took Bhabiji to Chandigarh on a leisurely trip. Bhabiji had never been there, and she enjoyed the experience. I took some time from the trip to visit my old alma mater, Panjab University. A couple of my former classmates were now senior faculty in the department. It was lovely seeing them.

I was back in White Plains by the third week of January 1977, the return trip home from India far more uneventful than my travel there.

***

Though my attitudes toward belonging might have changed somewhat after gaining citizenship, my career continued on the same track as before. I enjoyed leading my team of engineers, even as I kept my eyes open for new opportunities. One such opportunity arose in 1976, just six months before I returned from India, when Stauffer needed someone in a supervisory position in the Licensing-Engineering Department (LED). By this time, Stauffer had developed several proprietary technologies for manufacturing phosgene, vinyl chloride monomer (VCM), polyvinyl chloride (PVC), and chlorinated solvents. Phosgene is an important building block in the synthesis of pharmaceuticals and isocyanates; the latter are precursors to polyurethanes, used in coatings and adhesives. Polyurethane foam is used as cushioning in bedding, furniture, and automotive interiors. PVC is used in building and construction applications, such as flooring, windows, roofing, and wall coverings. Chlorinated solvents, such as methylene chloride, chloroform, and carbon tetrachloride, were typically used in industrial processes to dissolve and clean other materials, as in paint stripping, metal cleaning, and dry cleaning. Environmental and safety constraints progressively reduced their use toward the turn of the century. They were going strong in the 1970s, however, and there was a huge demand for Stauffer's technologies.

Stauffer licensed these technologies worldwide. The LED handled all such details. It was charged with keeping these technologies constantly updated, preparing engineering packages based on these technologies, and transferring these packages to client companies. Such an engineering package contained sufficient information for an engineering and construction (E&C) company to prepare the detailed design and construct a manufacturing plant, as well as for the manufacturer to successfully operate the plant.

The LED department had an opening in mid-1976 for a supervisory position, principal process engineer; the position was the first rung in engineering management. I competed for and was offered the position. The promotion was deeply satisfying. It was the realization of the future possibilities that Len Wender had mentioned to me three years earlier.

Moving from corporate engineering to licensing engineering may have involved moving my office only by two hundred yards, but it was akin to living in a different world. Whereas my previous activity was all inward-focused, the work in the new department involved very extensive interactions with our clients worldwide. LED made technical and commercial presentations to potential clients. While we prepared the detailed technical packages, some clients physically moved some of their employees to our location so they could be fully conversant with the technical details of the project. Once the new plants were built, we would be on site to provide start-up know-how and support. After commissioning the plant, we stayed in close touch for recovering operational data so that our technologies could be upgraded when warranted.

Stauffer's VCM and PVC technologies had been licensed to AkzoNobel in the Netherlands, BASF and Wacker Chemie in

West Germany, Chemopetrol in Czechoslovakia, Kemanord in Sweden, Société Nationale d'Electrolyse et de Pétrochimie (SNEP) in Morocco, Sadaf in Saudi Arabia, Arak Petrochemical Corporation in Iran, Formosa Plastics in Taiwan, Colcarburo in Colombia, and two companies in India—Indian Petrochemicals Corporation Limited (IPCL) and Reliance Industries. Here at home, these technologies had been licensed to Diamond Shamrock Corporation (Dallas), Vista Chemical Company (Houston), Shell Chemical Company (also in Houston), Oxymar, Inc. (Ingleside, Texas), and Borden Chemicals (Columbus, Ohio).

The carbon monoxide and phosgene technologies had been licensed to Union Carbide Corporation, Dow Chemicals, and General Electric. Stauffer's benzene hexachloride technology was licensed to entities in India and Pakistan.

The chlorinated solvents technology—also called Perc/Tet, that is, perchloroethylene and carbon tetrachloride—had been licensed to AkzoNobel in the Netherlands. In a landmark contract, Stauffer licensed this technology to Britain's Imperial Chemical Industries (ICI) in 1978—ICI would build the world's largest chlorinated solvents plant in the UK. After the licensing contract was signed, ICI sent a team of engineers to the United States. We took them on a tour of Stauffer's plant in Louisville, Kentucky. This is where the technology had been developed and proven on the commercial scale. Then we stationed the ICI team in our offices in Dobbs Ferry for the next several months as we prepared the detailed design of the new plant.

I was the manager of the process engineering team in LED, which prepared all technology packages for clients. The ICI project was one of the larger projects to come my way. Other projects required me to travel across the country. We worked very closely with the Process Research Group (PRG) of the Western Research Center in Richmond, California. New ideas would often be developed by the LED and then proven on the bench and pilot plant scale by the PRG. Close coordination was essential, and the two groups would meet frequently, once every two months or so. Since all the piloting was done in Richmond, review meetings usually took place at the Western Research Center, so I traveled extensively to the West Coast.

I made my first trip to Richmond within weeks of joining LED. The primary mission of the trip was to meet my counterparts, members of the PRG managed by Elliott Doane, with whom I worked closely. I also visited the Stauffer plant in Long Beach, which manufactured phosgene as well as VCM. While in Southern California, I made the time to visit Disneyland.

We, the PRG and the LED, had active joint projects for significantly improving our VCM technology. One such project was the development of high-temperature chlorination (HTC). We licensed the HTC technology to the Swedish company Kemanord, and I led the effort to design the new process. One of the products in the HTC reactor for Kemanord was a static mixer—in fact, the world's largest static mixer at the time. This happened to be one of the engineering products produced by Koch Industries, the family flagship of David Koch, my former colleague at Scientific Design, who had by this time returned to his family's company. I invited him to give a presentation on his company's products, including the static mixer.

Besides the regular cross-country trips to California, I traveled a fair amount all over the world and to other domestic locations. Thanks to the preponderance of Stauffer's Texas-based clients, I soon rediscovered my familiarity with Houston.

Shell Chemical Company was one of these clients. We were at a business dinner at a restaurant in Houston in 1978. Both the Stauffer and Shell contingents were large, about fifteen in all. As the evening wore on, alcohol flowed generously and tongues were loosened. Several people from both cohorts started teasing one Shell guy. I have long forgotten why he was being teased. I joined in the teasing, which was clearly unwise, since I didn't know the man.

Cornered, the man darted in a very strange direction. He focused on me, the only non-white person at the table.

"Why are the Indians so unhygienic?" asked the Shell man, leveling an accusing gaze at me. "I saw them relieve themselves out in the open when I visited India."

I was too stunned to think of a fitting response and didn't engage. Nor did anyone else, even though at least half a dozen people nearby, from both companies, heard him clearly. I was galled that nobody stepped forward and reproached the man for his racist attack. I have read of the "bystander effect"—the concept that when there is a group of people that witnesses a racist or a bullying incident, individuals are less likely to respond than in, say, a one-on-one situation. The group mentality allows us to diffuse the responsibility to those around us.

Let us for a moment forget the failure of others at the table to reproach the Shell employee for leveling the racist attack on me. What bothered me more was his absolute assurance that he could openly insult me and get away with it. His behavior was the epitome of white privilege. Although I wouldn't be surprised if subtle racism had occurred without my awareness throughout my professional life, I can recall only this one incident of overt racism.

One of the dinner attendees that night was my boss, "Larry," seated at the other end of the long table. He was the number two to the chief of the LED. Larry had weaknesses. He would get drunk at department functions and openly make passes at the department secretaries. I once observed him forcibly embracing and trying to kiss one of the secretaries after one such lunch.

The women's self-empowerment movement was barely

starting in the late 1970s, and it certainly hadn't yet made inroads into corporate America. I don't know if the secretary ever lodged a complaint with human resources or whether it would have made a difference. I too was complicit—I didn't bring his unacceptable behavior to the attention of his boss or the HR people.

Larry also suffered from an inferiority complex concerning those who were more educated than he. He held a master's degree in chemical engineering. He often made derogatory comments about the "exaltedness" of the PhD degree, sometimes in the presence of the three or so of us in the department who held the degree.

This issue impacted many of our interactions. One of them involved the mathematical model of a reactor system. He had developed this model when he was working in Stauffer's Louisville plant. The engineers of the LED used it heavily to predict the performance of reactor systems we designed for clients. Another colleague, "Mike," tried fitting the new data coming in from a plant to the model, but the data wouldn't fit. Larry was just as baffled as Mike.

I proceeded to unpack the model. It quickly became apparent that Larry had used the wrong reactor configuration in his model, what we call the "plug flow" configuration. It was obvious to me that the reactor systems in our plants actually came closest to the "stirred tank" configuration. I corrected all the mathematical equations and totally revamped the model. It felt good to discover that the revised model tracked the observed plant data very well.

When I took the news to Larry, his face was ashen. He never thanked me for correcting the model. If anything, he held it against me, as if I had committed a cardinal sin by showing up his inadequacy. But when the department started using my model henceforth, at least Larry had the decency to stay out of the way.

I was surprised that Mike had not identified the cause of the problem with Larry's model. He too held a PhD degree. That someone with advanced graduate education in chemical engineering would miss such an obvious point was beyond my comprehension.

***

One hot day in July 1977, I got a phone call out of the blue.

"Hello, hello." The caller had a high-pitched voice. He sounded nervous.

"Hello, this is Sardul. Can I help you?"

"Mamaji, this is Parminderjit." Maternal uncles are called Mamaji in Punjab, and Parminderjit was my nephew, the son of my sister Parkash.

"Hi, Parminderjit. Is everything okay at home?"

"Yes, Mamaji. But I am calling from a pay phone near your apartment."

"What the hell. Nobody said you were coming."

I was flabbergasted. I had applied to sponsor Parkash and her family two years earlier. Apparently, the application was approved but nobody told me about it. Along with her husband and three minor sons, she had the interviews at the US Embassy in New Delhi and they were granted immigration visas. They flew out of India and stopped for a week in England to visit with relatives. Through all this, it never occurred to anyone to call me before they flew to the United States. They claimed to have sent a telegram to me, which I hadn't gotten. What galled me was that they were not at all embarrassed.

It took me a lot of driving and phone calls in the next two weeks to get my sister's family settled in an apartment in Queens Village, New York. Her husband found a cook's job in a restaurant in Manhattan. The boys enrolled in the public school system and found part-time jobs.

***

I resisted idealizing relationships as the end-all for personal happiness. Anthony Storr's quote about marriage not being the ultimate source of happiness epitomized my approach to life and relationships. This had been my mindset in the three years since I broke off my relationship with Ratilekha in 1974. I had occasionally dated other women, but nothing turned serious.

Nothing, that is, till I met Rosemary.

Three months after Parkash's arrival, my friend Bob Rickman invited me one evening to accompany him to a wine-tasting party in Yonkers, New York. We were barely fifteen minutes into the party when I spotted two tall women. The one that caught my eye was very pretty and about five feet, eight and a half inches tall, on the extreme end of the height that I would consider in a partner; I was just about the same height as she was, but on a good day. I was taken by how she stood ramrod straight and had a joyful smile on her face as she spoke animatedly with the other woman. I admired her beautiful, long brown hair. As I approached her, though, it was her lovely hazel eyes that sealed the deal.

Her friend, Tina, was even taller than she was, perhaps clocking in at five feet, eleven inches. She was blonde and pretty too, but not in the way the brunette woman was.

I went over and introduced myself. As you may have guessed by now, this was Rosemary, who was to become the love of my life. We learned that we lived in apartments within half a mile of each other. She lived in Tompkins Manor, the same apartment building I had lived in two years earlier. I secured her phone number before bidding her a good night.

Our courtship was fast. The first movie I took her to was Henry Winkler's *Heroes*. At our meal afterward, Rosemary noted one of my many eccentricities. She was taken aback by the sight of me eating my fully loaded cheeseburger with a fork and knife. Attempting to lift the entire multilayered concoction called a cheeseburger and taking a bite out of this monstrosity was well-nigh impossible for me. To Rosemary, eating a cheeseburger with a fork and knife just wasn't done. More shocking revelations would follow in quick succession. Horror of horrors, I ate pizza that way, too, with a fork and knife. Purists in the pizzeria were tempted to flee.

"Love conquers all" may be a truism, but it is also true. We had fallen in love soon after we met. We got used to each other's litany of weirdness, mostly mine, literally in a couple of months. Of course, there was the chemistry that fueled the initial spark. But the key factor was compatibility. We could communicate and relate to each other with remarkable ease. We could share emotions and laugh and cry together. We could understand each other and validate each other's feelings. Both of us wanted to make a lifelong commitment.

I proposed to her in my kitchen in January 1978. No bent knee here. Not even the proverbial ring, which would follow in the next few months after I made sure of her preferences. When she came to visit me in the office, she would knock and hide outside, with just her ring finger showing through the door. How could I miss the sparkle of that diamond?

Once I rode out with Rickman to the Butternut Ski Resort in the Berkshires of Western Massachusetts for a day of skiing. Rosemary was visiting with her mother, Jane, at the time in Northampton, sixty miles east in the same state. I had already met Jane earlier at Rosemary's apartment in White Plains.

Rosemary met up with me at the ski resort. I rode back with her to Northampton in the evening. My body ached after skiing the expert slopes all day. She ran hot water in the bathtub and helped me with the bath. It was heavenly soaking in the tub and having Rosemary wash my back.

***

Rosemary's dad, Warren Harvey, had grown up in Northampton. He worked as an assistant in the law office of Calvin Coolidge, who went on to become the thirtieth President of the United States. Coolidge had previously served as the mayor of Northampton in 1910–1911. Rosemary's dad came from French Canadian stock. Warren's mother, Rosemary's grandmother, was called Meme by all the children and spoke heavily accented English.

(Rosemary, with her mother, Jane Condron Harvey, 1978)

As the eldest son in his family, Warren had to go to work right after high school. Missing college didn't get in the way of his learning, however. Rosemary remembers her dad as an avid reader of newspapers. He would pick up many on his daily walk to the local convenience store. I never got to meet Warren, though, as he passed away in 1975 after a long and painful illness.

The parallels between Rosemary's father and mine were striking. Both had to give up aspirations for college because of the pressures to provide for the family. Both read widely and were very well informed. And sadly, both had passed away before we met.

Rosemary's mother, Jane Condron, was born in the small town of Groton, New York. Jane's mother was of German descent, while Jane's father, Jack, was of Irish descent. He had worked most of his life at the local Smith Corona typewriter factory. I had the pleasure of visiting with Jack a couple of times before he passed away at the age of eighty-nine in late 1979.

Jane graduated from a teacher's college in Cortland, New

York. She taught for a few years in a high school on Long Island before meeting Warren. Rosemary was their only child, born in 1955 in New Haven, Connecticut, where Warren was working as a salesman. The family moved back to Warren's hometown, Northampton, soon afterward.

Jane stopped teaching after marrying Warren and became a homemaker. Getting back into the workforce after her husband's death turned out to be very hard. Her persistence paid off, though. She was working at the tax collector's office in the City of Northampton when I first met her in late 1977. She worked for the city until her retirement.

Jane's last couple of years were painful, though she still had the opportunity to be a loving grandmother to Rosemary's and my two children, Michael and Jeffrey. She suffered a stroke while living alone at her home in Northampton and spent her remaining time in a nursing home. I was struck by how courageously she adapted herself to the trauma of never seeing her house again. When Rosemary and I visited her just months after her stroke, we found her to be mentally as sharp as before. She seemed to be relatively content with her life in the nursing home. Sadly, she was diagnosed with lymphoma and died in 2004, within ten days of starting chemotherapy.

Rosemary's parents were people of moderate means. What they had in abundance, and passed on to their daughter, was an excellent moral code.

Rosemary attended the local Catholic school, where she graduated as the salutatorian of her senior class. She attended Smith College, located in Northampton. She studied psychology and liberal arts and graduated cum laude in 1977. She had interviewed with some of the companies visiting the campus and accepted an offer from Procter & Gamble, working in Westchester County as a sales management trainee.

I have particular regard for Rosemary's steadfast devotion to truth, her instinctive recognition of right from wrong, and her eye for excellence in every endeavor. I consider myself extraordinarily fortunate to have found her. The long wait was worth it. We were married on July 29, 1978, her dad's birthday, in Helen Hills Hills Chapel on the Smith College campus, followed by a reception at the Alumnae House. I was thirty-five and Rosemary was twenty-two.

I had considered buying a house when I was single. Meeting Rosemary brought my resolve to fruition. A couple of months before our wedding, we bought a house in the bucolic village of Katonah, twenty miles north of White Plains. We got to know each other well as we painted the interior of most of the rooms. It was grueling work. The good news? We still wanted to get married afterward.

(With Rosemary, at her friend Angela's wedding, October 20, 1979)

We have fond memories of our three and a half years in Katonah. It was home to a great many professionals. Some worked at the corporate headquarters of IBM in Armonk, New York, and others at the Pepsi headquarters in White Plains. Many worked in Manhattan, forty-five miles away.

The hub of social activity in the village was the "Katonah Newcomers Club." Even after the newcomers turned into established residents, they maintained their active participation in the club. We made good friends through that club.

Rosemary quit her job with Procter & Gamble early during her first pregnancy. Our son Michael was born on July 8, 1979, and Jeffrey followed on April 29, 1981, both at the Mt. Kisco hospital. Rosemary would stay at home to raise our boys until they were teenagers before returning to the workplace.

Rickman, the friend responsible for my attendance at the party where Rosemary and I met, was my best man at our wedding. He and his wife Patty lived in Brewster, about ten miles north of our home in Katonah. They divorced soon afterward. Rickman then found happiness on the ski slopes in California. A few years later, he married a fellow skier, and they bought a house in Walnut Creek, twenty-five miles northeast of San Francisco.

(Our first house, in Katonah, New York)

***

Readers may wonder why I didn't ask my own brother, rather than Rickman, to be the best man at my wedding. It was because Ranbir arranged to travel to India at the time of the wedding.

I hadn't seen my brother since my last visit in 1973. He left graduate school soon after that and took a job as a systems analyst with the Toronto Transit Commission in about 1975. He and Kuldip bought a house. He had gotten deeply interested in the life of Sikhs both in Canada and in Punjab. He had harbored strong feelings about "Sikh persecution"

(With my brother, Ranbir, my niece, Surbjit Parmar, and Michael, 1980)

from the days when we were students in Chandigarh.

Ranbir visited Rosemary and me in Katonah in 1980. He had stopped by on his return journey from another visit to India. He was very guarded and a bit sarcastic during the two-day stay. He also made deprecatory comments about my supposed "passion for accumulating dollars." One of his bags was packed with books. I casually opened it and started browsing, which upset him greatly. He didn't trust me anymore, and I sensed his hostility. Something was very wrong, but I didn't know what to do about it.

***

I felt stymied in my work life as well by the summer of 1981. I had earned a very significant promotion at Stauffer, but that was five years previously, and my current position included an unsympathetic boss. I started getting calls from executive recruiters. One recruiter presented a very enticing opportunity, so I agreed to talk to his client.

Rohm and Haas Company, headquartered in Philadelphia, had a sterling reputation in the industry as a "high-tech" company. It had a far larger R&D organization than Stauffer Chemical, even though they were about the same size in terms of sales.

I interviewed and received an offer to be a research section manager, which I accepted. My young family—Michael was two and Jeffrey was six months old—moved to an apartment in Bucks County while we had a house built in Yardley, a lovely village thirty miles north of Philadelphia. I started at the new job in October 1981.

CHAPTER 9

YARDLEY

Leadership is the art of getting someone else to do something you want done because he wants to do it.
   - Dwight Eisenhower, "The Federal Career Service: A Look Ahead," 1954

My office was located in Bristol, about twenty-four miles north of my new employer's Philadelphia headquarters. We rented an apartment in Bensalem Township and began looking for a home to buy. We concentrated our search north of Bristol, in townships such as Langhorne, Newtown, and Yardley.

The first thing Rosemary and I noted when we started house-hunting in Bucks County was that the houses were bigger and came equipped with more amenities than what we had in Katonah. The houses included central air conditioning, a feature we sorely lacked in the house in Katonah. After an exhausting couple of months of searching, with no clear winner, we opted to build a house instead, in Yardley.

The first year in Pennsylvania was a trying time for both Rosemary and me. Rosemary had a particularly difficult time managing in an entirely new milieu with no friends. She had the responsibility of caring for our two very young children. Foremost in her mind was the question, was she doing enough to care for our children and to support me as I tackled my new job? She came through wonderfully. She supervised the construction of our new house. George, the contractor building the house, was difficult at times. She reviewed the ongoing construction and made sure that George lived up to his commitments. He cut corners several times and she made him take corrective actions.

We ended up with a spacious home. It was worth the hassle Rosemary faced with the building contractor. For heating and cooling, we opted to install a heat pump for each level of our house. This was a novel technology at the time. The unit would work as an air conditioner in summer. In winter it would work in reverse, pumping heat in.

Our landscaper, who was recommended by the problematic contractor, also tried to cut corners many times, which Rosemary caught. He even had the gall, at the end of the job, to ask for a bonus.

A ten-minute drive from our house would transport us to another century, as it were. The small historic village of Yardley, nestled along the banks of the Delaware River, had managed to retain the charm and quaintness of colonial days. It was founded by William Yardley, who immigrated to America in July 1682 with his family. He had made an agreement with Penn before leaving England, to buy five hundred acres for

(Our house in Yardley, Pennsylvania)

ten pounds. William Penn, of course, was the founder of Pennsylvania and the designer/developer of the city of Philadelphia.

One outstanding feature of the village was Lake Afton, home to a large flock of ducks. I remember the countless mornings Rosemary and I took our boys to the lake to feed the ducks. An image that persists in my mind is the long line of ducks as they would occasionally cross the adjoining road. All traffic would come to a standstill, drivers waiting patiently for the flock to finish crossing the road.

The lake would freeze in winter, and the skaters would come out in force. I don't quite know what happened to the ducks, but they would surely return in spring. Ice skaters made for a lovely sight. Little could the old Yardley family have known, when it dug the pond for its grist mill three hundred years earlier, of the joy the pond would bring to countless residents and visitors.

(Lake Afton in Yardley—A typical ice-skating scene in winter)

***

The sixteen-mile commute to my office in Bristol was reasonable. I had thrown myself into the midst of a brand-new company culture, a host of totally unfamiliar technologies, and an enormous gaggle of strangers. My entire previous career of twelve years had been in engineering. I had interacted with research, but now I was smack in the middle of it as a manager. I had to learn fast.

Rohm and Haas had the reputation at the time of being a high-tech company. Its research division was a mammoth organization, nothing like what I had seen at Stauffer. For a $2 billion company, a research force of five to seven hundred scientists and engineers was truly exceptional. The company sought to emulate the example of its famous and much larger neighbor, DuPont, headquartered in Wilmington, Delaware. The proximity of the companies allowed for some movement of professionals between the two. The person who would lead the Research Division at Rohm and Haas, Robert E. Naylor, was recruited from DuPont several months after I joined the company. Naylor didn't even have to relocate.

The company was founded in Esslingen, Germany, in 1907 by Otto Haas and Otto Rohm. Haas moved to Philadelphia and established the American company in 1909; Rohm stayed behind to steer the German affiliate. The main products of Rohm and Haas were specialty materials. Advanced chemistry allowed end-use products to have a particular characteristic: for example, low-odor water-based paints and sunscreens with greater SPF.

One product, in particular, gave widespread name recognition to Rohm and Haas—Plexiglas. It is made from the chemical polymethyl methacrylate, which was invented in the early 1900s by Rohm. In 1933, Rohm produced a stable, transparent, hard, shatterproof polymer that Rohm and Haas registered under the Plexiglas trademark. Plexiglas is very versatile and is widely used for light and instrument casings in cars and to make appliances and eyewear lenses. In sheet form, it is used in windows and bathroom showers.

Even fighter planes during World War II had parts made of Plexiglas. In fact, the company's CEO during my tenure was Vincent Gregory, Jr., who flew those fighter planes in the war. Long before he joined the company, he noticed that the bubble canopies of his planes were made of Plexiglas, perhaps portending his future connection with Rohm and Haas. The company sold Plexiglas to Elf Atochem in 1998 (the equivalent of General Electric selling off its bulb-manufacturing business, which it has not, to date).

As CEO, Gregory was also connected to a high-achieving Indian American at Rohm and Haas, Rajiv L. Gupta.

After earning a bachelor's degree in mechanical engineering at the Indian Institute of Technology, Bombay, Gupta picked up a master's degree in operations research from Cornell and an MBA from Drexel University. He joined Rohm and Haas as a financial analyst in 1971 and was picked to be Gregory's special assistant in 1974. The pair developed a reputation at the company—Gregory for his incisive strategic insights and Gupta for having financial information about the company at his fingertips.

Working directly for the company's CEO in his early years provided enormous ballast to Gupta's career. He was groomed for high-level positions from early on. I first met him in the company's office in Paris in 1984. At the time he was director general of a subsidiary, Ducolite International. He brusquely referred to the formal "sanitized" reports and how the company's top brass in Philadelphia, including Gregory, relied on him for the real story. I was surprised; but in retrospect, perhaps he was telling me the truth.

Meeting Gupta was an inspiration. We had similar backgrounds as engineers trained in India who had moved to America for graduate education. Seeing Gupta ascend to such a high position supported my belief that America had been very fair to immigrants, including the ones who happened to be non-white. The country recognized talent and rewarded it.

Gupta was named CEO and president of Rohm and Haas in 1999 and stayed in the CEO role through the sale of the company to Dow Chemical Company in 2009. He netted $100 million from the sale.

Vijay Khanna was another Indian American immigrant, a fellow section manager in the Research Division. He had earned his doctorate degree in chemical engineering at the University of Michigan and had been with Rohm and Haas ever since, rising higher on the management ladder. He was well respected in the company, enjoying a good reputation not only as a professional but also for his athletic abilities. He was a good tennis player.

Khanna was on the panel of Rohm and Haas employees who interviewed me. I was motivated to accept the job offer partly because of my observation of how well the company had recognized Khanna's talent.

Khanna and I were both chemical engineers and Indian immigrants who had earned a PhD in the United States. Our families socialized. Khanna and his wife, Jyotsna, had two sons, as did Rosemary and I. While Khanna made his mark in the technical profession, his older son Rohit would shine in national politics.

***

My own political awareness grew during our time in Yardley, which roughly coincided with Ronald Reagan's tenure as president. My political sympathies had always lain with the Democrats, but I was not very well informed about politics. The presidential election in 1976 was the first time I ever voted. I had even licked envelopes in the district campaign headquarters of Jimmy Carter in White Plains. Before that, when I wasn't even eligible to vote because of my immigration status, I had worked for Bobby Kennedy's presidential campaign in Indiana in 1968.

But Reagan's defeat of Jimmy Carter in 1980 was a big blow to Rosemary and to me.

I was struck by the racist tones of Reagan's campaign. I would never forget how he chose to kick off his presidential campaign in 1980 in Philadelphia, Mississippi, the town still notorious in the national imagination for the Klan lynching of civil rights volunteers James Chaney, Andrew Goodman, and Michael Schwerner sixteen years earlier. His dog-whistle to the constituency of Southern whites couldn't have been any louder.

Reagan trumpeted his racial appeals in blasts against supposed welfare cheats. He repeatedly invoked the story of a "Chicago welfare queen" with "eighty names, thirty addresses, and twelve Social Security cards, who is collecting veteran's benefits on four non-existing deceased husbands. She's got Medicaid, is getting food stamps, and is collecting welfare under each of her names. Her tax-free cash income is over $150,000." Often, Reagan placed his mythical welfare queen behind the wheel of a Cadillac, tooling around in flashy splendor. Newspapers actively sought to find such a person. Reagan was asked for particulars. Shockingly, the "Chicago welfare queen" was never located.

For Reagan, conservatism and racial resentment were inextricably fused. For his reelection campaign in 1984, he returned to Philadelphia, Mississippi, this time to endorse the neo-Confederate slogan "the South shall rise again."

Reagan's economic policy, especially tax legislation, was geared to enrich the very top rungs of society. American income inequality began to rise roughly in concert with the ascendance of Reagan to the presidency. According to an April 23, 2014, publication of the Economic Policy Institute, the share of all income claimed by the top 1 percent of Americans grew from 33.5 percent in 1979 to 38.1 percent in 1988, the last year of Reagan's presidency.

I had grown up very poor, and I was a brown person in a mostly white America. My sympathies were naturally with the people at the bottom of the economic heap. I harbored a visceral hatred of racism of any kind. In the eight years of Reagan's presidency, I could not look at the man's image on television without flinching and getting angry. It is true that I personally didn't experience overt racism, protected as I was by my education, my position in the corporate hierarchy, and the affluence of the community where we lived. But one didn't have to go far to witness victims of racism and poverty in the country, such as the Central Park jogger case in April 1989, in which five young black and Hispanic men were tried and wrongly convicted for the rape of a white woman. The case only later became a prime example of racial profiling and inequality, achieving notoriety at the time partly because of the national discourse about violence against women.

***

Rear Admiral Grace Murray Hopper (1906–1992) was one of the first women flag officers of the US Navy. She coined the term "debugging" in 1945 when she and a colleague took apart a broken computer only to find a moth inside. The moth was removed and "debugging" entered the lexicon. "Amazing Grace" is perhaps more well known for saying, "You manage things. You lead people." With this pithy yet penetrating observation, she immortalized the difference between management and leadership.

In my years as a supervisor at Stauffer, I had pondered this difference. Management gurus of the twentieth century had stressed the rudimentary components of management—planning, budgeting, controlling, etc. Admiral Hopper pointed out how leadership was different.

Now that I had a management role at Rohm and Haas, I realized that I needed to lift my sights above the process of management and strive to become a leader. While management is a set of skills, leadership is an art.

I was responsible for a group varying in size from six to twenty professionals. Occasionally, the group would include chemists besides the normal contingent of chemical engineers. The group was charged with developing the manufacturing process technology for agricultural chemicals, which included herbicides, insecticides, and fungicides. I worked with a sister group, which was comprised entirely of chemists. The chemists developed the basic chemistry and reaction pathways in the laboratory. My process engineering group would scale them up and transfer the process technology into manufacturing plants. My job required extensive travel, within the United States and to our operations in South America and Europe.

Most of our chemical engineers were relatively young, anywhere between one and fifteen years out of university. The bulk of them held master's degrees, with a smaller number holding bachelor's degrees and a handful holding PhDs.

The Research Division at Rohm and Haas had been vastly expanded and upgraded about a decade earlier in response to a very deliberate strategic decision by the company's leadership to emphasize research and make R&D the backbone of their competitive advantage. The idea was that the company would develop its own new products rather than acquire them from outside. The Research Division would ensure that these products were the most efficient for the intended markets and that they were produced using the most efficient process technology, with high quality and the lowest manufacturing cost. While my group was located adjacent to the company's large plant in Bristol, the bulk of the Research Division was housed in a sprawling campus twenty-five miles to the west, in Spring House, Pennsylvania.

A majority of my work was geared toward the manufacture of new products. I was also responsible for the company's old manufacturing processes and for updating them by insertion of the latest technology. My focus in the first couple of years was on the family of diphenyl ether herbicides. The most promising product in this family was Blazer, which had proved particularly effective as a post-emergent herbicide with major crops such as soybeans. It continues to be in use today; it is prominently listed in the *2016 Herbicide Guide for Iowa Corn and Soybean Production*. Blazer had many derivative products, which proved particularly effective in niche agricultural markets. My group developed the manufacturing processes for Blazer and its derivatives.

In late 1984, toward the end of my third year at the company, I was called in by my boss's boss. He told me that I would get an additional assignment of about one-half of the projects, and the corresponding staff, of a fellow manager. This gentleman was approaching retirement, and the director wanted to make sure that his key projects would continue to receive top-level attention. My staff ballooned to more than twenty. This expression of confidence in me by my superiors was greatly uplifting.

One major product area that I inherited from my retiring colleague centered around an old fungicide, Dithane. The company had been making it in numerous countries (including France, India, Colombia, and the United States) for decades. We took a fresh look at large sections of the manufacturing process and developed new process technologies for them. Our flagship plant was located at Lauterbourg, in the Alsace region of France, where we would check out new technologies. We partnered with other technology companies in France, West Germany, and Switzerland.

This aspect of my new project load gave me the opportunity to travel extensively around Europe. The city of Strasbourg, the official seat of the European Parliament—it also meets in the cities of Brussels and Luxembourg—was only forty miles away from our Lauterbourg plant. I developed a taste for Alsatian wines. Rosemary even accompanied me a couple of times, as we enjoyed taking time off in Switzerland and Paris.

(Rosemary, with the snow-covered mountains of Switzerland as the backdrop, 1985)

The first four years at Rohm and Haas were good for my development as a leader. I acquired confidence in leading large projects across the many functional and geographical boundaries they presented.

But a catastrophe lay in wait.

***

Our lives were jolted in the spring of 1986. Rosemary developed a head cold, which stretched from days to over a week. Her primary care physician tried various cold medications, but none worked. Out of desperation, he sent her to an audiologist, who found 25 percent hearing loss in her right ear.

Her physician was alarmed. He dispatched her immediately to see an otolaryngologist at Thomas Jefferson University Hospital in Philadelphia. An MRI revealed an acoustic neuroma next to her right ear.

Acoustic neuromas are benign tumors that form on the auditory nerve, which leads from the inner ear to the brain and transmits sound and balance information. These tumors begin in the cells that form a protective lining around the body's nerve fibers. Generally, they grow slowly, so it is possible Rosemary's tumor had been growing for quite some time. At the time it was discovered, it was already developed, though we did not know whether it was benign or malignant. It was later confirmed to be benign. Her symptoms were significant—ringing in the affected ear (tinnitus), pressure in the ear, loss of balance, and facial weakness as the tumor pressed against the adjacent facial nerve.

Medical technology has made enormous strides in the last three decades. Today, radiation may be recommended when tumors are small to medium. Stereotactic radiosurgery is a form of radiation therapy that precisely targets the tumors with high doses of radiation while sparing the surrounding tissues. Another modern tool in the doctor's toolkit is microsurgery, with the goal of preserving both hearing and the facial nerve.

Unfortunately, very few options were available at the time. We were never given the option of radiation, perhaps because the tumor wasn't discovered early enough. Immediate surgery was recommended. Rosemary was all of thirty years old. For her to be struck with such a serious illness at such a young age was calamitous for her and for our family. Jeffrey was five at the time, Michael was approaching seven.

A team consisting of the heads of the neurosurgery and otolaryngology departments operated on Rosemary for eight hours on June 10, 1986. The surgeons were able to remove the tumor but had to sacrifice the hearing nerve. The facial nerve was preserved, but it appeared to have temporarily lost most of its function. After she recovered from the operation, the right side of her face sagged. About 80 percent of the function returned to the facial nerve in the following four weeks. However, it took more than a full year for Rosemary to feel that she had almost full control of both sides of her face. She lost her hearing in her right ear for good.

I will never forget the children's reaction when they came to visit their mother in the hospital. It had been a few days since the surgery. Her facial nerve was almost useless at this time, and her right cheek sagged visibly, contorting her face. The boys hugged her first and then looked at her. That is when the shock set in. Jeffrey ran into the bathroom and wouldn't come out.

Michael looked bewildered.

"Daddy, what happened to Mommy? She looks so different."

Words failed me. I could do little to console our sons but gather them in my arms and hold them tight. Even as I write this, the scene flashes before my eyes. It is hard to control my emotions.

Our sons' reaction was devastating to me. But I had to keep it together and try to restore their spirits. Even more importantly, I needed to give my all to Rosemary to buck up her spirits. She had seen the reaction on the children's faces. I could only imagine her pain and anguish.

While we awaited her recovery in the next few days, a serious complication emerged. Her spinal fluid was leaking profusely through her nose. It turned out that the neurosurgeon hadn't properly patched up the section of her brain that had been operated on. I got the shocking news at work and drove the twenty-four miles to Philadelphia in a haze. I found Rosemary in her hospital room with Kleenex stuffed in both nostrils. She was agitated, both because of the discomfort and perhaps even more so because the leak was an indication that more surgeries lay ahead.

The next eight months were a time of profound distress for my wife. The children missed their mother as she was in and out of the hospital. The surgeons would operate to try to find and patch up the leak. She would be discharged from the hospital. We would attempt to make her as comfortable as possible at home. The children would get their mommy back. But then, in a matter of a few days or a few weeks, the cursed leak would return, sometimes more torrential than the last time. Off she went back to the hospital for yet another attempt by the surgeons. I lost count of the times an ambulance had to be summoned to take her from Yardley to Thomas Jefferson Hospital in Philadelphia.

Perhaps the saddest day for me in 1986 was July 4 of that year. I had just walked out of Jefferson Hospital at night. The City of Brotherly Love was lit up with fireworks. I felt utterly desolate in the midst of the celebration of the nation's birthday. I felt like I was in a deep pit that I would never climb out of.

We learned through the grapevine of a highly reputable neurosurgeon at Johns Hopkins University Hospital in Baltimore, Michael J. Holliday. In January 1987, we drove 130 miles to Baltimore in a fierce snowstorm. The nurses were kind enough to let me stay with Rosemary in her hospital room for a couple of nights. Dr. Holliday operated on her and was confident enough to discharge her from the hospital on the third day.

Upon Rosemary's homecoming from Baltimore, our sons presented their mother with a cake with the inscription "Welcome Home, Mommy." By then, her facial nerve had restored most of its function, permitting her to smile at their warm greetings.

(Rosemary's homecoming from Johns Hopkins University Hospital, Baltimore, late January 1987)

We monitored Rosemary's nasal discharges with dread after returning home. We had been disappointed too many times after the operations at Jefferson Hospital to let our guard down. We dared not allow ourselves to fully relax. Days passed into weeks. There were no more leaks of the spinal fluid. Dr. Holliday had been successful in a single try.

Joy made its way back into our household after the operation in Baltimore proved a success. We were happy again. I felt like an immense weight had been lifted off my chest.

Perhaps it was my desire to blot out the memory of this painful episode in our life, but in the three decades since, I have never been able to remember her "good" hearing side, as we take seats in a restaurant, for example. She has to remind me to sit on her left. I am embarrassed, and I think it is callous of me. The memories of those horrid eight months come flooding back.

***

I could never have managed the household, cared for our sons, and attended to my job in those eight tumultuous months without our guardian angels—the scores of relatives who helped take care of us. Rosemary's mother Jane and her aunt Ann Powers took turns staying with us. My sister Gurmit's son, Gurtej, stayed with us the bulk of the summer of 1986, before starting graduate school at the University of North Carolina at Chapel Hill in the fall. My niece Surbjit, my sister Surjit's daughter, came down from Toronto to help. My eldest sister, Parkash, came over from Queens for a couple of extended stays. My side of the family in the 1980s was primarily located in Toronto and Queens, though my sister Gurmit and her husband Sarjit didn't emigrate until the early 1990s, settling down in Boise, Idaho, to be near Gurtej after I had sponsored them for immigration to the United States. My brother, Ranbir and his wife, Kuldip, lived in Toronto. While Ranbir had been working for the Toronto Transit Commission, Kuldip had found a job as a caregiver at a daycare nursery school. Ranbir had sponsored our sister Surjit's family for immigration to Canada from England, where they had been living since the mid-1960s. Surjit, her husband, Darshan, and their four children moved to Toronto in late 1975. Darshan found a blue-collar job.

The summer before Rosemary's illness, one of Surjit's daughters, Surbjit, had come to live with us in Yardley for several months. She had been having difficulties with her parents in Toronto. I suppose there were the inevitable clashes between parents with old-world expectations and teenage daughters who wanted to go out and meet young men.

We had our house painted that summer. The painting crew had a handsome young blond man, James Schuler. Jim and Surbjit were drawn to each other immediately. But Jim appeared to be shy, so Surbjit took the initiative in suggesting a date. When she returned the following summer to help me during Rosemary's illness, she and Jim picked back up their relationship. Their courtship led to marriage and a beautiful daughter, Sonia. Surbjit and Jim now live in New Hampshire.

Things weren't going as well for other members of the family.

While Ranbir held his job with the Toronto Transit

Commission, he was getting deeply consumed by the politics of our original home state of Punjab, as I noticed later when he visited me in 1980. He tried to start a magazine that would focus on Sikh affairs in Punjab.

Parkash's eldest son, Inderjit, had stayed behind in India when Parkash immigrated to America with her husband and three younger sons in 1977. Inderjit joined the rest of the family in Queens two years later. He had a severe speech disability and had difficulty finding a job because of it. So, he and Ranbir considered the idea of him joining Ranbir in Toronto to help him put out the Sikh-focused magazine. Ranbir had even started the paperwork.

Then Inderjit died in a subway accident in New York City in 1981. Most of our family saw the tragedy for what it was, an accident. But Ranbir saw it differently. He theorized that our nephew's death was the work of "America's intelligence services," who didn't want Inderjit to help Ranbir publish the magazine. He wrote up his "theory" and distributed copies of the paper at the Sikh temple in Toronto, as well as at bus and subway stations in the city. How Ranbir connected the idea of publishing a magazine in Canada for an audience in India to the American intelligence services boggled my mind.

Within days of his return to Toronto after services for Inderjit took place in New York, Ranbir had a nervous breakdown. He shook violently. He would remove his turban and pass notes to his wife, suggesting that intelligence agencies had planted monitors in the turban. Kuldip suggested admitting him to the hospital, which he refused. But she did have him examined by a team of psychiatrists at the local hospital. Their diagnosis? Paranoid schizophrenia.

Ranbir refused to take his medication. He wrote notes to Kuldip, saying he was no longer taking his prescription, since it was all a plot by the intelligence services to poison him and thus cripple his project to publish his magazine, which they—

the combined intelligence services of India, Canada, and the United States—viewed as a grave threat. He warned her not to say anything out loud because the house was bugged by intelligence agencies.

I talked to him on the phone. He bitterly complained how "they" were out to get him. When I counseled him to diligently take his medication so he would get well, he broke off all communication with me. He successively accused me, Surjit's family in Toronto, and, ultimately, Kuldip, of betraying him.

Despite this, Ranbir retained a sharp awareness of his financial needs. He filed for disability pay with the Toronto Transit Commission. Kuldip called it quits a few years later. They sold their house and divorced. He isolated himself and lived alone in Toronto.

I thought I might be able to reach him through a letter. His response broke my heart. He accused me of betraying him and listed the times ever since we lived on the farm as boys when "you sought to harm me."

I was so alarmed that I flew to Toronto. He agreed to see me but would say nothing. I brought up the times on the farm when we planted acres of wheat together. I reminded him of how he would help me with difficult problems when we studied chemical engineering in Chandigarh. But none of these common threads ignited recognition of our previous mutual trust and caring.

I wonder if I could have done something differently to help my schizophrenic brother. Such mental illnesses are not 100 percent curable, but they are definitely treatable. Psychotherapy, stress reduction, healthy living, and taking prescribed medications improve the patient's chances of a better outcome.

Yet one of the biggest challenges in getting Ranbir treatment was his anosognosia, the medical term for the illness that interferes with your ability to know that you are not well.

Not accepting that you are psychotic has enormous consequences, including inhibiting your cooperation with treatment.

Months turned into years and years into decades. Ranbir stayed totally cut off from the rest of the family. He wrote pamphlets bitterly criticizing the Canadian and US governments for purportedly killing our nephew Inderjit and a host of other criminal actions. I heard from relatives in Toronto that Ranbir was distributing these pamphlets around town. He had added the names of his relatives, including me, to the list of people who cooperated with the intelligence agencies that sought to harm him. I decided it was best to leave him alone so he wouldn't feel provoked or threatened. I wouldn't see him for many decades.

Ranbir's illness has tormented me all my life. When I last saw my dad, Bauji, in 1972, he shared his worries about Ranbir. "There is something very wrong with him," he told me. I had seen Ranbir several months earlier in Fredericton, Canada, and I assured Bauji that Ranbir was well. But I could see the deep sadness in Bauji's eyes. The thought haunts me that I didn't do enough, that I failed my brother and Bauji, too.

***

I had made a point of continuing to attend to my professional duties at Rohm and Haas throughout the eight months of Rosemary's illness. I had to take blocks of days off at critical junctures. But my head could never be 100 percent on the job. The stress and the worry were too much. Most of the time I had the surreal feeling that I was in two places at the same time. I would be in an important meeting and the image of Rosemary lying distraught in her hospital bed would drive the reality of the meeting out of my mind. My job required extensive travel, which I could no longer undertake. My focus wavered and my performance suffered.

I was passed over for a promotion during this period.

I was starting to feel a degree of disconnect with my employer. I had two choices: I could dig deeper into my job with Rohm and Haas. Or I could start elsewhere if a higher-level job were to come my way, though the latter option would most likely require relocation.

Thankfully, I didn't have to seek out new positions. Probably because of my career trajectory thus far, executive recruiters never stopped calling through my six-year tenure at Rohm and Haas. An attractive opportunity was brought to my attention in late 1987. It was a higher-level position, at a much larger multinational company, in Charlotte, North Carolina. I was interested.

CHAPTER 10

HORNET'S NEST

Let's get out of here; this place is a damned hornet's nest.
- Lord Charles Cornwallis, October 1780 in the battle at Charlotte, NC

After sixteen days of frustrating Revolutionary War battles in and around Charlotte against the outnumbered American militia commanded by General William Lee Davidson, Lord Charles Cornwallis was deeply annoyed and frustrated. He may not have said the exact line that is attributed to him above, but he said something to that effect.

Charlotte, at the time, wasn't much of a town, much less a city. Colonel William Davie's small detachment from General Davidson's militia bore the brunt of the fighting against the British. Colonel Davie described Charlotte as a town of "about twenty houses, built on two streets, which cross each other at right angles, at the intersection of which stands the court-house."

The Battle of Charlotte didn't have a lasting adverse impact on Cornwallis's career. Six years later, in February 1786, he was appointed the commander-in-chief of British

India and the governor of the presidency of Fort William, the same Fort William where my dad served as the SSO in 1949. I had first come across the name Lord Cornwallis when I studied Indian history as a teenager.

The Charlotte of twenty houses that Colonel Davie saw had been chartered as a town only twelve years earlier, in 1768. The European settlers who chartered the town named the new hamlet after King George III's wife, Queen Charlotte, and gave the surrounding county the name Mecklenburg in honor of the queen's birthplace in Germany.

The town had certainly grown in the 207 years since. When I arrived in Charlotte in October 1987, it was the premier metropolitan city in the Southeast, second only to Atlanta. It was one of the largest banking centers in America. We weren't surprised that the first NBA franchise in Charlotte would have an angry hornet as its mascot, given Lord Cornwallis's pronouncement. What did surprise newcomers, and the city was full of them when I moved there, was how Charlotte defied most other cities by calling downtown "Uptown." A rich international culinary scene flourished around the city. A majority of homeowners in the community where we chose to live were also transplants from the Northeast.

***

I started on my new job, director of process technology, with Sandoz Chemicals Corporation (SCC) in October 1987. SCC was part of a much larger multinational company, Sandoz Corporation, headquartered in Basel, Switzerland. In 1996, Sandoz would merge with Ciba-Geigy, another multinational based in Basel, to form Novartis.

Swiss companies had a very strong foundation in organic chemistry. Sandoz was a global behemoth with a presence in a great many countries. It had one dubious distinction, however. One of its chemists, Albert Hoffmann, first synthesized LSD (lysergic acid diethylamide) in 1938.

The strength of Sandoz lay in organic synthesis. It developed numerous dyes and molecules with pharmacological activity. The pharmacological group formed the foundation of Sandoz's biggest division, Sandoz Pharmaceuticals. As by far the largest group within Sandoz, its pharmaceutical division set the company culture. Process engineering was not the company's strong suit. The Sandoz processes may not have been optimal, but the manufacturing costs for pharmaceuticals were often a minuscule fraction of the prices these products commanded.

SCC was heavily focused on textile dyes. It had a sizable paper chemicals business, too, and another group of products described roughly as specialty chemicals. The specialties business marketed pigments and chemicals for leather processing.

All of the SCC product lines, in contrast to Sandoz Pharmaceuticals, commanded relatively low selling prices. Low manufacturing costs and consistent quality were the key requirements. The leadership at SCC recognized that induction of process engineering was essential to meeting both requirements. My mission was to set up the process technology function, which would be a part of the company's R&D function. I had been hired by "Elias," the vice president of R&D.

We would scale up the new processes developed by R&D's chemists and facilitate their introduction to one of the three manufacturing plants—Mount Holly in North Carolina, Martin in South Carolina, and Fair Lawn in New Jersey. I planned to replicate what I had seen of corporate research at my previous employers. In the other jobs I had, the entire research function, including process engineering, had already been fully developed. At Sandoz, I was instead charged with creating the process engineering function and making it work harmoniously with the existing groups.

The research group was located at the Mount Holly plant, where I was stationed, while Elias operated from the company headquarters in Charlotte, fifteen miles away.

***

I stayed in a bachelor apartment with a forty-minute commute from my office in Mount Holly, while the rest of my family stayed behind in Yardley until we could find a new home. Rosemary and I liked a house in the Park Crossing community, in southeast Charlotte. But the seller needed the house for another six months, so we executed the formal purchase and rented it back to him until he could move out.

In the meantime, I rented a larger apartment for the whole family. We drove down from Yardley on New Year's Eve, December 31, 1987, and stayed the night in Richmond, Virginia. Rosemary, the boys, and I arrived at our apartment in Charlotte on January 1, 1988. We barely had time to stock the refrigerator and unpack before we were hit with a debilitating snowstorm. Longtime residents couldn't recall another snowstorm of such ferocity. And while we were accustomed to driving in snow and on icy streets, most Charlotteans were not. Rosemary had a few close calls while driving with the children in the car. The natives drove either too fast or too slowly.

Despite that rocky start, we eventually settled into the home we had purchased. Among all the houses we have owned since our marriage—we are now living in our fifth—the house in Charlotte was the most beautiful. As residents of Park Crossing, we had full access to its pool and club. Our kids made heavy use of the pool.

The city enjoyed a progressive reputation in the late 1980s, both socially and politically, when we settled there. I met and

(Our house in Charlotte)

shook hands once with the black Democratic mayor of Charlotte, Harvey Gantt. He would contest the election for the US Senate from North Carolina in 1990 against the white Republican incumbent, Jesse Helms.

Helms ran the "White Hands" TV ad in the 1990 Senate campaign. It was designed to inflame white voter anxiety over his black opponent. It showed a pair of white hands balling up a rejection letter while a voice said: "You needed that job and you were the best qualified. But they had to give it to a minority because of a racial quota." Helms's scorched-earth campaign tactics worked, and he won the election.

Even white Charlotteans who were otherwise easygoing and friendly seemed quite unwilling to consider a black man for the US Senate. I would occasionally chat with one of the mothers at our sons' baseball games. When I brought up the matter of voting for Gantt, she looked shocked.

"Can't vote for them," she said, meaning black people, astonished that I would give Gantt serious consideration.

Not much had changed since Helms began his political career when he was an unabashed segregationist. Affiliated with the Council of Conservative Citizens, an outgrowth of the White Citizens' Councils that promoted white supremacy, he had stated in 1960 that forced busing and racial integration were unwise.

Charlotte's public schools became a model of integration by 1980, despite Helms's efforts—one of the most integrated school systems in the country. They did not have a good academic reputation, though. We visited some of them and were dissatisfied. In reaction to mandatory busing, several parochial and private schools had sprung up. We considered two of them—Providence Day School and Charlotte Country Day School. They were good but pricey.

We chose the parochial school St. Ann Catholic School. Many kids in Park Crossing went to St. Ann's. The school didn't provide busing, so the neighborhood mothers formed carpools.

Rosemary got busy with activities revolving around our children, especially at the school. She realized early on that our boys' knowledge of math far exceeded the offerings in their respective grades. A genetic component appeared to be at play; as a child, I couldn't get enough of math, and that love had been passed on to our sons.

Math SuperStars was an enrichment opportunity designed for self-directed learners in mathematics, conceived and coordinated by the Florida Department of Education's Mathematics Department. Its goal was to enhance students' appreciation and knowledge of mathematics, with particular emphasis on problem-solving skills.

Math SuperStars started out at St. Ann's as a workshop attended by some of the elementary school teachers. One of the attendees, Judith Akins, who taught second-grade math, recruited Rosemary to organize and launch the program at the school.

Rosemary prepared a proposal for the school-wide introduction of the program, which Mrs. Akins presented to the principal. They got approval to start the program at the beginning of the 1989/1990 school year. All school grades, one through six, participated in the program. Michael and Jeffrey would start participating in the program as fourth and third graders, respectively.

Rosemary enlisted two parent volunteers from each class to help her grade the student answer sheets. A student's performance was graded in terms of the number of stars per worksheet. She set up a wall of stars in the school, showing all participants.

To raise donations, she presented the program to local businesses. The donations were used to offer prizes to program winners. Ninety percent of the students signed up for the program in the first year. Of the 340 students who signed up in the second year, the retention rate by the end of the year was 75 percent. The program was wildly popular.

Rosemary soon started another program, Family Math, introduced as a complement to the Math SuperStars program. It offered a hands-on approach to learning math and solving problems through evening workshops involving parent-child participation.

Among all her endeavors throughout her life, Rosemary is most proud of what she accomplished with the Math SuperStars program. I remember seeing her grade reams of papers at night. Her role wasn't too different from that of a teacher. There was one important difference, though. She had volunteered. She got paid in the currency of love and the satisfaction of her charges.

***

Our boys' interests extended beyond math. They were both avid fans of baseball and basketball. Our family got caught in the craze for the Charlotte Hornets. George Shinn, an entrepreneur from Kannapolis, North Carolina, wanted to bring an NBA team to the Charlotte area. The original franchise was

(In Charlotte, with Jeffrey and Michael, December 1990)

established in 1988 as an expansion team, owned by Shinn.

But first, the team needed a name. Shinn decided to sponsor a contest and had fans vote on six finalists. More than nine thousand ballots were cast. Hornets won by a landslide, beating out Knights, Cougars, Spirit, Crowns, and Stars.

The Hornets played their first game on November 4, 1988, losing to the Cleveland Cavaliers. I attended an electrifying game on December 23, 1988, when the Hornets defeated the Chicago Bulls. This marked the first time that Michael Jordan returned to North Carolina, his home state, to play basketball. He earned a standing ovation when he was introduced. As the game resumed, though, we were solidly behind our beloved Hornets.

Charlotteans were proud of our Hornets. This was the first time I ever felt an emotional attachment to a professional sports team. I remember standing in line in the middle of the night at the Charlotte Coliseum in the fall of 1989 to get season tickets for the upcoming second season.

Charlotte got its football franchise a few years later. The Carolina Panthers was announced as the National Football League's twenty-ninth franchise in 1993.

***

While Rosemary supported the boys in their challenges at school and play, I faced a big challenge of my own at Sandoz. I was expected not only to establish the whole new discipline of process technology at the company from scratch but to do so while all other interacting parts had been functioning for quite a long time. It was akin to grafting a new limb onto a body. It can work, but the body may reject it. Elias, vice president of R&D, and I knew going in that either outcome was possible.

What is novel about process technology? How does it differ from chemistry?

Imagine the chemist toiling away in his lab, checking out new reaction pathways in a flask. The agitator he uses to stir the contents of the flask is energetic enough to provide rapid and thorough mixing of the contents. If the reaction produces heat, he can surround the flask in a cooling bath. Conversely, he can provide heat by attaching a heating mantle. The reaction system he works with is small enough for him to control adequately.

Now imagine the chemist wants to carry out the same reaction on a commercial scale. His first instinct may be to do it in a giant flask. But the flask contents may greatly overheat in the center, given that the agitation is no longer as effective and cooling is likely to be very inefficient.

A chemical engineer determines the best commercial-scale reactor configuration. It may be a long tubular reactor cooled by running a coolant through a jacket around it. It may be a series of small stirred, jacketed reactors. It may be more efficient to cool the reactor contents by pumping them through an external cooler.

The chemical engineer addresses issues of safety, too. He makes sure the commercial reactor does not lead to runaway reactions, causing explosions. Just as important, he designs a system with minimal capital and operating costs.

How did companies like Sandoz manage to produce and sell all their products without the direct application of process technology? They had produced them on a commercial scale by using common sense, without adopting the systematic approach enabled by process technology. Their operations worked, but they were not generally cost-optimal. It didn't matter much in the pharmaceutical sector since the profit margins are vast. For the sort of products SCC marketed, however, manufacturing costs did matter.

But Elias and I made a couple of mistakes along the way.

At the time I was hired, the R&D professionals worked in a somewhat dilapidated part of the Mount Holly manufacturing plant. The R&D building looked shoddy and was cramped for space. The adjacent administration building, which housed the plant manager and his top lieutenants, was far better equipped and had a much more "executive" look.

The plant manager had offered to house me in the administration building. He wanted to get the new director of process technology on his side, including getting the new hire situated physically very close to him. Elias went along with his proposal, starting me out in a far better office, in a better building, than my fellow directors in R&D.

Elias should have exercised better judgment. Putting me in an executive office immediately induced jealousy and ill will among my colleagues. Perhaps I should have quickly picked up on the optics of such a move and asked Elias to house me in the R&D building. But changing offices so soon after starting would have been awkward.

We made another mistake. While only a small fraction of the scientists in the R&D organization held doctorates, I tried hiring PhD chemical engineers for many positions in process technology. Perhaps my ego got the better of me. It didn't sit too well with the others within R&D. Some sympathetic colleagues told me of people making snide remarks about the attempted "elitism" of process technology.

There were structural problems as well. My colleagues in R&D were used to speaking with marketing and manufacturing directly. They had developed relationships over time. They resented having to turn over those interfaces to me. Elias couldn't just order their cooperation. They needed to be convinced.

We did receive early cooperation from some sections of the company. Some people at SCC were open-minded about process technology. Others extended cooperation because Elias, an expatriate from the parent company in Basel, was perceived to be powerful. One important supporter was the vice president for operations, Ray Ankers. His support was crucial because the three manufacturing plants reported to him. But after my first eighteen months on the job, Ankers was moved into a staff job and the plant managers pretty much stopped offering their cooperation.

Organizations, like individuals, often feel threatened when they face a big change. But I had gone in with a bit of naïveté, fully expecting cooperation throughout the company as I set about fulfilling my mission. To the prevailing culture at SCC, process technology was indeed a big change in the way of doing things. At the very least, it introduced a new layer in the research process, which necessarily lengthened the product introduction process, leading to longer lead times for new products. I needed to convince the people at SCC that the benefits would outweigh the costs. For that, I needed quick success stories. How do you produce quick success stories when you have to first hire the entire staff and build the infrastructure?

Elias and I slogged away. Recruiting was tough work. It took almost two years to staff the critical positions. The prevailing pay scales at SCC made it hard to attract talent from other parts of the country, especially the Northeast and the Midwest.

We had several successes in my first three years. We helped in the successful market introduction of a new line of textile dyes. The specialty products group appreciated our efforts in bringing to market several products, especially for the leather market. But there were delays, too, caused principally by incomplete infrastructure and inadequate staffing. My group got handed the blame. The lack of support from my R&D colleagues hurt.

It was dawning on me then that a report card of unvarnished success under the circumstances would be impossible. I was operating in a milieu of dominant chemistry culture, where support for process technology wasn't a natural instinct.

To make matters worse, Elias had been losing support from his contacts in the Basel headquarters. One of his principal initiatives suffered a bad fate. He had been able to upgrade facilities for R&D by moving to a swank new building in the University Research Park adjacent to the University of North Carolina at Charlotte. But after a couple of years, he was not allowed to renew the lease. R&D had to relocate back to the plant, a blow to morale.

After three and a half years at Sandoz, the denouement arrived. In the early summer of 1991, I was informed that I was no longer a good fit and my job was terminated.

It was a trying time for me, even though Rosemary came through with full emotional support. Throughout my education and career, I had known mostly success. The few failures had stung. The memory of failing the engineering drawing course in my freshman year at Chandigarh never left me. Now, suddenly, I was hit with failure again. It wouldn't do to blame others, though it was tempting. I had to reach deep into myself. Unless I understood where and why I had fallen short, I would be unable to recover and resume my upward trajectory. I willed myself to learn from this experience.

***

Sandoz provided me with a generous severance package, which included outplacement services. I continued to dress up every morning and go to the office provided by outplacement in Uptown Charlotte. Outplacement included professional counseling, secretarial help, unlimited phone calls, and office space. I had a full-time job: to find another professional position.

The outplacement service subscribed to all the national and business newspapers and magazines such as *Fortune* and *BusinessWeek*. We could dart out to the nearby public library in Uptown Charlotte as needed, since, of course, this was before the advent of the internet and LinkedIn.

One particular advantage of having access to outplacement was how it served as a relief valve and brought me face-to-face with many other laid-off executives. There were former vice presidents and even a smattering of company CEOs that availed themselves of the help. We had free give-and-take. We were free to tap into the experiences of colleagues—how they successfully identified opportunities, prepared for interviews, and so on. Setbacks of others also constituted valuable lessons for the rest.

We would seek to buck up a colleague's spirits after a bad interview or loss of an expected job offer. The employees of the outplacement service were a valuable resource as well. They were a great sounding board and a source of ideas for continuing our job search.

I made a couple of very good friends at the time I was going through outplacement. It was a valuable learning and building experience for me.

One temporary opportunity came my way within weeks of starting the search process. I connected with Angus Chemical Company in Chicago, which had a manufacturing plant in Ireland. To my enormous relief, I won a six-month consulting assignment in Cork, Ireland.

***

The Angus assignment applied a balm to the open wound of losing the job at Sandoz. It allowed me to quickly reengage in professional work and ease the pain and humiliation of my experience at SCC.

The leadership at Angus headquarters in Chicago was concerned that the plant in Cork wasn't being run optimally and may have been cutting corners in the area of safety. I reported directly to the vice chairman of the company in Chicago, who hired me, while I would work closely with the local plant manager in Ireland.

I won't dwell too much on the details of the assignment. It went smoothly. I tried to be respectful of the local management and be wary of their sensitivities. Visitors from Chicago were often ham-handed with the locals. I did my best to avoid this sort of behavior. I made several recommendations during my stint; a majority of them were approved and implemented in the plant. Interestingly, I didn't find much difference between how professional activities were carried out in Ireland and in the United States.

Angus flew me home once every four weeks and rented an apartment for me in the city of Cork. My immediate challenge was to master driving the stick-shift rental car I had. The last time I had driven such a car was at Notre Dame, twenty-five years earlier. The other challenge was more serious: conditioning my mind to drive on the left side of the road. I got the hang of both after about a week.

I absolutely loved Ireland and the Irish people. They were gentle and polite. On weekends, I would drive to other Irish cities or explore the countryside. One trip that I particularly enjoyed was a weekend in the city of Galway on the west coast. Given my early devotion to Bobby Kennedy, I was touched by the memorial sculpture of JFK that the Irish had put up in Eyre Square. The older Irish folk I met in bars still retained vivid memories of the day in June 1963 when Jack Kennedy visited the city and made remarks at Eyre Square. Their faces lit up when they talked about it.

A trip to Dublin on another weekend was memorable. I reconnected with Noel Murphy, a fellow graduate student from Notre Dame. He returned to Ireland soon after completing his doctoral work in late 1968 and had been teaching at University College, Dublin, from where he would retire in 2002.

Murphy picked me up from my hotel and gave me a tour of Dublin and its outskirts. He showed me the rich peat bogs just outside the city. It was nice to revisit the old days and hear of his life since then. He was kind enough to host me for dinner at his home, with his teenage son and wife. He had maintained one tradition from our graduate school days. He and his son were Notre Dame football fanatics. They would videotape all the home games and claimed to have watched all of them!

I arranged for Rosemary to visit me on her first trip to Ireland. Her mother, Jane, was kind enough to agree to take care of the children for a week. Jane hopped onto a train from Northampton and made the eight-hundred-mile journey by rail to Charlotte. She was deathly afraid of flying and had never set foot on a plane in her entire life.

Rosemary and I had a lovely week together, almost like a second honeymoon. We hit most of the tourist spots near Cork and farther out west, near the coast. Our tour of the Blarney

Castle & Gardens was particularly memorable. We climbed the Blarney Castle and took turns contorting our bodies into position for a kiss of the famous stone, supposed to grant you the gift of gab. It is a scary experience if you make the mistake of looking down from the ninety-foot height, which I did.

(Rosemary outside the Blarney Castle, near Cork, Ireland, fall 1991)

Sometimes, in the midst of my happiness in Ireland, the reality of my joblessness would hit me out of nowhere. It would happen sometime late at night when I was alone in my apartment. The fact that I would have to return to Charlotte to resume my job search stung. The opprobrium of being asked to leave Sandoz was torture. Mercifully, I had a job to do in the Angus Chemical plant. I would wake up in the morning, head out to the office, and allow myself to be pulled into the lovely embrace of Ireland. Life would go on.

***

During the assignment in Cork, I reconnected with David Koch. The last time I saw him was when I invited him in 1977 to Stauffer Chemical Company to give a presentation on the products marketed by Koch Engineering Company.

While in Cork, I came across an article Koch had written in the magazine *Chemical Engineering*. He described an airplane accident that occurred at the Los Angeles airport on February 1, 1991.

Koch was a passenger on a USAir flight that had originated

in Syracuse, New York. Upon its descent, the Boeing 737 landed on top of a turboprop aircraft serving a SkyWest flight that taxied for takeoff on the same runway. Twenty-three out of the eighty-nine people on board the Boeing were killed, as were all twelve on the SkyWest flight; most of those on the 737 succumbed to asphyxiation in the post-crash fire.

His article included several recommendations for the airline industry to improve safety during post-accident evacuations. Tellingly, he identified himself only as a chemical engineer. He eschewed the use of big titles, such as his then title, president of the Chemical Technology Group of Koch Industries.

I called him in August 1991 at his New York office to inquire after his well-being. We spoke for about twenty minutes. Koch still had a bad cough, a result of smoke inhalation in the accident. He said the smoke had seared his lungs. The call gave us the opportunity to catch up on the goings-on in the previous fourteen years.

***

The six months of the assignment in Cork flew by swiftly, and I was back in Charlotte. I returned to the outplacement office in Uptown and renewed my contacts. Some clients of the office had successfully moved on, though the vast majority of them were still there.

The next twelve months were a hard slog. There was no income and our savings were depleted. I had to turn to my sister Parkash for a sizable loan. She sent the money with no questions asked. Later, when I tried to pay it back with interest, she would only accept the principal. This is what characterized Parkash—great generosity, not only in fiscal matters, but generosity of spirit too.

My job search concluded successfully at the end of 1992.

Earlier that year, I had learned through my networking contacts that the leadership of a small company in Virginia, named Lee Laboratories, was in flux. It had recently been acquired by a large German pharmaceutical company, Boehringer Ingelheim Corporation (BIC).

One morning I made a cold call to the president of Lee Laboratories and, to my surprise, he picked up the phone and spoke with me. He didn't have a specific need but, because "things are so fluid here," he invited me to come visit. I flew out to Petersburg, Virginia, about twenty miles south of the state capital of Richmond.

I met the top management of the company, including "Fritz," a young German from the BIC headquarters in Germany, who headed R&D at Lee Labs. Nothing came of this introductory meeting.

I received a call from a recruiter several months later. A lot had changed since my last visit to the company. The recruiter was seeking to fill the position of director of engineering. Lee Labs had by now been officially renamed Boehringer Ingelheim Chemicals Corporation (BICC). The company had hired a new president, Michael "Mike" Zaleski, to replace the man I had made my cold call to. Zaleski was seeking to fill the newly created engineering director position.

I had a head start among the candidates being interviewed since I had already met many players at BICC. My second round of interviews went well, and I was offered the job, which I accepted. What made the offer even sweeter was that the position paid almost 40 percent higher than the one I had left at Sandoz.

I started working for BICC on January 21, 1993, eighteen months after I had left Sandoz. Though I was not destined to climb the ladder at Sandoz, another Indian American would, as the company underwent many interesting changes in the following twenty-five years.

***

The leadership of the Swiss pharmaceutical giants, of which Sandoz was a prime example through the last century and the early part of the twenty-first century, had come from Swiss schools and connections. Marc Moret, the CEO of Sandoz during my time, retired in 1992 and was succeeded by Daniel Vasella.

Though Vasella earned his stripes independently as a physician in Bern and as the head of the US pharmaceutical subsidiary of Sandoz, it didn't hurt that he was married to Moret's niece. Vasella would go on to lead the combined Novartis after Sandoz's 1996 merger with Ciba-Geigy. He turned over the reins of the company in 2010 to his hand-picked successor, Joseph Jimenez, an American from Silicon Valley.

The company announced Jimenez's retirement in February 2018, a few months after Vasant Narasimhan had been named his successor as CEO of Novartis. He was just forty-one at the time. I could never have imagined when I worked at SCC that an Indian American would one day ascend to the peak of Novartis.

Dr. Narasimhan is a first-generation American, born to Indian parents. They originate from Tamil Nadu, having immigrated to the United States in the 1970s. The family is a glowing example of immigrants to the United States who have made impressive contributions to their new home country.

CHAPTER 11

OLD DOMINION

Our auntient Collonie of Virginia, one of our own Dominions.
        - King Charles II of England, 1663

With these words, King Charles II was acknowledging a gift of Virginia silk that Governor William Berkeley of Virginia presented to him in 1663. Charles II was grateful to the colony because Virginia recognized him as the monarch in the interval between 1649, when the Parliamentarians executed his father, Charles I, and 1660, when the exiled Charles II was restored to the throne. The name "Dominion" started evolving into "Old Dominion" during the American Revolution.

When Rosemary, the boys, and I moved to Virginia in 1993, the state was controlled by the Democrats; they controlled the governorship as well as the two houses of the Virginia Legislature. The Democrat Douglas Wilder had been elected governor in 1989. He was the first elected African American governor in Virginia's history. He couldn't run for reelection in 1993 because Virginia limits governors to a single term. Wilder was succeeded by the hard-core Republican George Allen. Allen would later become a US Senator, and an incident during his reelection campaign highlights the antipathy of some powerful Americans to immigrants, especially immigrants of color.

On August 11, 2006, at a campaign stop in Breaks, Virginia, a worker from the campaign of his opponent, James Webb, had been filming the event as a "tracker." Allen singled him out and called him "Macaca," which is a derogatory term in North Africa, meaning monkey. The tracker, S. R. Sidarth, was the dark-complexioned son of Indian immigrants who had been born and raised in Fairfax County, Virginia. The "Macaca moment" quickly went viral.

I was so steamed by the racial insult that I protested in a letter to the *New York Times*, published on August 17, 2006. Here is an excerpt from the letter, which was printed under the title "The Ugliness Within."

> Mr. Allen appears to have no qualms belittling others who come from a background different from that of his nearly all-white audience. Has he forgotten that his own mother, who speaks Arabic, French and Italian, migrated to the United States from Tunisia?
>
> Mr. Allen has offered an "apology" to Mr. Sidarth. He would do better to look into his soul and recognize the ugliness that dwells within.

Republicans would go on to control the state of Virginia for the next twenty-five years. Their reign ended when the state decisively turned blue in 2019, with Democratic control restored to the gubernatorial office as well as to the state's house of delegates and the state senate. In fact, an early indication of the impending change came in 2008 when Barack Obama won the state of Virginia in his first run for the presidency. But, in politics, nothing is forever. The Republican candidate, Glenn Youngkin, won back the governorship in the state election of November 2021.

***

I moved to Virginia in the last week of January 1993 to take up my new job at BICC. The company put me up temporarily at the Holiday Inn in Chester Township, about twelve miles north of my office in Petersburg.

I moved quickly to search for a house. Rosemary would come up from Charlotte on weekends to look at available homes. At five hours one-way, it wasn't a very convenient drive, but we were able to quickly zero in on the area and then found a house we liked.

The house we bought was in the Salisbury section of Midlothian. The development had been built in a huge wooded area, a substantial part of which was left undeveloped. Salisbury Country Club was less than a mile from our home, and we drove by it every time we went shopping. The Club was big on golf, a sport I never took up. Our younger son, Jeffrey, held his first job there at the age of twelve.

(Our house in Midlothian, Virginia)

We had considered, and rejected, the option of me living in an apartment for three months to allow the kids to finish out the school year at St. Ann's in Charlotte, and then we could search for a home and relocate sometime in the summer of

1993. But Rosemary and I wanted to keep the family together, so everyone relocated to Midlothian in mid-March 1993. The kids were enrolled in the public school system immediately.

(With Rosemary in our Virginia home, late 1993)

A majority of our neighbors in Salisbury were native Virginians, very unlike our Park Crossing neighborhood in Charlotte, which had mostly transplants. The environment was more sober and quieter than in Park Crossing. I decided I preferred the quieter environment. I got to treasure the forty minutes of my commute to work. It allowed me to just chill out and get my mind away from the daily firefighting chores on the job and to think longer term.

(Michael and Jeffrey in Midlothian, Virginia, October 1993)

***

Some of my thoughts during those commutes obviously were about my career and how I had come full circle with my position as director of engineering at BICC. I had started out as a process design engineer at Scientific Design Company. I continued in the engineering function at Stauffer Chemical. I ascended to higher management levels through the research function, first at Rohm and Haas, and then at Sandoz. Now I was making a lateral executive move back to engineering, heading the entire engineering function for BICC.

Boehringer Ingelheim was founded by Albert Boehringer in 1885 in Ingelheim am Rhein, Germany. The company was, and continues to be, owned by three families—the Boehringer, Liebrecht, and von Baumbach families. Boehringer's initial venture was a fairly mundane one, the production of tartaric acid for use in baking powder. The company became heavily invested in research in 1917 when it hired a future Nobel laureate, Heinrich Otto Wieland, to set up the research department. By the time I joined, the company was active in pharmaceuticals, biopharmaceuticals, and animal health.

A major project during my tenure at BICC was the design and construction of a brand-new facility for the manufacture of the active ingredient for the drug Viramune (generic name nevirapine). It was one part of a powerful "triple-drug cocktail" that helped change AIDS from an automatic death sentence to a chronic, but often manageable, disease. The triple cocktail treatment is also known as highly active antiretroviral therapy (HAART). Like Lazarus being raised from the dead, this cocktail treatment returned many AIDS patients who were debilitated and dying to relatively healthy and productive lives.

Viramune had been developed in the laboratories of Boehringer Ingelheim in Germany. We were racing ahead between 1993 and 1996 to put in place the manufacturing capacity for this, the second drug in the cocktail, fully anticipating Federal Drug Administration (FDA) approval, which would come in 1996.

BICC's president, Michael Zaleski, was a handsome man. He was twice married. His second wife was a beautiful woman, much younger than her husband. Originally trained as a chemical engineer, Zaleski had come up through the ranks as a salesman and a marketer. He was easygoing and had a certain charm about him.

Zaleski needed to staff critical parts of his organization. He also needed to kick off plans for the market introduction of a great many new pharmaceutical products. These were the priorities of his bosses in the Danbury, Connecticut, headquarters of Boehringer Ingelheim's American affiliate. The Petersburg facility, where I was based, would be the critical hub that would manufacture the active ingredients of these products.

Many of these new products were coming out of the research pipeline. Their manufacture fell within the purview of the FDA. We were obligated by law to conduct qualification of all new equipment, instrumentation, and facilities. Such qualification included installation (IQ), operation (OQ), and performance (PQ).

To get the full flavor of qualifications, let us wade into the weeds briefly. Before you even get to IQ, OQ, and PQ, if you're acquiring a new piece of equipment, you need design specifications that define exactly what's in that piece of equipment—everything from the type of power source it will utilize to the exact materials used in its construction. Once you have your final approved design specifications, you order the equipment. When it comes in you are now charged with developing your IQ, OQ, and PQ.

For installation qualification, we first look at the equipment material. For example, if we specified passivated 316 stainless, we test to verify it is in fact 316 stainless and that there are no further residues from the passivation process. For the motor driving the equipment, we confirm that the power output and the power requirements are consistent with our specifications and that the room the equipment is installed in can accommodate that power source. Once you have completed your review of the installation and everything is in order, you can trust that the equipment is going to operate the way in which it was designed.

Common sense, you say. We just needed to verify that we got what we ordered, and that it operated and performed as we had designed it. Who would quarrel with that? Nobody except the head of R&D, Fritz, who was also Zaleski's deputy.

Fritz was cantankerous and obdurate. He had failed "up" from his previous job at Ingelheim headquarters. His father wielded influence in Ingelheim and got Fritz moved to Virginia.

Fritz was deeply opposed to carrying out the detailed qualifications, "because they were unnecessary." The effort needed to carry out these qualifications did in fact require a serious outlay of resources, but the FDA had made them mandatory. Still, Fritz ordered the staff not to undertake this work.

I remember the exasperation of the head of quality assurance as he sought to assure Fritz of the need to do this work. Even Zaleski had to intervene forcefully. But Fritz, with his passive-aggressive style, was relentless, even managing to hold off his own boss. Finally, he acquiesced and grudgingly got out of the way. But his opposition cost us months of valuable time and sowed unnecessary discord.

Fritz loved to be in control. When I was searching for a house in the first few weeks after joining BICC, Fritz wanted me to focus my search close to the office in Petersburg. He had this notion that company employees should live close to the plant and pop in often, even in their time off. He considered this a manifestation of employee loyalty.

But Petersburg had poor-quality schools, I argued. He had a ready solution. "Your kids should go to the private school where my children go." I was shocked. He expected me to finance private education for my children out of my own pocket, merely so I could be available to spend my time off at the office. Many expatriate European employees had generous allowances for putting their children in private schools, which I am sure Fritz enjoyed as well. Nevertheless, Rosemary and I elected to live in a community thirty miles away, with good schools.

***

It would be easy to attribute Fritz's idiosyncrasies to his background, coming as he did from a completely different culture than I had. Yet I had many interactions with people from the parent company's headquarters in Ingelheim, not that this was even my first experience with a European company. I traveled several times to Ingelheim. I also attended seminars at resorts away from Ingelheim. Sandoz had attuned me to the culture of large European companies, and Boehringer Ingelheim didn't offer any surprises.

What do I mean by company culture? First, Germans and the Swiss were far more hierarchical than Americans. The top person would speak for the group in a meeting, while his underlings at the table surveyed the scene idly (and, yes, they were always "his" underlings). In the United States, everybody in a meeting is expected to contribute. Most times, people can't wait to get their two cents in. Second, people in Europe kept the office doors firmly closed, which is very contrary to our open-door policy in America. In fact, the first CEO of Bank of America, Hugh McColl, made it clear that a closed office door without justification was a firing offense. Third, Europeans were very status-conscious in the use of titles, such as the honorific "doctor." Curiously, they wouldn't return this courtesy to American visitors.

This debate concerning who is rightfully entitled to use the title "doctor," while not new, was recently brought into sharp relief by an opinion article in the *Wall Street Journal* that appeared on December 11, 2020. It reprimanded the soon-to-be First Lady, Dr. Jill Biden, for the use of the honorific.

The author, Joseph Epstein, who holds a bachelor's degree, questioned anyone not a physician who would want to be addressed as "doctor." The tone of the article was insulting. Epstein's opening sentence addressed the first lady by several names, including "kiddo." In response to the huge, indignant upsurge of criticism, the *Journal* doubled down. Paul Gigot, the editor of the *Journal*'s opinion pages, justified Epstein's reference to Dr. Biden as kiddo because others call her that, specifically her husband, the president. I am sure the president also has other endearing names for his wife—honey, sweetheart, and so on—though Epstein refrained from using those in his article.

I had already addressed this subject when I worked at BICC, perhaps influenced by my observation of the differences between American and European uses of the honorific "doctor." The *Richmond Times-Dispatch* published my letter, "Scholars Can Claim 'Doctor' More Fairly Than Physicians," on August 3, 1996. The paper recognized me as the "Correspondent of the Day" and later as the "Correspondent of the Week." At the end of the year, the paper invited me and Rosemary to attend a gala reception, at which the name of the "Correspondent of the Year" was revealed. Alas, that wasn't me.

I have reproduced the letter in full here:

> In your otherwise laudable editorial, "The Heir Apparent" (July 24), you take a dig at holders of the PhD degree

who claim the title Doctor. I think a clarification is in order.

That only physicians have the right to use this title has it backward. Derived from the Latin word docent, meaning to teach, the word doctor means "teacher" or "scholar." By no stretch of the imagination does it mean "physician." From Roman Times through the Middle Ages until into the 18th Century, the honorific "Doctor" applied only to eminent scholars, e.g., Martin Luther, known universally in the 16th Century as "Dr. Luther."

Jealous of the respect shown to scholars, medical schools in the 18th Century—particularly Edinburgh in Scotland—began the practice of addressing their graduates as "doctor." Physicians appear to have successfully misappropriated this title since then.

I think the standard for claiming this title is evidence of scholarship. Holders of earned PhDs have done all scholarly work in the form of a dissertation following a grueling course of graduate studies. Physicians cannot claim such evidence of scholarship, though they are required to master an impressive amount of technical detail.

Along the theme of your editorial, I agree that inherited titles such as those of British royalty should not demand automatic respect. However, I see no problem with the use of earned titles, such as "Doctor" by the recipients of the PhD degree.

***

Rosemary had long ago given up a professional career in favor of raising our children. She had quit her sales job with Procter & Gamble in 1979, a few months before Michael was born.

A couple of years after moving to our Midlothian home, when Michael was sixteen and Jeffrey was fourteen, she took steps to reenter the workforce. She worked as an area sales supervisor at a department store chain, Proffitt's, for eighteen months starting in 1995. She moved on to America One Communications, a division of Capital One Services, in late 1996 and worked there till early 1998. She had multiple successive roles at America One—sales specialist, sales facilitator, and trainer.

Rosemary worked exceptionally hard while the family lived in Virginia. Besides her full-time jobs, she also shouldered the bulk of parental duties. I was often unavailable, as I traveled heavily for my job with Boehringer Ingelheim.

But I wasn't totally absent from parenting duties. I introduced our sons to skiing at an early age. We went a few times to a ski area just west of the border into West Virginia, the Snowshoe Mountain Resort. I am proud to say they picked up on downhill skiing faster than I did when I first attempted skiing at Hunter Mountain in New York state in 1972.

(Jeffrey, Rosemary, and Michael at home in Midlothian, July 1996)

***

My engineering department undertook numerous other projects, though none with the scale and the sweep of the one to manufacture nevirapine. Toward the end of 1996, our capital budget started drying up. There just wasn't much else left to build. My job looked more and more like a dead end, and I began taking calls from executive recruiters.

One position brought to my notice was director of R&D at the Nutrilite Division of the multilevel marketer Amway. I had a negative image of Amway in the past, with stories in the press accusing Amway of running a Ponzi scheme. But I was greatly impressed during the job interviews by the company's emphasis on R&D. The good impression was apparently mutual because Amway offered the job to me.

One sore point was the location—Nutrilite was headquartered in Southern California. My family had always lived on the East Coast, and it was quite a jump to move clear across the continent. Amway was most generous with its relocation policy, however. I have been lucky that all relocations in my career have been fully paid for by my new employers.

Rosemary and I decided on a compromise. I would accept the offer and live in an apartment for a year. The rest of the family would stay behind in Midlothian. This would allow Michael to graduate from high school. Amway agreed to fly me home for weekends once every three weeks.

Jeffrey still had a year to go in high school in the summer of 1998 when we relocated the family to Orange County. Requiring Jeffrey to finish the last year of high school in California was a heart-wrenching decision for us. He had even worked out an alternative scenario, in which he would stay behind in Midlothian with family friends for a year. Eventually, he was a good sport and agreed to move with the family.

I started my new job at Nutrilite in June 1997, following two strings of long interviews in Southern California and in Ada, Michigan, the corporate headquarters of Amway. The faith I had in myself must have been evident during these interviews. Losing my job at Sandoz had hit me hard. The following eighteen months had been difficult, although getting the six-month consulting opportunity in Ireland softened the blow. I spent four years at Boehringer Ingelheim, from January 1993 through May 1997, a tenure that put me firmly back in the saddle, my confidence fully restored.

There is an interesting postscript to the BICC plant in Petersburg. I saw a news item in late 2013 in the *Richmond Times-Dispatch* reporting that the company had decided to shut down the plant by the end of 2014. I wondered about the hundreds of millions of dollars in investment sunk into the plant. But multinational companies have to assess the global picture, and it was quite likely that Boehringer Ingelheim found less-expensive ways of sourcing its active ingredients elsewhere.

There, too, was the human factor, disruption in the lives of hundreds of workers. I had been away for seventeen years. I didn't personally know who among the people I had worked with was still there and was impacted by the shutdown. Nonetheless, I was saddened by the turmoil unleashed on so many lives.

CHAPTER 12

Pinnacle

> *It is not on the pinnacle of success where men and women grow most. It is often down in the valley of heartache and disappointment and reverses where men and women grow into strong characters.*
> - Ezra Taft Benson, Conference Report, Stockholm Sweden Area Conference, 1974

My apartment, in the city of Orange, was twelve miles south of my Nutrilite office in Buena Park. I had another office in Lakeview in Riverside County—about half of my department operated out of Lakeview. The commute to Lakeview was much longer, a sixty-mile distance. I would divide my time roughly in half between the two offices.

Living alone in California allowed me to focus almost solely on my job. Sometimes, I could go home more frequently than the once-per-three-week agreement with Amway. I could occasionally schedule meetings at Amway headquarters in Ada toward the end of the week, followed by a weekend with the family in Midlothian.

Selling our house in Midlothian and buying a house in Orange County in mid-1998 turned out to be far harder than anticipated. Virginia had a housing glut, whereas Southern California suffered from a very lean housing inventory. We finally found a home in Anaheim Hills, which would require commutes of twenty and forty-five miles to my offices in Buena Park and Lakeview, respectively.

While our house in Charlotte, North Carolina, was the most beautiful among the five houses we have owned, our home in Orange County comes a close second! It is spacious and airy. It was built such that we can fully avail ourselves of the wonderful sunlight that is so special to Southern California. Natural light permeates most parts of the house. You have to have a really good excuse to feel down in such an environment.

(Our house in Anaheim Hills, California)

I have now lived longer in the house in Anaheim Hills than in any other place on earth. This house can truly be called our home, where we shall stay as far into the future as I can see.

Are there shades of gray in our sunlit piece of paradise? There is the occasional temblor, and there are fires. One serious earthquake, magnitude 5.5 on the Richter scale, occurred on July 29, 2008. Its epicenter was twenty miles from our home, near Chino Hills, and its hypocenter was nine miles deep. It resulted in no deaths or significant destruction, though. Merchandise was scattered and knocked off the shelves in stores. Our beds danced a bit on the floor. Some floor tiles on the first floor of our home got uprooted and others were cracked. Mercifully, the house escaped structural damage.

The year 2008 brought us another natural calamity—the Freeway Complex Fire. The Freeway Fire first started shortly after nine a.m. on November 15, 2008. It was fanned by the Santa Ana winds, with the Landfill Fire igniting approximately two hours later. These two separate fires merged a day later and ultimately destroyed 314 residences in Anaheim Hills and Yorba Linda. It was a scary experience, what with embers falling within one hundred feet of our house. These embers would ignite bone-dry vegetation, allowing the fire to jump several hundred feet in a single leap.

Life in Southern California remains vastly preferable to me to living anywhere else on earth, the occasional earthquake and fire notwithstanding. Steps can be taken to reinforce houses to better withstand the impact of earthquakes. Some elementary precautions lessen the risk of being caught up in the brush fires. I feel truly fortunate to be enjoying seventy-degree balmy weather during most of winter while two-thirds of the country lies smothered in deep snow.

***

I couldn't lie around in the sun every day, though. There was work to be done. Nutrilite's Buena Park facility included R&D and a tablet manufacturing plant. The facility also housed the corporate offices of Nutrilite, including the usual corporate functions such as human resources, purchasing, and marketing.

Nutrilite had another sprawling complex at Lakeview, sixty miles to the east, in Riverside County. The Lakeview Complex housed an agricultural farm and a manufacturing plant. The Lakeview plant processed the produce from the farm (such as alfalfa, spinach, and watercress) into concentrates. Some produce was dried and ground. Other produce was juiced, and the juices dried and ground. All concentrate production was shipped to Buena Park to be processed into the finished form of the dietary supplement products we sold, such as tablet, softgel, powder, and capsule.

Almost one-half of Nutrilite's corporate R&D was based in Lakeview. It carried out leading-edge work, with a special focus on establishing the impact of concentrates' active ingredients on different human wellness factors.

Nutrilite acquired two large organic farms, one in the state of Washington and another in northeastern Brazil. The Washington farm grew herbs while the one in Brazil was dedicated to the production of acerola berries, a rich source of vitamin C. The company already owned another farm, not far from Guadalajara in Mexico. The latter was the source of numerous crops and vegetables, which were all processed and shipped to Buena Park to be incorporated into finished nutritional products.

Corporate R&D had several components—nutrition research, product and process research, regulatory control, quality assurance, quality control, and so on. Product and process research, led by myself and my colleague "Martin," comprised almost eighty professionals. It was spread out almost evenly between Buena Park and Lakeview.

The histories of both Nutrilite and Amway, which eventually became one organization, are intertwined. It started with Carl Rehnborg, who had been sent to China as an accountant for an American oil company in 1915. He didn't have much formal education but is said to have been a gifted individual who had a unique way of looking at problems. The massive malnutrition in China prompted him to develop ideas on supplementing food with multivitamins. On his return home in 1927, Rehnborg set up a rudimentary laboratory in his house in California. Based on the findings of his research, he founded California Vitamins in 1934, renaming it Nutrilite Products Company in 1939.

Rehnborg got a big sales assist in 1945 when two multi-level marketers, Lee S. Mytinger and Will Casselberry, joined forces with him in moving his products. However, they soon ran afoul of the FDA, which impounded their inventory in 1948 on the charge of false advertising. Apparently, Mytinger and Casselberry had been claiming that some of the Nutrilite products cured diseases. The case went all the way to the United States Supreme Court, which decided in favor of the FDA in 1950.

While that litigation was pending, two young marketers in Michigan got their start in 1949 as independent distributors of Nutrilite using the multilevel marketing (MLM) approach. Concerned about the FDA dispute, Jay Van Andel and Rich DeVos steered clear of the controversy and launched a new company in 1959. The American Way, later shortened to Amway, would use the MLM system for other household products, too.

Meanwhile, Rehnborg severed his connection with Mytinger and Casselberry and marketed his products directly before hooking up with Amway in 1959. He had steadily expanded the operations of Nutrilite and established a manufacturing plant in Buena Park. His son, Carl Samuel, graduated in chemical engineering from Stanford University in 1958 and later received a PhD in biophysics from the University of California, Berkeley. Dr. Sam, as he was called, joined forces with his father and stayed at the helm after Carl's death in 1973. Amway bought a controlling 51 percent interest in Nutrilite in 1972 and bought the rest of the company in 1994. Dr. Sam was shifted to the position of president and CEO of Nutrilite Health Institute. He retained high visibility both inside the company and around the world as its principal ambassador.

I got to know Dr. Sam fairly well. I can't quite forget his speech at the opening of the new vitamin powders manufacturing plant at the Lakeview Complex in early 1998. We had invited former president Gerald Ford, enjoying retirement in his Palm Springs home at the time, to the inauguration. Ford's speech was lackluster and rather formulaic. But Dr. Sam brought the crowd to life. He had a mesmerizing speaking style. He laid out the history of Nutrilite and how, against great odds, his father had succeeded in availing the nutritional constituents of fruits and crops to enrich countless human lives.

Nutrilite was closely controlled from Amway headquarters in Ada. A position with complete responsibility for running all of Nutrilite, such as CEO or president, did not exist. I reported to the R&D executives in Ada. Various support functions, such as quality assurance and quality control, reported into their respective silos in Ada as well. The plant managers of Nutrilite reported to a local head of manufacturing operations, who in turn reported to the head of worldwide operations in Ada.

The operations chief at Nutrilite, John Lindseth, was an affable and likable executive. In relaxed settings, Lindseth would turn on his singing talent. Such attitudes of camaraderie and friendliness were encouraged at the company.

Nutrilite had a four-day workweek, which was wildly popular. The short workweek had its genesis in the energy crisis of 1973 as a way of saving energy by requiring employees to drive to work one less day. Once in place, the policy could not be abandoned without arousing employee discontent. There was some grumbling from Amway employees in Ada about this, but because headquarters had a five-day workweek, most Nutrilite executives worked on Fridays anyway.

Amway had entered the Chinese market about five years before I came on board. MLMs faced skepticism from the local authorities. Multilevel marketing was officially denounced as an "economic cult," and in 1998 the government banned all direct selling. Direct selling was made legal again only after China was admitted to the World Trade Organization (WTO) in 2005. Admission to the WTO came with restrictions on the endless recruiting of new distributors.

Long after the ban and legalization of direct selling in China, on January 8, 2018, the *New York Times* took a critical look at the operations of American MLMs in China. The article—"Amway Made China a Billion-Dollar Market. Now It Faces a Crackdown"—reported widespread corruption among Chinese authorities, which had facilitated the very recruiting practices officially frowned upon.

From my ringside seat inside Amway, I can state that the company brought to bear a formidable level of science and technology in researching and manufacturing its products. The quality and depth of its R&D were head and shoulders above those of its competition, particularly in the MLM world. Its label claims were soundly supported by the scientific evidence.

Amway underwent a cataclysmic internal convulsion in 2001. Dick DeVos and Steve Van Andel, sons of the founders, had been running the company for a few years before I joined. The generational change had not gone over too well. A major company-wide restructuring and downsizing in 2001 resulted in a very significant reduction in the workforce. The cutback was brutal and extended across all levels. I lost my position, as did my boss and many other fellow executives. Thankfully, Amway was very generous with its termination packages.

My frame of mind after my second job loss was one of equanimity. When Sandoz terminated my job ten years earlier, it caused a severe shock. Regardless of the mitigating circumstances, the firing was an indication of my failure. It took the consulting assignment in Ireland, the camaraderie of my colleagues in outplacement, and then my accomplishments at Boehringer Ingelheim to rebuild my confidence as an executive. That confidence came in handy as I tackled the challenges at Nutrilite/Amway, and it also changed how I reacted to my layoff.

I had greatly improved my executive skills since the days of Sandoz. I now had a much better sense of the needs and perceptions of others in the company. As I formulated goals for the department, I took care to be sure that they were in alignment with the larger objectives of the organization. I had also developed a gentler touch with my own employees. In short, my experiences had taught me to be a great deal more harmonious with the company at large and within my own department.

I left Amway with a lightness of spirit. Amway had been happy with my performance. The two terminations differed starkly. At Sandoz, it resulted from my performance. At Amway, it was a result of the performance of the top leadership.

There was another reason, too. In 1991, I was the sole breadwinner for our family of four. But Rosemary had a good professional job in 2001. Her income and my separation package would allow me to explore my options in a more tranquil frame of mind, rather than feeling the desperation of running through our savings.

I took on consulting gigs in the following eighteen months. The most meaningful, and personally rewarding, was a six-month assignment at Shaklee Corporation, headquartered in Pleasanton, California. Shaklee maintained its corporate R&D facility in Hayward, thirty miles east of San Francisco.

I had networked to connect with James Greene, vice president of R&D. Many years earlier, Greene had worked for Amway in Ada, Michigan. Not only was Greene a thoughtful and considerate boss during the temporary assignment, but I made a lifelong friend. Greene arranged to pay for my room and board during the week and flights home for the weekends.

***

Even though being apart for long periods while I worked elsewhere wasn't ideal, the separation was worthwhile, since it allowed Michael to graduate from high school in Midlothian. For a year after moving to Orange County in 1998, Rosemary was hip-deep in managing numerous projects around the house. She had the full interior and the exterior painted and new wall-to-wall carpeting installed. She had a lot of electrical work done, including the installation of a surround-sound system in the family room. The lawn and the landscaping we inherited required upgrades. She hired the services of a new gardener and started on the exterior projects.

But Rosemary's higher priority by far was to do all she could to make Jeffrey's transition to Canyon High School in Anaheim Hills as smooth and productive as possible. We had yanked Jeffrey out of his high school in Virginia before his senior year. She felt obligated to help Jeffrey get a good start at the new school. She got deeply involved in his sports programs and arranged for him to attend a volleyball camp in Newport Beach. Fortuitously, he met the University of California at Irvine (UCI) volleyball coach at the camp. A few months after Jeffrey started his senior year, Rosemary helped him navigate the college selection and admission process. She drove him to numerous universities in Southern California for campus tours.

Jeffrey was accepted by UCI, where he selected computer science as his major. Even though the campus was only twenty miles from our house, he wanted to have the full college experience, including living in university dorms and joining fraternities. From September 1999 onwards, we saw a lot less of him as he immersed himself in campus activities. He threw himself into college life with complete abandon. In his junior year, he was elected president of the 30,000-student body, which was a singular honor.

To compensate for a very active life in college activities,

including his fraternity, Kappa Sigma, something had to give. He ended up changing his major to political science. Jeffrey graduated in 2004 with a degree in political science and a minor in computer science.

My mind goes back to how Bauji motivated me to work very hard in college by suggesting a worthy goal of bettering my life eventually by immigrating to America. The immediate requirement was very clear to me: I needed to build an excellent academic record. It's possible I may have been projecting my own life experiences on Jeffrey rather than letting him discover his own. In the process of growing up, though, he discovered what he liked and what he excelled at it. His parents' goals could not be his goals.

Michael elected to take a gap year and got a job at Best Buy. The following year, he enrolled at the local community college, Santiago Canyon College. After two years of community college, he transferred to the Fullerton campus of California State University (CSUF). Michael graduated with a bachelor of arts in business administration, with a finance concentration, in 2004.

With the house renovations completed and the boys' paths well charted, in the summer of 1999 Rosemary focused on restarting her career. Leveraging her background as a trainer at Capital One in Virginia, she landed a position as training manager in commercial sales and marketing with PacifiCare Health Systems (PHS), headquartered in Cypress. She nearly doubled her salary from the job in Virginia, which came as a pleasant surprise to both of us, and the twenty-mile commute to her office in Cypress was manageable. This was the start of an intensely busy phase of her career.

Rosemary moved into a project management job at PHS in January 2001 and won a huge promotion to the position of director of disease management in September 2005. She managed a department of over twenty professionals in this job.

The insurance giant United Healthcare acquired PacifiCare in 2007, and Rosemary transferred to the Optum Division of United Healthcare that January as associate director of disease management, quality and standards, and clinical programs. The acquisition brought a change to Rosemary's work routine. She could work from home. The company equipped one room in our home with all the gadgets she would need to communicate with her peers around the globe. The time she would otherwise have needed for getting ready in the morning and commuting to work she used to plunge vigorously into the day's work within moments of waking up.

***

After the Shaklee assignment ended in mid-2002, I was casting about for new opportunities, both in consulting and for full-time employment. I made a cold call to Valeant Pharmaceuticals' executive vice president and worldwide head of manufacturing and supply, John Ireland Cooper, one morning. He invited me in for a face-to-face meeting at his office in Costa Mesa. He liked my background and skill set. He confided in me that he had been in the position for only a few months and numerous areas of Valeant under his command were still unknown entities to him. He needed someone to go and find out about them.

Headquartered in Costa Mesa, Valeant was founded in 1960 as ICN Pharma by a colorful character, Milan Panić. Panić was a promotor; he had actively promoted his Horatio Alger story of "founding the company in his Pasadena garage." He built ICN through numerous acquisitions in Eastern Europe, Russia, and Latin America and boasted a revenue of $670 million in 2001. Panić also retained his roots and connections in the former Yugoslavia. He served as Serbia's prime minister from July 1992 until March 1993, when he lost out to Slobodan

Milošević, who went on to rule over Serbia and eventually was tried for war crimes at The Hague.

Panić's hold on ICN turned shaky in the late 1990s as he and his board came under sustained attack. A new board took control in June 2002 and booted him out. The board renamed the company Valeant Pharmaceuticals International Corporation and hired a new set of top executives, most of them from GlaxoSmithKline (GSK). The GSK contingent included Cooper, incoming president Timothy Tyson, and executive vice president of marketing Wesley Potter Wheeler.

Valeant hired as CEO Robert O'Leary, who had been the CEO of PHS, where Rosemary was working at the time. O'Leary ceded the CEO position to Tyson in January 2005 but retained the board chairman position for himself. Sadly, he would die a year and a half later, at the age of sixty-two.

In our first meeting, Cooper proposed a three-month consulting assignment on very generous terms, which I accepted with alacrity. That meeting would help my career reach its pinnacle.

The organization Cooper oversaw was a behemoth, with over five thousand employees spread over numerous manufacturing plants on multiple continents. He wanted me to take a close look at three technical centers: one in Humacao, Puerto Rico, another in Mexico City, Mexico, and the third one in Rzeszów, Poland. He also wanted me to get familiar with a technical center in Basel, Switzerland.

Cooper rotated his quarterly review meetings with his direct reports between locations. These direct reports were the respective global manufacturing supply (GMS) heads for regions such as North America, Latin America, Europe, and Asia. The direct report list also included the heads of various service functions within the GMS organization, such as finance, purchasing, engineering, and product development. Each of them held the rank of vice president, except for one, who was a senior vice president.

The position heading product development was vacant at the time. He made it clear throughout the company that he regarded me as the acting vice president of product development, even though I had come in as a consultant.

The first Valeant quarterly meeting after I came on board was scheduled to be held in Mexico City in January 2003. That would be my effective start date. This was also an efficient way of introducing me to his staff and for me to get a snapshot of his vast operations by participating in the review.

After Cooper and the other review attendees left, I stayed behind for a deep dive into the operation of the local technical center. The director who led the center had a good command of English. However, most of his professional employees, not to mention the support staff, such as technicians, mechanics, and the administrative assistant, spoke very little English. I was forced to go through the director for information I needed from specific employees. Still, I insisted on presentations by each professional on the projects they were leading, notwithstanding the inconvenience of translation.

During this initial review, I focused on the skill sets of employees and their active projects. I had talks with the leadership of the Latin American Region (LAR), which was headquartered in Mexico City. I tried to understand the LAR's expectations of the technical center and what it needed.

I followed up with similar visits to Humacao, Rzeszów, and Basel. Humacao was the main sourcing center for the North American Region. Rzeszów and Basel were the principal suppliers for the European Region.

I wrote up the final report for Cooper. I recommended that the technical centers in Mexico City, Humacao, and Rzeszów be reorganized into a single function. Cooper accepted my recommendation and asked me to run the proposed Global Physical Product Development (GPPD) function as its vice president. The directors of the three technical centers would report to me directly.

Cooper and I had developed an excellent relationship during my three-month assignment. It was one of mutual respect. This and the acceptance of my report by the top echelons of Valeant facilitated his offer of the full-time position.

While my groups in Mexico City and Humacao were focused exclusively on the finished dosage delivery form of pharmaceuticals, such as tablets, caplets, and injection ampoules, the group in Rzeszów carried out the development of new active ingredients, also called drug substances, as well. The work on new active ingredients was chemistry-intensive, and only the Rzeszów group had this unique capability within Valeant.

The Polish group was better accomplished and better qualified to carry out product development than the two other groups. However, the language barrier was a big handicap. A few key people in the Polish group were fluent in English, though, and I soon came to appreciate the good work that the group was doing.

I realized that the missions of the three GPPD groups were not identical, and they thus needed to be treated individually and deftly. I encouraged cooperation between the three groups and was heartened by their willingness to give each other a helping hand. This was unexpected, given that they knew nothing of each other before we integrated them into the new corporate function of GPPD.

I made some personnel changes as the first order of business. The director in Rzeszów wasn't well regarded at the country headquarters in Warsaw. I got an earful during my visits, mostly concerning her unwillingness to openly communicate her work with the other stakeholders. I replaced her, not without considerable shedding of tears by the woman. I took her out to lunch and tried to explain gently why the change was needed. She wasn't being let go. She could perfectly well work her way to other positions of equivalent responsibility. She calmed down in a couple of days and accepted my decision.

I continued the personnel changes at the other two technical centers, too. The headcount in the Mexican group was way too inflated in relation to the workload. Overall, for the entire GPPD function—all three technical centers—I had inherited a combined headcount of a little over one hundred people, mostly degree-holding professionals. I was able to whittle it down to about seventy-five in eighteen months.

While this part of my job, especially replacing the director at Rzeszów, was new to me, I found out that I had the skills for it. I loved the job. I had been preparing for it throughout my career.

I shall give an example. As I stated, the technical centers reporting to me were in three different countries: (1) Humacao in Puerto Rico, which is part of the United States, (2) Mexico City in Mexico, and (3) Rzeszów in Poland. There are vast cultural differences between even the two Spanish-speaking locations, Humacao and Mexico City. Poland and the United States have even less in common. I vividly remember the frustration of the plant manager in Rzeszów as he tried to express himself in English. "Dr. Minhas, I would much rather be speaking in Russian rather than English," he exclaimed at one point. It wasn't just the language, either. As a Slavic nation, the Poles have a far greater affinity to their eastern neighbors, such as Ukraine and Russia, than to the nations to their west.

How did these differences manifest themselves in my dealings with the three technical centers? For one thing, my jokes went over very well in Humacao, less so in Mexico City, and elicited blank looks in Rzeszów. Many executives leaven their communication with jokes. I just had to be aware of what worked where.

The Poles were far more hierarchical. My instructions to the director were accepted with more alacrity than by his counterpart in Humacao. The latter expected an explanation and at least an attempt on my part to achieve his buy-in. The reaction of the director in the Mexico center lay somewhere in between.

Employees everywhere appreciate it when the boss makes an effort to learn something about their culture. These are the intangibles that help to lubricate the official discourse. I saw results quickly with the Poles I worked with as I learned the rudiments of Polish history and their system of government.

This awareness of the need to relate to different cultures and the ability to do so was the part of my earlier career that likely most helped me prepare for the Valeant position. I had traveled and interacted extensively with people around the globe while in the Licensing-Engineering Department of Stauffer Chemical Company. Such interactions continued unabated in my subsequent jobs. I got to understand a fair amount about the cultures of diverse areas of the world, especially Latin America and Europe. By the time I arrived at Valeant, I could reach into my tool kit effortlessly when I needed to communicate with the locations in Mexico, Puerto Rico, and Poland.

In 2006, Cooper faced two serious situations. His wife, Cathy, had been diagnosed with a grave illness. He needed time away from work to take her to specialists and be with her in her time of need. And professionally, he had become disenchanted by the machinations of an executive in the direct report team of Timothy Tyson, the CEO. Cooper and this individual had worked together previously at GSK and didn't get along. Now this executive was in a more powerful position and sought to frustrate Cooper's initiatives.

Cooper resigned from Valeant in the middle of 2006. Since he was my mentor and booster at the company, I didn't have a sufficient support base left behind. I followed him out at the end of the year.

Over the course of a year, Cathy was fully cured of her illness, and Cooper felt free to look for employment elsewhere. He accepted a position in August 2007 with Novartis Pharmaceuticals and relocated his family from Orange County to Raleigh, North Carolina. Sadly, Cooper died on November 28, 2007, as a result of a heart attack. He was only fifty-two.

Cooper was an extraordinary human being. While most people are focused on power and money, he cared deeply about values such as charity and volunteerism. It didn't matter to him what racial group he was helping in his private capacity. This tall, blond, high-level executive took weeks off every year to go do missionary work in the poorest regions of the globe and offer help and comfort to the poor and the afflicted. After tending to AIDS victims in Africa, he would return home emanating a glow of satisfaction.

Though Cooper was a Republican and I was a Democrat, still we could find common ground quickly on a great many issues concerning our nation. We became good friends after we left Valeant. His untimely death took away a piece of the heart from all of us who loved him. I was privileged to have known him.

Cooper was quick to perceive my skills and strengths when I was between jobs and offered me a coveted opportunity without hesitation. Then he trusted and supported me. His friendship taught me the value of humility and the need to look beyond myself to the needs of others. I was overcome when his son Joshua, who was making the funeral arrangements, called to say that his family wanted me to be one of his pallbearers. I flew out to North Carolina to pay my respects to Cooper, who left a mark on all who came into his life.

At Cooper's funeral, I met Larry Allgaier, the CEO of Novartis Consumer Health and Cooper's boss. When I hung out my shingle as a business consultant in 2007, I consulted for many nutritional supplement, personal care, and pharmaceutical companies. One of the more significant assignments was with Novartis as a direct result of meeting Larry. Even after his death, Cooper was still supporting my career. I retired for good at the end of 2010.

***

Despite being affected by the death of a mentor and friend, nothing could have compared to the earlier loss of my mother, Bhabiji. She had stayed behind in India after my father died. It was two years after my sister Parkash emigrated before she would travel to the United States in 1979. Leaving the family home in Dhandaur, Bhabiji stayed with Parkash in Queens Village, New York. But for the occasional arthritic flare-up, Bhabiji enjoyed good health. Up until the age of ninety-two, she was fully functional. Her mental faculties were sharp and her memory keen. She climbed up and down the stairs from her room on the second floor several times a day. Although she didn't speak English, she was able to enjoy popular American TV shows. One of her favorites was *General Hospital*. She knew full well the story arcs of the leading characters, Luke and Laura.

Bhabiji had a stroke in 1996 and lost most of her vocabulary, as well as part of her mobility. Amazingly, she could still climb up to her room a few times every day. She completely lost mobility in the last year of her life. She died at the age of ninety-six in 2000.

Of all my siblings, Parkash was by far the most giving, in love as well as practical help. She voluntarily shouldered the responsibility of caring for Bhabiji for twenty-one years. In the

1979–1981 time span, our sister Surjit had Bhabiji stay for brief periods at her home in Toronto, Canada. Ranbir would have her stay occasionally at the house he and Kuldip owned. Bhabiji was happiest when she was with Ranbir.

I tried to have Bhabiji stay with me a couple of times, when we lived in Yardley and, later, in Charlotte. But language was a barrier that rendered communication between Rosemary and Bhabiji very hard. Jeffrey developed a rapport with his grandmother through sign language. He thought she was funny. I was amused to see how they were able to communicate through signs. But it was clear that her stay with me as a longer-term option wasn't viable. Bhabiji was happy to return to Parkash's house.

For all her caretaking, Parkash herself had suffered from tuberculosis. After our mother's death, Parkash was in and out of the hospital. In 2004, I received the terrible news of her death when I was on a business trip to Warsaw, Poland. She was seventy-three at the time.

Unlike my ongoing relationships with my sisters, especially Parkash and Gurmit, my brother and I were not able to maintain our childhood bond. Our contact vanished in the early 1980s, as his paranoid schizophrenia worsened after I last saw him in 1982. He had cut off communication with me. Even his wife, Kuldip, was unable to live with him for very long after his breakdown. She divorced him within a few years of my last seeing him.

Years later I came upon a one-page screed authored by Ranbir in 2002. I reproduce it in full to give the reader a glimpse into how the disease had ravaged his mind. All of us who loved him watched helplessly over the years as Ranbir descended further into madness.

Torture Operations
I am daily tortured by the American secret police (CIA and FBI).

American intelligence has planted electronic devices in my teeth. One is the listening device planted in 1980. The second device, planted in April 1987, tells the position and direction of my face.

During my sleep, American intelligence operatives enter my room and inject my body with pain-causing drugs. One or more parts of my body are always kept in pain, often intense pain. These parts include mouth and jaw, neck, shoulders, arms, back, lower back, legs and heels. Intelligence has been doing this for years.

Four of my large teeth have been broken by intelligence in my sleep in the last few years, causing intense continued pain.

American intelligence keeps bombing my residence all day and night with a variety of sounds. Since 1987.

The cabinet door in the washroom has been opened by remote control hundreds of times. Scores of times it was opened in my presence.

People are used daily by the American secret police to instigate violence. More than one hundred thousand people have already been used in torturing me and in laying traps of instigating violence.

American intelligence steals most of my mail, both incoming and outgoing.

New tortures are kept inflicted on me in rapid succession every day.

American intelligence keeps me in total isolation.

With continued isolation, traps, tortures (both mental and physical) and other disinformation, the American intelligence keeps me in a state of mental exhaustion and exasperation at all times.

These are some of the ways used by the American intelligence to torture me.

Managements of Canadian news media (such as CBC-TV, Globe and Mail, Toronto Sun and Toronto Star) are under the instructions of American intelligence not to report the news of its torture operations.

I am 61.

> Signed
> Ranbir Singh
> 280 Sammon Ave., Unit 301
> Toronto, Ontario, Canada
> M4J 1Z7
> (No telephone)
> 1 July 2002

That he suffered so much over the last decades of his life breaks my heart.

CHAPTER 13

Retirement

To be able to fill leisure intelligently is the last product of civilization, and very few people have reached this level.
  - Bertrand Russell, "Conquest of Happiness," 1930

After retiring in 2010, I pondered ways to fill my leisure intelligently. The inspiration came after a visit to India with Rosemary.

I hadn't been to India in twenty years; I last visited on family business in 1991. Rosemary had never visited India. Now we would have the opportunity to enjoy our travel through India as American tourists.

I was keenly looking to observe changes over the previous two decades. Rosemary wanted to observe firsthand what she had read and learned from me about India. Through a travel agency, we arranged to stay at luxury hotels. We would fly between cities and had the services of a chauffeur-driven car as we took in the sights of each city. The availability of a driver would free us up to observe the everyday India of crowded and bustling cities and towns. We planned to talk extensively with the drivers, tour guides, and the occasional man on the street.

With New Delhi as our point of entry and departure, we traveled through the North Indian states of Punjab, Rajasthan, Madhya Pradesh, and India's most populous state, Uttar Pradesh. The first difference I observed was the ubiquity of motorcycles and how the highways, the roads, and the city streets were choked with automobile traffic.

(At Sahelion Ki Bari, the Queen's Garden, in Udaipur, Rajasthan, December 2010)

The tourist sites were lovely. We particularly liked the city of Udaipur in Rajasthan. It was relatively clean, and its palaces, the lake, and the gardens were breathtakingly beautiful.

The economic advancement since I had last been there was evident. People appeared to eat better and live better. But India's lack of cleanliness dismayed me. The attitudes toward the need for good hygiene were unchanged. So was the poverty of the bottom strata of society. Nobody made an effort to hide it.

(At a traditional dinner near Jaipur, Rajasthan, with mandatory turbans, December 2010)

It was all there, in your face. What bothered me most was people's willingness to settle for mediocrity. In nice homes and office buildings, we would find frayed interiors and very messy bathrooms in urgent need of repair. But nobody seemed to mind and life went on as normal.

The discovery of the average Indian's tolerance for mediocrity hit me hard. The brief life I had lived in India before moving to America was a cocooned one. My family did strive for excellence on the farm. I strove for excellence in school at Chandigarh and Kharagpur. I had never been exposed to the life of an average Indian, in the bustling towns and shanties and in the marketplace. Ironically, here I came face-to-face with it when I returned as a foreigner in his own land.

What if I had not emigrated? Would I have been encompassed by the same convenient Indian culture of "doing just enough"? My sense of "best" was challenged consistently in the American academy and industry. It inspired me to make contributions to my profession, which were not limited to just a single country. I doubt I would have been as productive if I had never left India.

Surprisingly, Rosemary was a lot more tolerant than I was of these blemishes on the face of India. She is naturally a great deal more generous toward and understanding of other peoples and cultures. She also may have been extra sensitive to my feelings. She noticed that I was bothered, and she tried to ease some of my pain.

I wrote up my impressions of the visit and had my essay published by one of the leading English newspapers of India, *The Hindu*. The response was massive, amounting to almost two hundred comments and emails.

The success of my first publication inspired me to take to writing to fill my leisure intelligently. I trust I measured up to the expectation laid out by the philosopher Bertrand Russell.

Over the next eight years, I wrote a total of fourteen opinion pieces, which were published in several newspapers and magazines. I explored many issues, including global warming, gerrymandering, the Electoral College, income inequality, and immigration. One of these essays, "An American Success Story Is One About Immigration," was published by the *Orange County Register* on August 17, 2018. It inspired me to write this, the story of my own life.

As I was delving deeper into writing, lots of changes were underway all around me.

***

Ronald Reagan made the following statement at a campaign rally in Fullerton, California, on November 1, 1988: "Orange County is where the good Republicans go before they die."

Among the many dignitaries present at the rally that day was Congressman Bob Dornan. "B-1 Bob" typified the Republican leadership in Orange County—pugnacious and intensely anti-Hispanic.

Dornan, whose nickname comes from his relentless crusade for the California-made bomber, represented the 46th Congressional District from January 1985 through January 1997. He was considered unbeatable until he was beaten by Loretta Sanchez in 1996. The 46th District centers around the heavily Latino city of Santa Ana, and the demographic changes finally caught up with B-1 Bob.

The sprawling Orange County had been reliably conservative through most of the twentieth century. It was the bastion of defense and aerospace workers. It was also steeped in right-wing politics. A regional leader of the John Birch Society, Herbert Philbrick, was a former FBI agent. He had railed against "big government and liberalism," which "would lead to Soviet domination."

Philbrick's message took hold in fertile ground, and Orange County would soon have thirty-eight chapters of the John Birch Society, which called President Eisenhower a "communist tool." John Wayne was a member. So was B-1 Bob. Leaving no doubt about its political leanings, the county renamed Santa Ana Airport, the main airport serving the county, John Wayne Airport in 1979.

The county's deep pockets funded right-wing candidates throughout the country. Governor Pete Wilson was a prominent supporter of Proposition 187, which would deny public services to immigrants in the country illegally, including attendance at public schools. The proposition passed with a two-thirds majority in 1994.

Proposition 187 turned out to be a political inflection point in California and in Orange County specifically. It fired up the activists among the Latino community as well as the California progressives. Their efforts led to the 2011 California DREAM Act, which gave undocumented students access to college. The state also provided them with driver's licenses and limited the ways local law enforcement could interact with Immigration and Customs Enforcement (ICE).

In the meantime, the demographics of the voting population were changing fast. The last time a Republican presidential candidate carried California was George H. W. Bush in 1988. The last time the Republican Party won any statewide seat was in 2006, when Arnold Schwarzenegger was reelected governor and Steve Poizner was elected insurance commissioner.

I had arrived in Orange County in 1997 when the furious reaction to Proposition 187 was in full swing. The twenty-five years of my residence in the state—1997 through the present (mid-2022)—have seen a complete political transformation.

Orange County was the last one in the state to turn blue. In 2018, Democrats made a clean sweep in all four congressional districts (39th, 45th, 48th, and 49th) then held by Republicans. My own district, the 45th, elected Katie Porter, who would go on to earn a considerable national reputation in

Congress in her first term.

However, political trends aren't always linear, and regions don't always go straight from deep red to deep blue. In 2020, Republicans recovered two seats they lost in 2018, in the 39th and 48th Congressional Districts. I suppose we can mark the county of my residence purple for now.

One particular California politician had a spectacular rise.

Kamala Devi Harris is the daughter of immigrants. Her mother, Shyamala Gopalan, arrived in the United States as a graduate student from India in 1958, about twelve years before the first wave of Indian immigration and just seven years before me. She went on to earn a PhD in endocrinology at the University of California, Berkeley. Kamala's father, Donald Jasper Harris, immigrated from British Jamaica and earned a PhD in economics from the same university. Gopalan died in 2009. Dr. Harris is a professor emeritus of economics at Stanford University.

Kamala Harris steadily rose in California politics. Her first elected position was as the district attorney of San Francisco, where she served from 2004 to 2011. She won the statewide office of the attorney general of California in 2010. Between 2017 and 2021, she served as the US senator from the state. Harris was sworn in as the Vice President of the United States on January 20, 2021—the first female, the first black, and the first Asian American vice president.

Harris has proudly recognized her two heritages, which shaped her career. She is the daughter of a woman from India and a black man from Jamaica. She has actively maintained her connections with her mother's family in India. While growing up, she accompanied her mother to India many times and formed a special bond with her maternal grandfather.

While Harris is the child of an immigrant from India who rose to the pinnacle of American politics, there are many other promising up-and-coming progeny of Indian immigrant parents. Remember my colleague at Rohm and Haas, Vijay Khanna? His son, Rohit "Ro" Khanna, has served as the US representative from California's 17th Congressional District since 2017. He has developed a special reputation in the progressive ranks of the Democratic Party. I fully expect this youthful forty-six-year-old to rise higher in national politics.

Another child of Indian immigrants who has made his mark in California politics is Amerish "Ami" Bera. His father, Babulal Bera, emigrated from India in 1958. Ami Bera was raised right here in Orange County, in the city of La Palma. He earned an MD from the University of California, Irvine. He was elected the US representative for California's 7th Congressional District in 2012. He has represented the 3rd district since January 2013.

I also want to acknowledge the non-political contributions made by the immigrants and children of immigrants mentioned here. Shyamala Gopalan and Donald Harris contributed to America through their research in cancer and economics, respectively. And Ami Bera served as a physician before going into politics.

***

Perhaps such hard work characterized the immigrant struggle, or perhaps it was a coincidence. But in my family, I was absolutely not the only one with a strong internal drive to achieve. Starting in early 2007, Rosemary enjoyed the opportunity to work from home with United Healthcare as the associate director of disease management. She continued in that role even after I retired.

Since Rosemary worked from home for close to a decade after I left a traditional office, I became aware of how she conducted business, especially in the numerous group phone calls she took daily. Even with her office door closed, I could sense the tempo of her work. She had a thoughtful, supportive style. She assumed positive intent with others, which went a long way toward resolving disagreements and conflicts. I was impressed with how she exercised self-control and situational awareness. I often marveled at the way she kept a cool head in tense situations and was able to cut through the clutter.

I regarded her as a very natural fit for her management position. But she started to think that she would be more comfortable in a staff role. She felt that the effort expended on the personnel side of her job was disproportionately high. She requested a move, and in March 2011 she took a staff position as the senior clinical program consultant for value realization.

I think she was guided to this decision by her innate modesty. She doesn't derive satisfaction from being a boss as do many other people, including, I am afraid, me. She received performance ratings of "excellent" for each of the eleven years she worked for United Healthcare.

I found her putting in more than sixty-five-hour workweeks in her new role. Her work-related stress permeated our lives. We had to decline invitations for Thanksgiving dinners two years in a row because she was working right through the holiday weekends. I tried to persuade her that she no longer needed to work and that we would be all right financially. She relented and retired in August 2016.

Her retirement allowed us to spend more time with our family, including our sons, as they pursued their own goals. We have gotten to watch our three grandchildren growing up. That is a privilege not too many grandparents can claim. At this juncture of our lives, nothing gives us more pleasure than knowing and loving our grandchildren.

Jeffrey, our younger son, was offered a job right after graduation at UCI's Office of Alumni Affairs. As I write this in June 2022, Jeffrey has risen to the position of executive director of Alumni Affairs at UCI.

(Michael and Jeffrey, 2012)

Jeffrey met Maggie, the young lady he would marry, while they were students at UCI. They were married in 2007. Maggie proceeded to earn a master's degree in education from Pepperdine University and taught for a couple of years in the San Clemente school district. She, and most of her young colleagues, were caught up in the massive wave of retrenchment in 2008 that coincided with the Great Recession. Since then, she has successfully built her business as a photographer.

Maggie has a famous lineage. Her maternal grandfather, Richard "Red" Blanchard, Jr. (June 1920–June 2011), was a musician and a radio personality. He performed on the radio in California from the mid-1940s to the mid-1960s. In his comedy-oriented shows he developed a unique style, described by the *San Diego Daily Journal* as "zany, screwball and funny."

Maggie's mother, Becky, flew with Blanchard to San Francisco for his induction into the Bay Area Hall of Fame on October 1, 2008. I could still see flashes of the once-bright red hair from which Blanchard's sobriquet was derived when I first met him in 2008 at Becky's house, even though his hair had thinned considerably. Becky inherited her father's red hair.

Maggie and Jeffrey have three children. Logan was born in July 2008, followed by Charlotte in October 2011. Carter arrived in April 2015. We are grateful to Jeffrey and Maggie for prioritizing stability and managing to stay in Orange County all along. My inability to put down roots in one place before moving to California was a matter of great regret to me. Rosemary and I consider ourselves fortunate that Jeffrey's family has always lived in Orange County and that we can be a part of their lives.

(Charlotte with Maggie, Carter with me, and Logan with Rosemary, in front of Jeffrey and Michael, 2016)

Michael, our eldest, also stayed close. After his graduation from Cal State Fullerton in 2004, he started out as a financial advisor with a position at Ameriprise Financial. On the fine points of investing, his knowledge is encyclopedic. He is perhaps the best among his peers in drawing up a financial plan for a client. Michael has a sharp, highly intelligent mind. He was able to earn good grades despite not studying much. We

(Logan, Carter, Maggie, Charlotte, and Jeffrey on Easter, April 2, 2021)

are proud of his strengths—his impeccable honesty and his sense of empathy for others.

***

My retirement sounds like an idyllic life: travel, grandchildren, time with my wife. But it hasn't all been easy. I have had several back surgeries on account of spinal stenosis. The last one, and the most serious, was in December 2021, when the surgeon fused the vertebrae from T10 through L3.

During the weeks of recovery following a back surgery in 2014, images of my brother kept flashing in my mind. I hadn't seen Ranbir in thirty-two years. Every few years I would turn to Surjit for news of our brother. She still lived in Toronto as well and would have her husband drive her to the building where Ranbir lived. She never talked to the building manager, who was also the owner of the building, about Ranbir's well-being because "the contact may scare Ranbir off to flee, rendering him homeless." I thought this was poppycock. Anyhow, she would walk past the building at night, on the side Ranbir's apartment faced. The light in his apartment would be turned on sometimes, which satisfied her that Ranbir was perhaps doing all right.

The dissatisfaction with the lack of news and the sense of dread about my brother that had been building up in me for decades came to a head as I recovered from surgery. Within two months, I flew to Toronto.

Surjit offered to accompany me to his apartment building. The building manager knocked at Ranbir's apartment and drew him out with a ruse—that he needed to discuss something that couldn't wait. After his initial reaction of shock on seeing us, Ranbir calmed down and complained that authorities had installed electronic devices in his body to cause him immense pain. He also disclosed that he had been diagnosed with bone cancer, which neither I nor Surjit knew about, but he did not associate his pain with the cancer. He blamed it on "American intelligence," just as he had done in that diatribe I found among his papers.

He agreed to see me again two days later. When I returned, I tried to hug him when he opened the door. He blanched and pulled back, saying that he needed to tell me something. "I don't trust you. Now get out of here," he growled. After he slammed the door shut, the grief of seeing my brother's wasted life was so overwhelming that I wept. The building manager came over and tried to comfort me.

I followed up with another visit to Toronto four years later, in May 2018. The building manager tried to draw him out again, but Ranbir never fully opened the door. He was civil enough, but he looked angry at the sight of me. Ranbir spoke of how he had been hospitalized with pneumonia recently and that he was receiving chemotherapy for his bone cancer.

He was very suspicious. He demanded to know why I came to see him. As I took my leave, I reminded myself that in spite of his off-putting behavior, I was at least able to see him. The time comes when you have to just let go.

But I could not let go for very long. Our lives had been so closely interwoven throughout the first twenty years of my life. I remember moments of kindness, such as the time when I was eleven, and I received a deep gash on my finger while cutting animal fodder with a scythe. He quickly took me to the nearby water source, washed the wound, tore up a piece of his turban, and wrapped it tightly around my finger. There were no words spoken, but I could see the concern in his eyes.

Then there was the time I encountered my first serious setback as a student, failing the engineering drawing course in my freshman year. He spent the summer and early fall helping me grasp three-dimensional spaces so that I could better meet the challenge of the subject. Thanks exclusively to his help, I not only passed the second time, but did so with a high grade.

Despite our separate lives for the many decades since we were children and students together, he was, and is, deeply embedded in my psyche. He appears in my dreams with great regularity.

I dreamt of seeing Ranbir in a casket on the night of September 26, 2018. Within an hour of waking up the next morning, I received a call from Surjit. When I saw her name on the caller ID, my heart sank. I knew Ranbir was no more. He had died on September 26, just nine days shy of his seventy-eighth birthday.

We cremated Ranbir on October 11. A surprising number of mourners gathered for the service. My nephew Ranjit, one of Parkash's boys, had driven up with his family from New York. My cousin Gurdip came with his two adult sons from Kitchener, Ontario. Even though I was overcome with grief, I kept hold of myself as I spoke to the gathering. I was the only one to speak.

My sister Gurmit was unable to attend Ranbir's service. Her health would not permit travel from her home in Santa Clara, California. She had lived there with her daughter, Sumeet, after her husband, Sarjit, passed away in 2014. She turned eighty-seven on December 31, 2021.

Gurmit has slowed down physically. She has lost some memory and some of her cognitive edge. I used to fly up to the Bay Area to see her. These visits were interrupted by COVID-19 in 2020 and 2021. Rosemary and I drove up and saw her in late May, 2022. Her deterioration across the board was jarring, and saddening.

Gurmit and Parkash always gave me unconditional love. With Parkash gone, Gurmit remains my sole link to the memory of my family. I treasure the time I have spent with her.

Despite the outsized role my close relatives play, others

who occupy a place in my life continue to claim my attention. Three people stand out—Peter Skelland, Donald Schaller, and David Koch.

***

Peter Skelland, my thesis advisor, left to teach at the University of Kentucky in Lexington within months of my departure from Notre Dame. He left there in short order for the Georgia Institute of Technology, where he taught through retirement.

He wrote two textbooks—*Non-Newtonian Fluids and Heat Transfer* and *Mass Transfer*, the former while he was still at Notre Dame. The latter was a seminal textbook that would be used in chemical engineering schools across the globe.

Our paths crossed again in 1990 when I was on a business trip in Atlanta. He had retained his full head of silvery hair and his suave good looks. He joined me for a drink at my hotel and invited me to visit his office at Georgia Tech the following day. I spent most of the day at Georgia Tech. He introduced me to his fellow professors.

Skelland shared with me some of his background from before we met. He had developed severe tuberculosis while he was an undergraduate at the University of Birmingham in England. He was hospitalized for two years before finally being cured of the disease. He was immensely grateful to the United Kingdom for two major life experiences—to the British Health Service for curing him of tuberculosis and to the Education Ministry for financing his undergraduate and graduate studies. Out of this gratitude, he decided to retain his British citizenship forever. To this day, well into his nineties, Skelland remains a British citizen, even after residing in the United States continuously since 1962.

I reconnected with him in 2017, when he was eighty-nine, and have followed up with a few more phone conversations since then. I learned new things about him each time. He had divorced his wife Peggy, who I had met at Notre Dame long ago. He had a brief stormy marriage with someone he met in Kentucky. And he married for the third time at the age of eighty.

To be honest, I didn't like some of Skelland's politics. He was a Trump apologist. I was shocked when he told me that "Rush Limbaugh is a national treasure." In a conversation in January 2021, I asked him to help me understand a conundrum. It was the generous welfare state of the United Kingdom that educated him and helped cure him of tuberculosis. How did he reconcile that with his deeply conservative politics, which sees a limited role for government? He didn't give me a satisfactory answer.

However, we have not allowed politics to get in the way of a warm personal relationship. I was saddened to learn that January that Skelland had been using a wheelchair since he fell in the kitchen a year earlier. While he tried to keep up his usual good cheer, I could sense an overwhelming sadness and even dread in him. He appeared to have given up. "I think I shall forever be confined to the wheelchair," he confided, as he contemplated turning ninety-three in a few weeks.

Skelland was not the only old colleague with whom I would reconnect after losing touch over the years. The same happened to my friend from Stauffer Chemical Company, Donald "Don" Schaller. We would resume our friendship seamlessly.

A few years after I left Stauffer in 1981, the company fell on hard times and let go of much of its workforce. The steadfast Don was one of the few survivors. Not only did he survive; he flourished. Stauffer changed hands a few times and was eventually sold to AkzoNobel of the Netherlands. Don rose to the position of senior vice president before taking early retirement when he had not yet turned sixty. Interestingly, he always managed to keep his office in Dobbs Ferry, right through his retirement.

Don's younger daughter's family moved to Orange County in 2016. Don and his wife Carmela would visit frequently, sometimes twice a year. He and I have met many times since, taking advantage of his daughter's relocation to my area.

Don and I most recently met at a Starbucks in Anaheim Hills on April 7, 2021. It felt great to be able to shake hands and remove our masks after a bleak, year-long period of the pandemic. Both of us had received our rounds of COVID vaccinations.

Our friendship has truly matured since we first met forty-nine years ago as colleagues at Stauffer. I admire Don's decency, intelligence, and humanity. I can't think of another person whose friendship I treasure as much.

Though David Koch wasn't exactly a friend, still he kept appearing in my life over a fifty-year period.

I last spoke with Koch on the phone in 1991, when I was stationed in Ireland and read about his airplane accident at Los Angeles International Airport.

My next, and last, contact with him was an exchange of emails in December 2012. As Koch rose higher in his family's company and as his political profile grew, I had imagined that his accessibility would be severely limited. But he responded to my email right away. He remembered me well.

David and his older brother Charles, the chief executive officer of the flagship Koch Industries, supported libertarian causes to minimize the role of government in Americans' lives. They opposed the Patient Protection and Affordable Care Act and the Dodd-Frank Wall Street Reform and Consumer Protection Act.

The younger Koch, David, has been maligned for his support of regressive political causes, perhaps in all fairness. But I prefer to retain my memories of the "good" David. He was generous with his guidance when I was a green process engineer at Scientific Design Company in 1969. Thanks to him, I was able to grasp some complex aspects of process design within months of starting my career.

Even the political profile of him that emerged since my phone conversation in 1991 is a nuanced one.

Koch had been reported as being skeptical about anthropogenic global warming, but when I questioned him about that when we emailed, he denied saying that "global warming is a hoax." Instead, what he wrote to me is this:

> I believe global warming is happening—the question is, what can be done about it without destroying economic growth in all advanced countries. If the government significantly reduces the use of fossil fuels by mandate, then these economies would be seriously harmed. There is a direct correlation between the consumption of fossil fuels and the standard of living in all advanced countries.

It is hard to find fault with Koch's stance. Perhaps he should have been open to the potential of renewable energy sources, whose cost of energy production has been dropping sharply. The worse I can say is that Koch was too cautious in fighting global warming.

Koch was commended by President Barack Obama in July 2015 for his bipartisan efforts to reform the US prison system, which he maintained unfairly targeted low-income and minority communities. During his lifetime, Koch pledged or contributed more than $1.3 billion to medical research, education, arts, and public policy. In recognition of his philanthropy, he was awarded the Laureate Award at the Lincoln Center Spring Gala in 2017.

I was saddened when Charles Koch announced David's death at the age of seventy-nine on August 23, 2019.

The Power of an Atlas

***

In line with some of the issues that Koch took a stand on, I have been sensing that the democracy I have experienced and admired in the fifty-six years of my residence in America is in grave peril. The election of our first non-white president, Barack Obama, unleashed a wave of nativist and racist fury. These nativist forces would deploy their built-in advantage in the Electoral College in 2016 to elect another president, Donald Trump, by a minority of the American population.

Immediately after taking power, Trump proceeded to decimate the country's efforts to combat global warming. He encouraged domestic terrorist groups, such as the Proud Boys, the Oath Keepers, the Three Percenters, QAnon, the Hammerskin Nation, and the Boogaloo Movement, each of them a white supremacist group. These groups provided the foot soldiers to Trump when he incited them on January 6, 2021, resulting in their insurrectionist takeover of the United States Capitol the same afternoon. This was a stunning attack on our democracy.

(Me, in the thick of the pandemic, June 7, 2020)

Immigration, which has been the lifeblood of our country, has been under sustained attack by Trump and his white supremacist supporters. They claim that the white identity is under threat by immigrants, who seek to replace its culture. Their chant—"You will not replace us!"—insinuates that growing minority populations threaten to overtake whites of European heritage in American society.

As an immigrant myself, I was deeply concerned with efforts under the Trump administration to drastically reduce legal immigration.

CHAPTER 14

IMMIGRATION—THE DEMAGOGUE'S PLAYGROUND

> *We have become not a melting pot but a beautiful mosaic. Different people, different beliefs, different yearnings, different hopes, different dreams.*
> - Jimmy Carter in a campaign speech, October 1976

America's history is a tapestry of innumerable threads, many deeply inspiring and others, such as the bigotry I saw on Arun's face, greatly dispiriting. American hospitality is symbolized by the Statue of Liberty. It was evident in the admission of hundreds of thousands of Vietnamese refugees beginning in the 1970s.

Then there is the ugly strain of racism and nativism in the outpourings of the far-right groups. This was detailed by the historian Richard Hofstadter in his essay "The Paranoid Style in American Politics," published in the November 1964 issue of *Harper's Magazine*. It's an outlook characterized by a sense of "heated exaggeration, suspiciousness, and conspiratorial fantasy," and focused on perceived threats to "a nation, a culture, a way of life." It regards its opponents as evil and ubiquitous, while portraying itself, in Professor Hofstadter's words, as "manning the barricades of civilization." The paranoid style described by Hofstadter infuses anti-immigration messaging today.

The two strains—hospitality and racism—have struggled for dominance ever since 1619, when the first slaves are said to have been brought to American soil. The struggle between the forces of rejection and acceptance seems unending. However, the arc of history has decisively trended up.

The unique nature of our country—that we are a nation of immigrants—was affirmed in none other than the Declaration of Independence, which was adopted by the Second Continental Congress in 1776. While listing the colonists' grievances against King George III, the Declaration referred to the roots of the American nation: "Nor have We been wanting in attentions to our Brittish brethren. We have warned them from time to time of attempts by their legislature to extend an unwarrantable jurisdiction over us. We have reminded them of the circumstances of our emigration and settlement here."

An editorial published in the *Daily State Journal* of Alexandria in 1874 praised a bill passed by the Virginia Senate appropriating $15,000 to encourage European immigration. "We are a nation of immigrants and immigrants' children," it said.

But the history of the nation since its founding has also been marked by a persistent tension between the founding dreams and the reality of its actions and practices. America has selectively honored the Bill of Rights; for almost two hundred years after the Declaration of Independence, these rights were understood to hold primarily for its white residents.

As racial attitudes softened toward America's non-white inhabitants, so did its willingness to lower barriers to entry from the non-white regions of the globe. But forces of retrenchment, since the passage of the most enlightened immigration law in 1965, are ascendant today. We need to ensure that the nation continues to avail itself of immigrants of all hues in order to maintain its record of innovation and economic growth.

Inhabitants of the newly independent United States of America fell broadly into three groups. The white Americans had been emigrating from European countries throughout the previous two hundred years. Most of the white population had been born in the New World but were the descendants of settlers who had fled England and other European nations. Eight of the fifty-six signers of the Declaration of Independence were themselves born in England, Ireland, Scotland, or Wales.

The other two groups were composed of several hundred thousand Africans and the Native peoples who had lived in the Americas for millennia.

Much of the African population, as well as its ancestors, had been forcibly brought across the ocean as chattel. The blight of slavery will never quite be wiped off the face of America. Frederick Douglass stressed that point when he gave a keynote address in 1852, at an Independence Day celebration held at Corinthian Hall in Rochester, New York. In this scathing speech, Douglass stated, "The Fourth of July is yours, not mine. You may rejoice, I must mourn.

"What have I, or those I represent," he went on, "to do with your national independence? The rich inheritance of justice, liberty, prosperity, and independence, bequeathed by your fathers, is shared by you, not me. There is not a nation on the earth guilty of practices more shocking and bloodier than are the people of these United States at this very hour."

The third group of people, Native Americans, didn't do much better than the Africans. The Natives' population was vastly reduced over the next one hundred years, primarily by exposure to the diseases brought from Europe by the white settlers. Native Americans were also victims of systemic persecution by America's white population. Nothing illustrates their suffering more tragically or clearly than the infamous Trail of Tears, the forced march beginning in 1830 during which four thousand Cherokee people died of cold, hunger, and disease.

The United States is rightly proud of the freedoms enshrined in our Constitution, guaranteed by our Bill of Rights, which was ratified in 1791. Yet Americans as early as the founding generation believed whiteness was a prerequisite for the exercise of republican virtue. Before the Civil War, there was a decades-long movement to send free and freed blacks back to Africa based on the theory that black people were unfit for and incompatible with democratic life.

But it was also the Bill of Rights that inspired Americans, white and non-white, to clamor for change. These voices grew louder after the Second World War and culminated in the passage of the historic Civil Rights Act of 1964, which outlawed discrimination based on race, color, religion, sex, or national origin.

***

Immigration laws have closely followed national attitudes toward race ever since the founding fathers enshrined the three-fifths clause in the Constitution in 1787. Just three years later, the United States Naturalization Law of 1790 was the first significant law regulating immigration, providing the rules the US would follow in the granting of national citizenship. This law limited naturalization to immigrants who were "free White persons of good character."

Irish and German immigrants had started migrating to America in colonial times, but the early Irish were mostly

Protestants from the north of Ireland who settled on the frontier, while the Germans were mainly religious refugees who clustered in Pennsylvania.

Between 1820 and 1860, almost two million people from Ireland and about 1.5 million people from the German-speaking states of Europe immigrated to the United States. The new Irish immigrants and about half the Germans were Roman Catholics; many were unskilled laborers. Differences in religion, language, and culture set the newcomers apart in a country that was still mostly British in ancestry and Protestant in religion. Some Americans bemoaned the new "foreign" influence on their "native culture," while others feared they would lose their jobs to immigrants willing to work for low wages. The Irish, especially, faced bitter prejudice. Help-wanted signs commonly added the advisory "No Irish Need Apply."

Rosemary's mother, Jane, had German Catholic roots. Jane's father, Jack, had Irish ancestry. She grew up in the small town of Groton in New York state, which was pretty much segregated by religion. The prejudice against Irish and Catholics was virulent in the first half of the twentieth century. It took me a while to fully appreciate Jane's sense of persecution and anger. For me, a migrant from India, it was inconceivable that a white family such as hers could have been the object of prejudice. I learned the lesson that in America, both the source and the recipients of prejudice have been fluid. Even the definition of whiteness has been malleable.

The Fourteenth Amendment, adopted on July 9, 1868, freed slaves, nullified the three-fifths clause, and codified American citizenship. The Citizenship Clause of this amendment provided a broad definition of citizenship, nullifying the 1857 Supreme Court decision, *Dred Scott v. Sandford*. The Dred Scott decision had held that the US Constitution was not meant to include American citizenship for black people, regardless of whether they were enslaved or free, but the Fourteenth Amendment conferred full citizenship on Americans descended from African slaves.

The Naturalization Act of 1870 was a direct outcome of the Fourteenth Amendment. Signed into law by President Ulysses S. Grant on July 14, 1870, it was notable for extending the naturalization process to "aliens of African nativity and to persons of African descent."

But there was a backlash within a decade. The 1882 Chinese Exclusion Act, which prohibited the immigration of Chinese laborers, was the first significant law *restricting* immigration into the United States. For the first time (and until 1943), federal law proscribed entry of an ethnic working group on the premise that it endangered the good order of certain localities. Never mind the uncommon skill and courage among the unsung immigrant Chinese who did the dangerous, backbreaking work over the decades, including blasting the Transcontinental Railroad through the Sierras and the Rockies.

***

Soon after the passage of the Chinese Exclusion Act, even whiteness no longer guaranteed a ticket to entry.

Immigrants, mostly European, kept coming in the nineteenth and early twentieth centuries, with and without permission, gambling their futures on the promise in our founding declaration that all have the right to "life, liberty, and the pursuit of happiness." However, an insidious xenophobic reaction was growing. Thomas Bailey Aldrich, who had edited *The Atlantic Monthly* from 1881 to 1890, sounded the alarm in 1892.

> Wide open and unguarded stand our gates,
> And through them presses a wild motley throng
> O Liberty, white Goddess. Is it well
> To leave the gates unguarded?

The *Washington Post* editorialized in 1906 that 90 percent of Italians coming to the United States were "the degenerate spawn" of "Asiatic hordes."

No less a personage than Calvin Coolidge, who would serve later as the thirtieth President of the United States, opined darkly in the *Saturday Evening Post* in 1921, "Biological laws tell us that certain divergent people will not mix or blend. The dead weight of alien accretion stifles national progress." The racial bigotry of the xenophobes was dressed up in the pseudoscience of racialized eugenics. The scientific arguments that Coolidge invoked were advanced by scholars from the nation's leading universities.

The zoologist Charles Davenport proposed that immigration be carefully controlled to improve human breeding. On February 9, 1921, the *New York Times* editorialized, "The need of restriction is manifest" for "American institutions are menaced" by "swarms of aliens."

The ideological bible of the eugenics movement was first published in 1916: *The Passing of the Great Race* by Madison Grant, the founder of the Bronx Zoo. He divided the white races roughly into three categories. Lower than the exalted "Nordics" of northwestern Europe were the dubious "Alpines." Lower than the "Alpines" were the contemptible and denigrated "Mediterraneans," the peoples of eastern and southern Europe. The book pointedly excluded Jews from membership in the white race.

Amid this cacophony, the Naturalization Act of 1870 was revised in 1906; the revision required immigrants to learn English in order to become naturalized citizens. It created the

Bureau of Immigration and Naturalization Service (INS) and firmly established race as a factor governing immigration by allowing only "free white persons" to become US citizens by naturalization. In a bow to the 1870 act, the revised act also allowed "aliens of African nativity and persons of African descent."

But the 1906 act proved to be just an intermediate stop. The confluence of the nativist voices in the public space and the pseudoscience of eugenics culminated in the Johnson-Reed Act, also called the Immigration Act of 1924. Setting a total immigration quota of 165,000 for countries outside the Western Hemisphere, it virtually ended immigration from Asia. Quotas for specific countries were based on 2 percent of the US population from that country, as recorded in 1890. Since most of the immigration from southern and eastern Europe had occurred in the 1890–1924 period, these populations had been poorly represented in 1890. The new law vastly reduced the immigration of Italians, Jews, Greeks, Poles, and other Slavs.

Four years before the Immigration Act of 1924, 76 percent of immigrants came from eastern or southern Europe. After the act, only 11 percent did. Greater than 95 percent of those immigrating from 1924 to 1965 were white. The deep immorality of the law is apparent in the denial of entry to millions of Jews trying to escape the tyranny of Nazi Germany.

***

In the light of the searing debate that was underway in the early twentieth century, the whiteness of even many Europeans was being questioned. A man from India, not dissimilar to me, forced his way smack into the middle of this debate.

Bhagat Singh Thind was a Sikh immigrant from Punjab, India. Thind arrived in Seattle in 1913 at the age of twenty.

Unlike me, he stayed fully turbaned and bearded all his life. Though still an Indian citizen, he enlisted in the US Army to fight in the Great War, mustering out as a sergeant two days before the Armistice was signed on November 11, 1918.

An amazing sequence of interactions with the US government followed. They would be comical if they hadn't visited so much suffering on Mr. Thind. Following his service with the army, he sought to become a naturalized citizen in the state of Washington. In a recent test of the revised Immigration Act of 1906, the US Supreme Court had ruled that "Caucasians of Aryan descent" had the right to become US citizens, and Indians at the time were anthropologically classified as Caucasians. Thind's application for citizenship was granted in December 1918—but it was rescinded by the INS within four days.

Five months later he successfully applied for citizenship in another state, Oregon. But the INS challenged the ruling. The case wound its way up to the US Supreme Court, which decided against Thind in 1923. The Court's judgment retroactively stripped all Indian Americans of citizenship for "not being Caucasian in the common man's understanding of the term." After an inexplicable three-year delay following the Supreme Court ruling, the INS revoked Thind's citizenship a second time in 1926.

Congress passed a law in 1935 allowing citizenship to *all* US veterans of the Great War. For the third time, and this time for good, Thind received his US citizenship, this time through the state of New York in 1936. The INS didn't dare challenge him again. Thind went on to earn a PhD in theology at the University of California, Berkeley. Dr. Thind is held in esteem by the Indian Americans who followed him to these shores, though I myself was unaware of his story when I first arrived in America.

***

The forty years following the passage of the Johnson-Reed Act of 1924 were characterized by immense change in the nation's societal mores and attitudes toward race. The Second World War proved a strong catalyst for change. Black Americans fought the Axis powers as full-fledged American soldiers, with freedoms they had never enjoyed at home. They ran into the buzz saw of segregation on return. The experience impacted not only the returning black soldiers but also many white Americans, one of whom was Harry Truman.

Truman had grown up in a family deeply supportive of segregation. When Truman was a US Senator, he wrote a letter to his daughter, Margaret, on April 7, 1937, describing a dinner at the White House with President Franklin D. Roosevelt. "They gave a real good meal at the taxpayers' expense—tomato soup, fillet of flounder, roast turkey, string beans, pineapple salad, chocolate ice cream and cake, candy and little cafe noir afterward," Truman wrote. "All these things were in courses, deftly placed and removed by an army of coons."

But Truman had been deeply disturbed by instances of violence and cruelty visited upon returning black soldiers and their families. He was haunted by an attack on Isaac Woodard, a black World War II veteran, who was pulled off a bus in Batesburg, South Carolina, and beaten and blinded by the police chief. "Truman referred to it often in public and private when justifying his support for civil rights," Kari Frederickson wrote in the book *The Dixiecrat Revolt and the End of the Solid South, 1932–1968*. Truman "had a special feeling for soldiers, and from that point on Truman took a different tack."

On December 5, 1946, Truman issued an executive order he called "Freedom from Fear," which created the President's Committee on Civil Rights, tasked with analyzing the state of civil rights in the country, investigating mob violence, and proposing legislation to protect civil rights.

Truman signed two historic executive orders on July 26, 1948. The first desegregated the armed services. He declared, "there shall be equality of treatment and opportunity for all persons in the armed services without regard to race, color, religion or national origin." The second desegregated the federal workforce.

These two orders set the course for civil rights for the rest of the century. Truman's moves were revolutionary in impact. He was the first American president to proclaim the equality of blacks. His actions also showed immense courage. He issued the orders in the summer of 1948, just weeks before launching his reelection campaign. An average politician would lie low and ride it out—get through the election and then do want he wanted to do. But not Truman.

Two other phenomena greatly affected mid-century white attitudes toward race—the civil rights movement, which bloomed in the 1950s and the 1960s, and the advent of television. Many white people were horrified by the images of police turning fire hoses and dogs on black protestors in the South.

The accelerating social changes climaxed in two historic pieces of legislation. The Civil Rights Act of 1964 ended segregation in public places and banned employment discrimination based on race, color, religion, sex, or national origin. The Voting Rights Act of 1965 aimed to remove legal barriers at the state and local levels that prevented African Americans from exercising their right to vote. President Lyndon Johnson signed both acts into law. Truman's legacy eased Johnson's actions, or as Johnson's aide, Bill Moyers, commented, "Truman's hand steadied his."

By the early 1960s, calls to reform US immigration policy had mounted, thanks to the growing strength of the civil rights movement. The Immigration and Naturalization Act of 1965 (the Hart-Celler Act) was signed into law on October 3,

1965—just one month after I came to the United States on a student visa—abolishing the earlier quota system laid down in the Johnson-Reed Immigration Act of 1924. Hart-Celler established a new immigration policy based on reuniting immigrant families and attracting skilled labor to the United States. Gone was the preferential treatment for white immigrants, especially from western and northern European countries. For the first time in history, the US opened its doors to all races and nationalities. Asians, for example, who had been locked out by the Johnson-Reed Act, were now welcomed on equal footing with Europeans. The new law would go into effect on June 30, 1968.

***

Without the changes enacted by the Hart-Cellar Act, my path to American citizenship might have looked very different, if it happened at all.

Within weeks of starting work in March 1969, my employer, Scientific Design Company, sponsored me for an immigrant visa. The green card arrived in less than six months. I applied for naturalization five years later and I was a freshly minted US citizen in 1974.

Perhaps fittingly, the presiding judge when I took my oath of citizenship at the local court in White Plains, New York, was an African American jurist. Blood coursed faster through my veins when I took the oath. It was an incredible feeling to be a part of this sometimes wayward but altogether magnificent nation.

Beyond allowing me to achieve a goal I had worked toward for twenty years, the immigration policy implemented in 1965 greatly changed the demographic makeup of the American population in the next five decades. New immigrants came increasingly from Asia, Africa, and Latin America, rather than Europe.

The US is now home to more immigrants than any other nation in the world. Our current foreign-born population numbers some forty-five million people, 14 percent of the total. About one in four people living in the US is foreign-born or the child of immigrants.

The racial composition of new immigrants has also undergone a sea change since the Immigration Act of 1965. A Pew Research publication from May 17, 2013, listed the share of the white immigrants admitted as permanent residents as 90 percent in 1964, 15 percent in 1992, and 9 percent in 2012.

Another Pew Research publication, on September 28, 2015, listed the white share of the US population at 84 percent in 1965. It declined to 62 percent by 2015 and is projected to drop below 50 percent sometime between 2041 and 2046.

***

These changing demographics have brought forth extreme resistance from the nativists. America under Donald Trump was ambivalent about greeting new arrivals—including those who come seeking asylum, as they are entitled to do—with open arms. It preferred to offer the cold shoulder, a detention center, and deportation. It came in proclaiming opposition, not only to illegal immigration, which few support, but to legal immigration, too.

The number of green cards handed out to migrants for all of 2016, the last year of the Obama administration, stood at 1.18 million. Under Trump, it dropped steeply to one-half, 580,000 in 2019.

The driving force behind the anti-immigration policy was Trump's senior advisor, Stephen Miller. His anti-immigration stance is ironic, considering that his ancestors arrived at American shores as refugees fleeing anti-Jewish pogroms in present-day Belarus. Miller's uncle, neuropsychologist David

Glosser, has called Miller an "immigration hypocrite" and the policies he helped create for the Trump administration "a complete repudiation of the American Dream."

The *Washington Post* published an interesting analysis by Jeff Stein and Andrew Van Dam on February 6, 2018. Even if immigration numbers were maintained at the level forced by Trump (reduced by 50 percent from the Obama years), the demographic changes now underway in the US will continue. It will just take five years longer to turn America into a majority-minority country, instead of the currently projected 2041–2046.

No matter how hard the forces of reaction try, the 1950s aren't coming back. Too many don't want them to. White nostalgia is about a world that never quite was, an idealized American past with the dirty bits brushed off.

***

Immigration has long been the lifeblood powering US economic growth. A joint report by the US National Academies of Science, Engineering, and Medicine, issued on September 21, 2016, revealed many important benefits of immigration—including economic growth, innovation, and entrepreneurship—with little to no negative effects on the overall wages or employment of native-born workers in the long term.

Though immigrants are only 14 percent of the American population today, they create about a quarter of all new businesses in the nation, while the immigrant share exceeds 40 percent of new firms in California, New York, New Jersey, and Florida. Overall, nearly one in five (20 percent) businesses nationwide are owned by immigrants. This share rises to roughly one-third in California and the District of Columbia and to more than a quarter in New York, New Jersey, and Florida.

Since 2000, immigrants have earned over a third of the American Nobel Prizes in chemistry, physics, and medicine.

The National Academies' report concludes, "Immigration supplies workers, which increases GDP and has helped the United States avoid the fate of stagnant economies created by purely demographic forces—in particular, an aging and, in the case of Japan, a shrinking workforce." Japan, an immigrant-unfriendly country, is facing an economic and demographic crisis. By 2050, it will have 23 percent fewer citizens than today, a magnitude of population collapses not seen since the great plagues of the Middle Ages. Japan has only itself to blame in its quest to remain racially homogeneous, primarily by strictly restricting immigration.

The National Academies' report concludes further, "Perhaps even more important than the contribution to labor supply is the infusion by high-skilled immigration of human capital that has boosted the nation's capacity for innovation and technological change."

There are numerous examples of such highly skilled immigrants from India who have contributed greatly to the United States. Vinod Khosla co-founded Sun Microsystems and became an important venture capitalist in Silicon Valley. Rajat Gupta rose to be the worldwide managing director of the global firm McKinsey & Company, a position he held from 1994 through 2003. Rajiv Gupta, the man I met and admired at Rohm and Haas, rose to the position of CEO of that company.

Pradeep Khosla has served as the chancellor of the University of California at San Diego since 2012. Padmasree Warrior served as the chief technical officer of Cisco before accepting the position of CEO at NextEv. Satya Nadella has been the CEO of Microsoft since 2014. Sanjay Mehrotra is the co-founder of SanDisk and has served as the CEO of Micron Technology since 2017. Sundar Pichai is the CEO of Alphabet

Inc. and its subsidiary Google. Arvind Krishna serves as the CEO of IBM. Shantanu Narayen has led Adobe as its CEO since December 2007. Parag Agrawal was named the CEO of Twitter in November 2021.

The shared characteristic of all these immigrants is this: they grew up and received their early education in India, just as I did. And though my relatives and I aren't populating lists of CEOs or heading universities, my family can lay claim to its own contributions made to America.

After earning a PhD in chemical engineering at the University of Notre Dame, I rose steadily through the ranks of corporate America. In my last corporate position before retirement, I served as vice president of Global Physical Product Development (GPPD) at Valeant Pharmaceuticals International Corporation, a multinational company.

I have led the design and construction of numerous chemical plants. I developed a great many product and manufacturing technologies in numerous fields spanning petrochemicals, agricultural chemicals, specialty chemicals, nutritional supplements, and pharmaceuticals. I am proud of my contributions as an immigrant to the United States.

My sister Parkash's three youngest sons were included in my sponsorship application for her in the mid-1970s. The youngest went on to receive an MBA from the Cooper Union in Manhattan and runs a successful tax consulting service. His older brothers went to work for the City of New York after graduating from high school. The eldest retired a few years ago from the New York City Transit Authority. The middle brother rose to the highest non-exempt level in the city's Sanitation Department before his retirement.

Despite my admittedly self-interested focus on Indian immigrants here, it is not only those from India who have contributed mightily to the United States.

Albert Einstein was a Jewish immigrant who made a

timely escape from Nazi Germany. Would we have had Google today but for Sergey Brin, who immigrated here from Russia? Nikola Tesla, an immigrant from Croatia, pioneered the distribution of alternating current, the dynamos, and radio technology. Elon Musk, an immigrant from South Africa, revolutionized the electric car industry. The rockets from his company SpaceX are the only launch vehicles available to NASA as of 2021 for transporting astronauts to the International Space Station.

Immigrants' roles in science and technology are frequently noted in this land of innovation. But the glamour of Hollywood would have been a shade dimmer without Charlize Theron, who migrated from South Africa, Maureen O'Hara, who immigrated from Ireland, or Natalie Portman, who immigrated from Israel.

American foreign policy was hugely influenced by German immigrant Heinz Alfred Kissinger, more popularly known as Henry, the fifty-sixth US secretary of state. Joseph Pulitzer, an immigrant from Hungary, founded the Columbia School of Journalism, a move that inspired the creation of the Pulitzer Prize after his death.

And in a more pertinent, timely connection, the biochemist Katalin Karikó, who immigrated from Hungary in 1985, pioneered the use of messenger RNA (mRNA), which led to the lightning-fast development of the lifesaving COVID-19 vaccines in 2020 by both Pfizer and Moderna.

***

Thus far, I have focused particularly on one type of immigrant—the kind who follows America's legal paths to immigration, despite how those paths have twisted and turned through the decades. One key issue today not covered by the Hart-Cellar Act is the presence of undocumented immigrants in the

United States. According to the Brookings Institute, estimates of the number of undocumented immigrants living in this country range from 10.5 to 12 million. Many of them have lived here for decades and have US-born, American citizen children. An often-overlooked fact pertinent to the discussion of immigration law is that illegal immigrants are taxpayers, paying payroll and sales taxes, while they are ineligible for most federal benefits, such as the Supplemental Nutrition Assistance Program (SNAP), known to most people as food stamps.

President Joe Biden sent to Congress sweeping immigration legislation on his first day in office. It provided a pathway to citizenship for the approximately eleven million people in the country illegally.

The president's immigration proposal, the US Citizenship Act of 2021, was fashioned after the Comprehensive Immigration Bill (S 744) of 2013, which was hammered out by a bipartisan group of senators known as the "Gang of Eight." It provided legal status to undocumented immigrants within the United States and passed in the Senate by a 68-32 vote but died in the Republican-controlled House of Representatives. The Speaker, John Boehner, refused to even bring it up for a vote.

Besides providing a pathway to citizenship for undocumented residents, the US Citizenship Act would reform the family-based immigration system by clearing backlogs, prohibiting discrimination based on religion, and clearing employment-based visa backlogs.

The House passed a narrower version of the president's immigration legislation on March 18, 2021. But the filibuster rule in the Senate, which required sixty votes to pass legislation, killed the bill. The stubborn opposition of two Democratic Senators—Joe Manchin from West Virginia and Kyrsten Sinema from Arizona—to carving out an exception to filibuster for the immigration bill doomed it. Another opportunity to enact this bill into law is unlikely till after the election in 2024, provided that the Democrats win complete control of the government, meaning the presidency and both houses of Congress by a comfortable margin.

EPILOGUE

Democracy is a form of worship. It is the worship of jackals by jackasses.
- H. L. Mencken, The American Credo: A Contribution Toward the Interpretation of the National Mind, 1920

Journalist and literary critic H. L. Mencken was known for his satire about America and American culture, but who knows what he would have said about the country of the twenty-first century. Former President Donald Trump's behavior in office gave new life to another quote from Mencken: "On some great and glorious day, the plain folks of the land will reach their heart's desire at last, and the White House will be adorned by a downright moron." So very prescient of Mencken!

The country is more divided today than at any other time in the fifty-six years I have lived in the United States. I don't mean to minimize the bitter division we saw in the years of the Vietnam War and the urban riots in the following decade. But the country never descended to the levels of tribalism it has in recent years. It all started with the end of "The Fairness Doctrine" in 1987, killed by strenuous efforts of the Republicans during the Reagan presidency. It opened the flood gates. Out poured the right-wing radio talk shows and radio personalities such as Rush Limbaugh. Fox News established a beachhead in cable TV. Some opposition was offered by left-wing radio and TV shows such as MSNBC. The emergence of social media poured gasoline on the smoldering embers of division.

On the positive side, Americans voted in November 2020 as if the nation was in peril, because it was. With an overwhelming margin of seven million votes, Americans affirmed their preference for Joseph Biden over Trump. President Biden is a caring, decent man who deeply respects our democratic values. He is the president we need, one who represents *all* Americans.

But Donald Trump left behind a poisoned brew of lies, racism, and a deeply conspiratorial mindset among his numerous followers. The end of his presidency shook American stability as even 9/11 did not. Trump reveled in lawlessness while glorifying law and order. So did his followers who attacked our Capitol in Washington, DC, on January 6, 2021. Unfortunately, these domestic terrorists represent only the tip of the malevolent Trumpian cult; the great majority of the Republican Party today subscribes to this dogma.

President Biden faced a steep challenge. Not only did he have to address the ravages of COVID-19 and the resulting economic desolation, but he was also charged with the very difficult task of rebuilding our nation, which Trump left in tatters.

I write this in mid-2022 at a very difficult time for our beloved country. Pressed by the three conservative justices appointed by Trump, the Supreme Court has greatly accelerated our divisions along policy and ideological lines, starting with its reversal of *Roe v. Wade*, a landmark ruling that had guided the nation for half a century. More rulings quickly followed, extending our fault lines to climate change, gun control, and voting rights.

But our Constitution has vested Congress and the president with final control of the nation's destiny. Congress can strip the court of its ability to hear certain cases and it can mandate a supermajority of justices to declare a federal law or previous decision unconstitutional. Congress can use the Guarantee Clause of the Constitution to defend the basic rights of citizens against a tyrannical Supreme Court and overbearing right-wing state governments. What we need to focus on is electing a Congress and president who will move in tandem to protect our basic rights.

It is important to remember our strengths. America has truly been "the city on the hill." Events of the recent past have led us to doubt our strengths. But we must not forget it, because it is true. The nation has found its way in the past crises. We shall do so again.

Why am I so sure? Because our nation lives by the Bill of Rights, a clarion call for liberty. Because our founding fathers set improbably high goals for governance. They serve as the beacons of light when we lose our way, as we did in practicing the institution of slavery, waging wars in Vietnam and Iraq, and, most recently, following the seductive siren of a con man. Thanks to these strengths, the nation has successfully found its way back from previous disastrous undertakings.

Lest we should forget, the nation also derives strength from its immigrants and the very idea that America is a nation of immigrants. Immigrants have an unbridled spirit. Their stories evoke optimism, belief in the future, the sharing of disparate pasts, and coming together, something we rarely see in most other countries in the world. We are a melting pot of so many nationalities—or, as Jimmy Carter said, "a beautiful mosaic." Immigrants renew the American spirit.

My own life story is a tribute to America's immigration saga. I am deeply grateful to America for offering me, a poor young man from India, an opportunity, based solely on my educational grades in that country. I hope I have repaid that debt many times over.

I am bereft of the sense of cynicism that tends to accumulate through generations. I and my fellow immigrants retain the idealistic spirit that our country was built on. We see what the nation is capable of achieving if we all put our shoulders together. We fervently harbor the notion that all Americans are in the same boat and we must row together and in harmony.

That Joe Biden's ascendency to the presidency has been paralleled by Vice President Kamala Harris, a daughter of immigrants and the first Indian American to be elected to that national office, is yet another tribute to America's immigration saga.

This is *my* country, no less mine than that of the fellow whose ancestors came here on the *Mayflower*. My face, and those of my children and grandchildren, comprise that mosaic that Carter said constitutes America. The dream inspired by that atlas, which Bauji presented me with such a long time ago, has come to fruition in full.

ABOUT ATMOSPHERE PRESS

Atmosphere Press is an independent, full-service publisher for excellent books in all genres and for all audiences. Learn more about what we do at atmospherepress.com.

We encourage you to check out some of Atmosphere's latest releases, which are available at Amazon.com and via order from your local bookstore:

The Great Unfixables, by Neil Taylor

Soused at the Manor House, by Brian Crawford

Portal or Hole: Meditations on Art, Religion, Race And The Pandemic, by Pamela M. Connell

A Walk Through the Wilderness, by Dan Conger

The House at 104: Memoir of a Childhood, by Anne Hegnauer

A Short History of Newton Hall, Chester, by Chris Fozzard

Serial Love: When Happily Ever After… Isn't, by Kathy Kay

Sit-Ins, Drive-Ins and Uncle Sam, by Bill Slawter

Black Water and Tulips, by Sara Mansfield Taber

Ghosted: Dating & Other Paramoural Experiences, by Jana Eisenstein

Walking with Fay: My Mother's Uncharted Path into Dementia, by Carolyn Testa

FLAWED HOUSES of FOUR SEASONS, by James Morris

Word for New Weddings, by David Glusker and Thom Blackstone

It's Really All about Collaboration and Creativity! A Textbook and Self-Study Guide for the Instrumental Music Ensemble Conductor, by John F. Colson

A Life of Obstructions, by Rob Penfield

Troubled Skies Over Quaker Hill: A Search for the Truth, by Lessie Auletti

ABOUT THE AUTHOR

SARDUL SINGH MINHAS was born into a family of farmers and soldiers in Punjab, India. At age eleven he was inspired by an atlas to one day live in America. As a boy he drove tractors and tended to cattle. He was home-schooled until the age of thirteen. He earned bachelor's and master's degrees in India and a PhD from the University of Notre Dame, all in chemical engineering. His career has spanned multinational companies in the chemical and pharmaceutical sectors. His last position was vice president of global physical product development, where he ran technical centers in Mexico, Puerto Rico, and Poland and oversaw a workforce of over a hundred engineers and scientists. Since his retirement in 2010 he has published fourteen opinion pieces on subjects such as Einstein, global warming, nuclear power, innovation, gun control, gerrymandering, electoral college, immigration, and the pace of change in India. He lives in Anaheim Hills, California with his wife, Rosemary.

Made in the USA
Columbia, SC
11 February 2023